The Stellar Approach

Simon Berkler
Ella Lagé

The Stellar Approach

How to Drive the Regenerative Transformation
of the Economy with Your Organization

Translated from German by Ben Hughes

Campus Verlag
Frankfurt/New York

The original German edition was published in 2024 by Campus Verlag GmbH with the title *Der Stellar-Approach – Wie deine Organisation zum regenerativen Wandel der Wirtschaft beiträgt*.
© 2024 by Campus Verlag GmbH. All rights reserved.

ISBN 978-3-593-51959-3 Print
ISBN 978-3-593-45912-7 E-Book (PDF)
ISBN 978-3-593-45911-0 E-Book (EPUB)

1st edition 2024

All rights reserved. No part of this book may be reproduced or transmitted in any form or by any means, electronic or mechanical, including photocopying, recording, or by any information storage and retrieval system, without permission in writing from the publishers.
Copyright © 2024 by Campus Verlag GmbH, Frankfurt am Main.
Cover design: total italic, Thierry Wijnberg, Amsterdam/Berlin
Illustrations: © Danika Baker-Sohn and Jana Stolz
Typesetting: Publikations Atelier, Weiterstadt
Printing office and bookbinder: Beltz Grafische Betriebe GmbH, Bad Langensalza
Beltz Grafische Betriebe is a company with a financial contribution to climate protection (ID 15985-2104-1001).
Printed in Germany

www.campus.de
www.press.uchicago.edu

"To understand how complex living systems actually work, and how we can apply these insights to our economy and to our organizations is the Great Work of our time. The Stellar Approach *offers a very useful field guide for the journey ahead.*"

John B. Fullerton,
Founder and President of the Capital Institute

"A pragmatic, light and encouraging approach! True sustainability needs many to lead the way – businesses will need to undergo a deep transformation that unlocks ambitious action. The Stellar Approach provides the necessary context on interrelationships and important tools for successfully developing regenerative skills across your own organization. This, alongside a deep redesign of businesses, is an important building block for helping humanity into the Doughnut. This book helps to break down the huge task into feasible steps."

Erinch Sahan,
Business and Enterprise Lead at the Doughnut Economics Action Lab

Check-in

Part 1
Shaping the Regenerative Change

20   Introduction

28   Between the "No More" and the "Not Yet"

34   No More: Is the System Broken?

52   Not Yet: The Dawn of a Regenerative Economy

74   The Transition: Changing the Rules While We Are Playing the Game

88   **How Organizations Can Contribute to Regenerative Change**

90   The Stellar Principles – Our Guiding Stars

103   The Stellar Approach Transformation Design

Part 2
The Stellar Approach

117   **Preparing for the Stellar Journey**

118   Packing the Equipment for Our Journey: The Stellar Practices

124   Inner Fitness Training: The Stellar Virtues

128   The Stellar Path: Context, Direction, and Impact

132   How We'll Make Our Way: Even the Longest Odysseys Begin with Small Steps

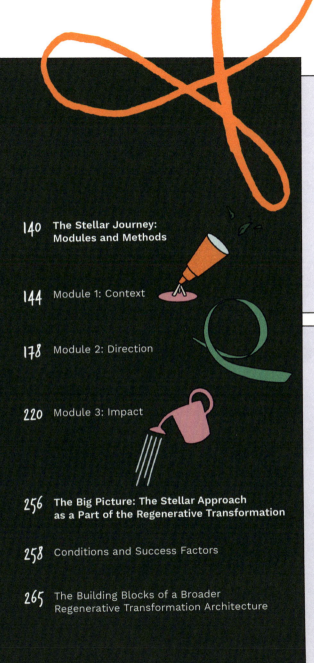

140	**The Stellar Journey: Modules and Methods**
144	Module 1: Context
178	Module 2: Direction
220	Module 3: Impact
256	**The Big Picture: The Stellar Approach as a Part of the Regenerative Transformation**
258	Conditions and Success Factors
265	The Building Blocks of a Broader Regenerative Transformation Architecture

Part 3
Food for Thought and the Way Forward

| 284 | The 5+1 Model: The Life-Centric Organization |
| 296 | Some Encouragement for Your Regenerative Development Journey |

Check-out

Appendix

303	Checklist for Workshops
306	Basic Concepts in Sustainability and Regenerative Economic Activity
317	References and Further Reading
324	Regenerative Glossary
340	Annotations
347	Image Credits
348	Contributors
350	About the Authors

Check-in

Whenever starting something new, we like to kick things off with a check-in. This is a short, simple ritual, where we say how we *are* at the moment and express anything else we feel is needed to start things smoothly.

So, let's begin: How are we? Looking at the state of the world today, we feel concerned. Often alarmed. Sometimes, when it all gets too overwhelming, we might even feel like giving up.

And it's not hard to see why: We find ourselves in a world where every passing day sees natural ecosystems damaged so severely that the very survival of humanity, as well as that of many other species, is gravely threatened. In a world where social inequality, already severe, only continues to worsen. A world where centuries-old historical privileges still shape the lives of many today. A world where – unfortunately – we're fast running out of time for countermeasures.

No wonder we sometimes feel powerless. But wait. That's not the whole story. We also feel excited. Hopeful, even. Because with the Stellar Approach, we're making a contribution to solving these problems. Because instead of waiting around for someone else to save the world, we're starting our own journey and heartening others to do the same. Because in this book we share how each and every one of us can help regenerate our battered planet and exhausted societies – one step at a time, in our own circles of influence.

Now, you may be thinking: "OK, but do we really need *another* book on sustainability?" And it's true that many books already cover various aspects of effective sustainability management. And more still make a compelling argument for why we desperately need a shift toward greater sustainability. But the way we see it, there's still a gap in the landscape that hinders progress: we need an approach that actually gives organizations *a roadmap* to guide them to their destination.

Our goal with the Stellar Approach is to bridge this gap. That's why in this book, you'll find a concrete, actionable toolkit to help any team or organization embark on their own journey of transformation.

Our focus is on organizations, or more specifically, *teams* within organizations. At its core, the Stellar Approach is a team development program that empowers them to contribute to regenerative change in their organization. The more teams come on board, the greater the resulting organizational shift will be. And the more organizations join in, the more profoundly the entire economy will change.

Of course, in real life, things are somewhat more complicated than that. The simple snowball dynamic described above is, in fact, not simple at all, but embedded in a complex multitude of dependencies. After all, were the solution uncomplicated, humanity would've likely already changed its course long ago.

This is why, in the Stellar Approach, we'll also delve into the dynamics of our current economic system. We'll explain how it's currently in the process of destabilizing itself, thereby contributing to our dire social and ecological predicament. What's more, we'll envisage a new, regenerative future – one that fosters the health and resilience of our societies and the planet as a whole. And finally, we'll describe what's needed to reach this beautiful vision.

The way we see it, this book is our contribution to the great debate on what kind of economy we actually want. Before we begin though, let's touch upon a few key ideas that could be considered the foundational premises of this book.

- **Acknowledging complexity:** Life is complex. We can make plans and predictions all we want, but what actually happens is dependent on interconnected system dynamics. And complex systems are famously unpredictable, as anyone who has witnessed recent world events can attest. But importantly, this does not mean that we should stop trying to steer in the right direction. Rather, it merely means that we shouldn't delude ourselves into thinking that in this social system we can somehow ensure every single step goes in that direction. That is an illusion.
- **Simplify without trivializing:** In order to communicate with each other as we navigate complex environments, we need to simplify. No model, concept, or theory can ever reflect reality perfectly but must always exclude or prioritize certain aspects of it. This also applies to the Stellar Approach. As we see it, simplifications are acceptable – and indeed, unavoidable – as long as the underlying complexity is not forgotten.
- **Radical development orientation:** Development is an essential part of life. And this development will continue whether we want it to or not. This simple fact leads to two important consequences: First, we should occasionally shift our perspective and question whether the current direction of development is the right one. Second, we need to embrace an organic and iterative approach to development, where even major developments consist of several small steps. After all, the prevailing wisdom is that it's easier to take a series of small steps than a giant leap.
- **Useful rather than right:** Based on the premises already covered, it's clear that we're not claiming, nor could we hope to claim, that our suggestions are objectively "right." For us, a much more meaningful criterion is whether they are useful in guiding development toward a desired direc-

tion. And in our case, the desired direction is making the economy more regenerative.
- **Practical relevance:** When discussing what could or should be changed in the economy, we acknowledge the need to share and compare our basic theoretical assumptions. Otherwise, we may find ourselves talking past each other, rather than with each other. Nevertheless, to us, it's just as important to provide practical tools that can be applied immediately. The Stellar Approach strives to balance both of these needs.
- **Beyond human supremacy:** This perspective is very important to us. We humans tend to consider ourselves the most intelligent species on the planet, while, simultaneously, we are doubtless the species that has wrought the most damage to our ecosystems. Even as we write about regenerativity in this book, we need to continually remind ourselves that ecosystems depend on many elements to enable life. And sometimes, the non-human lifeforms are wiser than us humans.

Finally, an important point we want to add: The discussion around how to further develop our economic system can quickly devolve into accusations of being politically one-sided, or even of promoting an ideological agenda. While it's of course impossible to avoid biases and projections altogether, we have made our best effort to write the Stellar Approach from a level-headed, matter-of-fact viewpoint.

We don't want to vilify the old nor glorify the new. We see our current economic system as, first and foremost, a mind-boggling cultural achievement. And at the same time, we consider it our duty to question it critically: Where has this system come from? What's useful about it, and what isn't? In what ways does it need an update or overhaul? These are the questions we need to ask if we want an economy that doesn't erode the basic necessities of life on our planet. It really is as simple as that. (But also kind of complicated at the same time.)

And on that note, we've checked in!

How we've structured this book

To help you navigate the contents of this book, we'll start with a quick overview of its structure.

Part 1 focuses on the regenerative change of the economy and on how organizations can contribute to this shift. In it, we examine our economic system and potential ways to develop it further. We also take a look at the basic transformation design that underlies the Stellar Approach.

Part 2 is dedicated to a detailed methodological description of the Stellar Approach. In it, we journey together through three workshop modules that pull together all the relevant tools and content into an easily digestible format. We also give tips on how to integrate the Stellar Approach into the broader sustainability transformation.

Finally, in **Part 3** of the book, we zoom out and adopt a systemic perspective. To create effective regenerative change, we need to go beyond the core contents of the Stellar Approach and consider additional design levels in organizations. We introduce six such levels that we regard as important going forward.

We recommend that you read the parts in sequence, as they build on top of each other. However, it's also possible to pick and choose the individual chapters that are of particular interest to you.

Why we wrote this book

For many years now, we've been exploring how organizations can contribute to the creation of a life-serving economy – an economy centered on life itself, mindful of all the processes of life on our planet. We're convinced that, in these dire times, each and every one of us is called on to make a positive difference in our respective circles of influence.

Of course, the Stellar Approach wasn't created in a vacuum. Rather, it builds on many brilliant ideas and concepts developed by others. But our aim isn't to merely provide useful tools and inspiration for the regenerative journey. We also want to encourage and embolden readers, because the regenerative transformation can only succeed if brave pioneers like you lace up their boots and join this journey.

To be clear, please don't consider this book complete, finished, or set in stone. Take the elements you find most useful and apply them in your work. Feel free to discard whatever isn't helpful. And should you find something missing or have ideas about how to make the Stellar Approach even more effective, just let us know! This way, future readers will benefit from your experiences, and you'll help them to do their part for the regenerative transformation.

Who we wrote this book for

The Stellar Approach is written for …

- Brave leaders on all levels who are ready to blaze a trail instead of waiting around for another 5–10 years to initiate a comprehensive, organization-wide transformation toward sustainability and regenerativity;
- Sustainability managers wishing to embed true sustainability and regenerativity throughout their entire organization;
- Organizational developers who plan and support transformation processes, and who have taken on the topic of sustainability;
- HR professionals wishing to understand what role they can play in the transformation toward sustainability;
- And last but not least, everyone who wants to do more than just talk, and instead take action and contribute to reshaping the economy. The pioneers, the innovators, the change-makers among us. The 3.5 percent of society that is needed to set off significant changes in the world![1]

Before we get started

We're at the end of the check-in, so it's a good time for you to ask yourself a few questions:

What does this book need to deliver, so that I would consider my decision to read it a resounding success? What are the big questions I wish to find answers to by reading this book?

Then, when you get to the end, flip back to this page to see if your expectations were fulfilled.

We hope that the Stellar Approach will serve as both a guiding compass and a practical toolbox, enabling you to start making an immediate impact in your circle of influence. There's much to do, so let's get going – one step at a time.

Part 1

Shaping the
Regenerative Change

Introduction

Let's start with a recap of the current situation: The good news is that sustainability[1] has emerged as a major issue in the world of business and the economy as a whole. The not-so-good news is that to get to this point took 50 years from the first widely publicized warnings about the danger posed by climate change.

But we're getting there. At the latest since the Paris Climate Agreement of 2015, sustainability has been steadily gaining ground as a relevant and publicly recognized issue of political, economic, and societal importance: The world is scrambling to find effective measures to curb the climate crisis. The EU has announced the *Green Deal*. CO_2 emissions are being priced, and new taxonomies and reporting standards for the economy are being rolled out. What's more, in many businesses, sustainability is such a high priority that it practically dictates the transformation agenda. Under the banner of "the sustainability transformation," companies have begun to set sustainability goals, draft decarbonization strategies, make implementation plans, and develop new business models.

So, you might now wonder, with all this happening is the problem effectively solved already? Can we roll our sleeves back down and get our hands undirty?

Not quite. Here's a less-rosy view of our current status: According to a study published in the prestigious scientific journal Nature, there's only a five percent likelihood that global warming can be limited to two degrees Celsius by the year 2100.[2] Meanwhile, biodiversity loss is happening at a dramatic and almost unstoppable rate. Social inequality is growing worse, a trend further exacerbated by the COVID-19 pandemic. The net-zero targets for companies, as well as for governments, are mostly still decades away from being hit. And according to the most recent estimate from the Social Progress Initiative, the UN's 17 Sustainable Development Goals won't be met before 2082 at the earliest.

"As we reflect on the past 20 years, it seems that everything has changed, and nothing has changed." This is how Business for Social Responsibility, a leading U. S. organization in the field of sustainable economy, described the situation in 2012.

Now, over ten years later, this conclusion may need to be more nuanced as the effects of the climate crisis have become much more visible everywhere, including in Europe and North America. Previously, the brunt of the force was felt by the Global South, which has long already suffered daily consequences from the consumption behaviors of the so-called developed countries.

But at its core, the statement still holds true: Sure, the topics of sustainability and climate protection are being discussed more broadly, and all the relevant players are ramping up their efforts. Yet, global energy consumption continues to break new records, and we're still failing to cut back global CO_2 emissions, halt the loss of biodiversity, or decrease social inequality.

Changing the rules while we play the game

Many people in the business world feel that "this sustainability thing" differs from other major challenges we've faced, like the one posed by digitalization over the last 20 to 30 years. This is because, on the one hand, the climate crisis poses a direct and existential threat to humanity.[3] And on the other because this challenge raises questions of whether societal and, above all, economic rules need to be fundamentally rewritten to meet key climate targets in the near future. Questions like: What would an economy look like that operates within our planetary boundaries, instead of constantly living beyond its means? An economy that promotes global justice rather than social inequality? Could such an economy even be considered the same one as today? And most importantly: how do we get there without jeopardizing social stability and sliding into societal chaos along the way?

It's kind of a paradox: we need to change the rules of the game while we're playing it. And unfortunately, there are no blueprints, master plans, or ready-made instructions for this. The only thing we know for sure is that, to succeed, we need the collective efforts of many players. We need the people who work *on* the systems and design legal frameworks: governments, politicians, and administrations. And we need the people who work *in* the system and can change it from the inside out: civil society, activists, citizens, as well as businesses and other organizations.

Transforming from the inside out

This is exactly where the Stellar Approach comes in. It offers a solution for organizations – actors within the system. It outlines a development path to a possible future state and helps organizations contribute, step by step, to solving the most pressing challenges, thereby also making their own business models more resilient. Importantly, the Stellar Approach recommends a direction to take, rather than dictating the outcome.

Sustainability and regenerativity are not end states to achieve, but processes to maintain. That's because no one today knows exactly what the economy of the future will look like. Many companies don't even know how they'll achieve the sustainability goals they've set for 2030 or 2045. In the Stellar Approach, we've adopted this unknowing and uncertainty into the solution: the organization embarks on a journey and learns along the way. What's useful is continued, and the less useful is discarded.

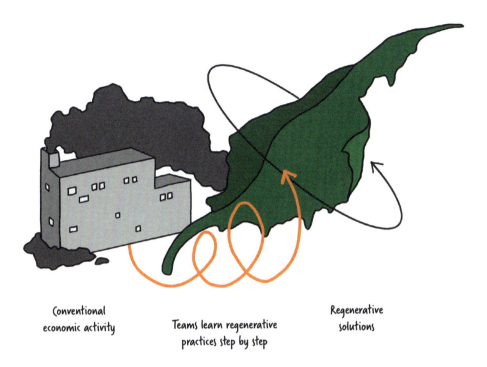

Conventional economic activity

Teams learn regenerative practices step by step

Regenerative solutions

At its core, the Stellar Approach is built for *teams*, regardless of whether they're functional, cross-functional, or leadership teams.

This is because teams are where the actual work of the organization happens. They are where decisions are made that can nudge the organization toward a more sustainable direction, or away from it. If all the teams[4] in an organization continually make their work more sustainable and regenerative, then the entire organization will also become more sustainable and regenerative. And when the established way of doing things is changed, so too changes the grand culture of the organization, thereby increasing the likelihood of further change. It's like a flywheel gathering momentum.

In the Stellar Approach, we use principles, practices, and virtues to help establish new patterns along the way. In the book, we gradually tie these three elements together.

Stellar Principles	The four Stellar Principles are our guiding stars. As design principles, they give a clear direction for the regenerative journey and help teams orient themselves along the way.
Stellar Practices	The seven Stellar Practices are the equipment that teams need along the way. With these practices, they develop the skills and habits necessary for the journey.
Stellar Virtues	The three Stellar Virtues are inner competencies that help individuals stay strong throughout the transition to regenerative economics.

Taking systemic dependencies into account

Even when working with individual teams, we still need to consider systemic dependencies. After all, teams themselves comprise multiple individuals who work together. What's more, teams don't exist in a vacuum – they're part of an organization and share the rationality of that system.

Meanwhile, the organization is part of the economic system and needs to meet the basic survival necessities of a business, at least if it operates in the private sector. And in turn, the economy impacts society and the planet. On the next page, you'll find a highly simplified illustration of these dependencies.

When companies embark on the path of sustainability transformation, they inevitably and repeatedly encounter fundamental questions that can only be answered on the level of the economy and society as a whole, or even that of the ecological system. Questions like: What about growth? Is an infinitely growing economy even possible in a finite ecosystem? To what extent are sustainability and prevailing shareholder interests compatible? Can the pursuit of profit and sustainability coexist, or must we accept that *trade-offs* are necessary? To what degree does increasing inequality threaten the social stability of the economy and society, and what can organizations do about it? These questions highlight how our current economic system opens up certain possibility spaces but also hampers access to others.

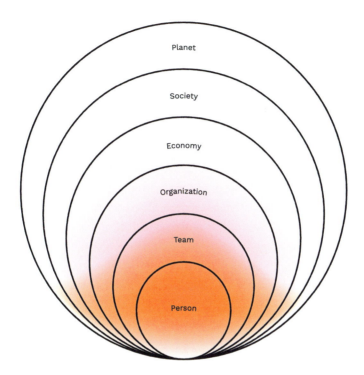

At the same time, we acknowledge that "the economy" is obviously not a static thing but constantly changing through new legislation and regulation. But more than that, change also comes from within, as individual players stretch the system's boundaries and do things differently than before, thereby establishing new patterns.

What kind of economy do we want?

It's an unavoidable fact that if we want companies to promote social justice and operate within our planetary boundaries, we need to update the core tenets of our economic system. Otherwise, they'll stand in our way, at least to a degree.

To make this update, we can't just skim the surface. We'll need to consider the fundamental system dynamics that companies currently operate under and envision a new, expanded space of possibilities. In other words, it won't be enough to just sketch out a new vision for *one* company – we need to open up new areas by expanding the canvas itself!

Of course, any profound shift will inevitably result in some goal conflicts. And these conflicts have to be identified and voiced so that we can take them and their consequences into account as we make informed decisions.

In the Stellar Approach, we operate on both the level of the organization and that of the economic system as a whole. The way we do this is by working with individual organizations, or more specifically, *teams* within organizations, to enable them to go in a sustainable – or even regenerative – direction. In this way, they can all do their part in updating the economy. This doesn't happen overnight, of course, but gradually, one step at a time.

Sustainable or regenerative?

In the Stellar Approach, we embrace the concept of a regenerative economy as a vision for the future. Later on, we'll dive deeper into what this means and what the differences between sustainable and regenerative economic practices are. But for now, here are the basics you need to know:

- Sustainable economics practices aim to mitigate the negative social and ecological impact of economic activity, reduce its ecological footprint, and thereby reach climate neutrality (Net Zero).
- Regenerative approaches focus on systemic solutions because they regard our economy, society, and planet as living, intertwined systems. The goal is to align economic activity with the fundamental principles of life, so as to support the processes that sustain life on Earth (Net Positive).
- Sustainable and regenerative approaches aren't mutually exclusive. In fact, we see sustainability as a stepping stone on the way to regenerative economic practices.[5]

In the next chapter, we'll examine our current economic system and how it might be further developed in a regenerative direction. What's more, we'll also review the current state of the world and the role of the economy in it. And we'll also venture a look into a regenerative future to see what a truly regenerative economy could look like and how we might get there.

Then, in the last chapter of this first part, we'll take a closer look at how organizations can undertake their own regenerative transformation. You'll learn about the Stellar Principles and how the Stellar Approach can support a gradual, step-by-step transformation of an organization.

A word of warning though: the thread that guides us on this journey is knotted with paradoxes. Periods of great change are always marked by contradictions and dilemmas, and we can't promise to fully unravel this tangled yarn.

What we can promise, though, is encouragement. Encouragement for you to take those first steps even when – or perhaps especially when – you can't yet know what the seventh and eighth steps will be.

Shaping the Regenerative Change

Between the "No More" and the "Not Yet"

"Regeneration offers a bold vision of the future we need to achieve, rather than the climate catastrophe we need to avoid."[1]

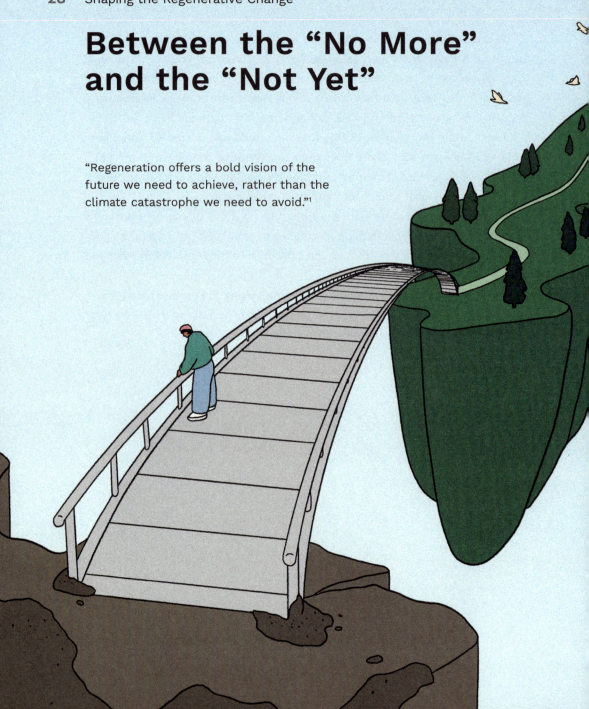

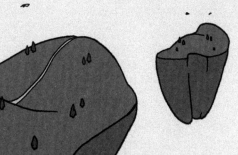

We, humanity, have led ourselves down an incredibly perilous path and now find ourselves at an important crossroads.

Today, global crises are cropping up at an alarming pace. Here's an incomplete and somewhat depressing list from the past 15 years alone: There was the financial crisis triggered by the Lehman Brothers, which was only mitigated by governments injecting huge sums of money into the financial sector. There's the climate crisis, already worsening for decades and now spiraling at an exponential rate toward a climate catastrophe. Social inequality is also worsening, with a handful of extraordinarily rich people possessing as much wealth as the poorest 50 percent of the globe. There's flagrant ecological inequality, where the richest 1 percent produce as much CO_2 as the poorest 66 percent[2]. There's the often unseen but dramatic and ongoing loss of biodiversity in the natural world. There's structural discrimination against marginalized and unprivileged groups, which, long ignored, is only today beginning to attract greater public attention. We experienced the COVID-19 pandemic, which stemmed from our own encroachment of animal habitats, spurring the rise of zoonotic diseases. Then there are geopolitical crises, where economic interests and the thirst for power seem to supersede all considerations for life on Earth. We also see various migration crises arising because parts of the Earth are becoming uninhabitable due to ecological, social, or military causes. And of course, there's the vague threat posed by artificial intelligence (AI), harboring both tantalizing opportunities and potentially uncontrollable risks.

Shaping the Regenerative Change

The numbers speak for themselves:

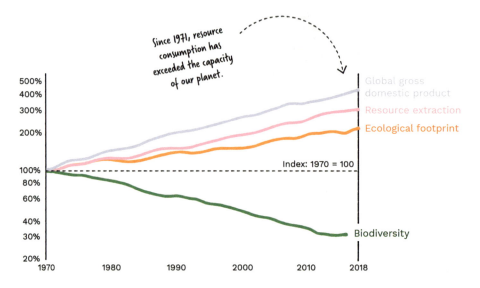

No doubt the generations before us also faced their own crises and a sense of impending doom. But there is something truly unprecedented about our current mess: its breadth and interconnectedness. Many of the crises listed above are *global* phenomena, transcending local and regional boundaries. And with the continuing devastation of the planet and its habitats, the stakes have gotten so high that human civilization, and eventually even human existence, is under serious threat. What's more, the interwoven nature of these crises means they can't be solved individually. Hence, they are often called "multiple system crises," with the terms "polycrisis" and "metacrisis" also frequently used.

Over the past few decades, the situation has gotten worse at an exponential rate, bringing a unique urgency to solving the problems. As just one of many examples, consider the climate crisis: Globally, compared to pre-industrial times, average warming is "only" 1.5 degrees Celsius or even slightly below it.[3] And yet, the effects of our current trajectory are already clearly visible around us. No one knows exactly what will happen if we hit 2.0 or even 4.5 degrees – it's basically impossible to make reliable predictions because the interdependencies between various tipping points in the global ecosystem can breed mutually-amplifying chain reactions. But it's clear that if we want to limit global warming to 1.5 degrees as per the Paris Climate Agreement, going forward the world can only afford to emit roughly 230 gigatonnes of CO_2 or CO_2 equivalents in total. And at the current rate of global CO_2 emissions, this remaining "CO2 budget" will last us less than six years.[4]

"It's the economy, stupid"

At this point, we've begun to accept that we're in a permacrisis. It's dawning on us that not only is a return to "normality" never coming, but in fact there was nothing normal about the past 50 to 100 years.

During this time, we've produced more energy than ever before in human history and achieved an unprecedented level of global productivity. But along the way we've also pushed our planet to the brink of collapse, created vast social problems, deferred problems to future generations, and ensnared ourselves in a growth trap that's proving difficult to escape from.

As individuals these problems can spark a range of feelings in us: Sometimes we're active and solution-oriented, at others incredulous and powerless. At times we're so overwhelmed we may even feel indifferent to the whole crisis. Of course, very few among us consciously *want* to see the extermination of entire species or the destruction of our planet. Yet collectively, this is exactly our impact every single day. It's as if we've engineered a system that's now taken on a momentum of its own, and there's no emergency brake to pull.

It would be overly simplistic to only blame the economy for all these global crises – the situation is far more complex than that. However, all of the crises mentioned above are related to our economic activities. That's why, in this first chapter, we will delve more deeply into the systemic dynamics of our economic system. To properly frame the concepts of "No More" and "Not Yet" mentioned in the chapter heading, we'll introduce the Three Horizons model.⁵ Just like all models, it is a simplification, but it can help us mentally map out what we see and think.

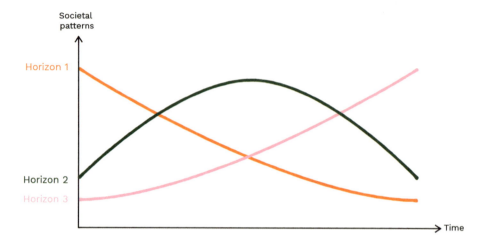

In the Three Horizons model, Horizon 1 (H1) represents the "No More" – the economy as we know it today, dominating everything else. (We can also call this paradigm *"business-as-usual."*) Our current dominant economic system can be described as neoliberal capitalism, finance capitalism, or asset capitalism. H1 systems were long seen as stable and reliable. But as the world has changed, some aspects of *business-as-usual* have begun to seem increasingly wrong and impractical. In the next chapter, we'll touch upon why the dominant capitalist economic system has always gravitated towards destabilization and crisis, and why an update is necessary – at least if we care about the survival of humanity.

"Horizon 3" (H3) represents the "Not Yet" – a new kind of economy that doesn't yet exist and still needs to evolve (*"business-as-the-world-needs"*⁶). This could be described as a sustainable economy, but in the Stellar Approach, we prefer the concept of a *regenerative* economy. In the next chapter, we'll explain what we mean by this. No one knows exactly what this kind of economy will look like or which societal shifts are necessary for it. So we need to come to terms with the fact that, although we understand the rough requirements for a viable, future-proof economy, we still need to figure out the specifics of how to implement them. The good news is that some early signs of H3 are in fact already evident today – sometimes called "pockets of the future."

Finally, "Horizon 2" (H2) represents the in-between. This bridge between H1 and H3 is where the transitional work happens, along with lots of experimentation and innovative breakthroughs. Some of these innovations are adopted by existing H1 systems and others lay the groundwork for new, radically different H3 systems. Typically, H2 is a time of uncertainty and upheaval because, effectively, the rules of the game are being changed in the middle of play. The Stellar Approach is a guide for navigating through this (H2) space, and it maps a structured development path from *business-as-usual* to *business-as-the-world-needs*. And it does all this without anyone knowing what exactly the future holds!

Reflection questions

At this point, take some time to spur your thinking by considering a few questions. Answer them from the point of view of the professional environments you know, meaning your own organization and any others that you're familiar with. Reflect on the following:
- What seems to be coming to an end? What no longer works?
- Where do I sense something new is emerging, and what's my part in it?
- Where am I contributing to a more sustainable or regenerative future, and where am I blocking one?
- What would I need in order to make an even bigger contribution to a regenerative world?

No More: Is the System Broken?

First off, we want to make it abundantly clear that the economic activities of the last two centuries have brought a swath of benefits to societal development.[7] Sure, there have been significant global disparities, but a lot of prosperity has been created. However, in recent decades, the collateral damage and dysfunctions plaguing the current economic system have become impossible to ignore.

We can see the symptoms of this daily. Our organic systems are sick, with flora and fauna under such immense stress that the ecosystems we share with them are jeopardized. Our social systems are sick, with growing societal inequality and polarization blocking collective solutions to global problems. And our mental systems are sick, with people increasingly sharing the stress of the severely burdened overarching system, as evidenced by the globally rising rates of depression and burnout.

So in effect, our current economy is on the one hand a problem solver, but on the other a problem exacerbator. And these two roles are often difficult to separate.

A (very) brief journey through recent economic history[8]

Let's rewind a bit: Before the Industrial Revolution, the consequences of economic behavior were often obvious and unavoidable. For example, if you didn't manage your resources responsibly, you probably wound up dead. Division of labor was a foreign concept, and economic activity depended largely on personal relationships. Essentially, the purpose of economic activity was to sustain your own life.

This all changed radically with industrialization. In the 18th and 19th centuries, early mercantile capitalism evolved into liberal-colonial capitalism, which gradually transformed into industrial capitalism. Then, from the post-war period up until the 1970s, the economy was heavily steered by the state. This brings us to our current era of neoliberal finance capitalism, which, in turn, is in the process of morphing into asset capitalism.[9] So what happened along the way?

As they have evolved, each of these forms of capitalism has had stabilizing but also destabilizing effects on human coexistence. And in periods of destabilization, the economic system was often bolstered by state interventions. But while these alleviated short-term problems, they often also sowed the seeds for new ones. And all through this, the two major issues with capitalism have never been resolved, but postponed time after time:

1. The rapid economic development of the last two centuries has been possible only thanks to massive energy use on a scale that exceeds the limits of our planet.
2. Growth under capitalism is driven by social inequality and exploitation that continues to this day.

Up until the 17th century, energy was mostly generated through natural processes. Agriculture was powered by the sun and rain, while longer-distance transport depended on muscle or wind power. A major shift came with European colonialism when the exploitation of people and resources in colonies made Europe enormously wealthy. Private ownership – of people, natural resources, and capital investments – was enshrined in law all over, while at the same time scientific research and technological innovation complemented each other to drive progress. Thanks to new technologies and capital investments, it became possible to produce energy at scale through the extraction and use of fossil fuels. Thus, in the 19th and 20th centuries, began the eras of "King Coal" and later "Big Oil."

The amount of energy derived from these fuels was enormous – equivalent to millions and millions of years of sunlight. This and other developments drove substantial societal changes, such as the abolishment of institutionalized slavery, increasing urbanization, and the rise of the middle class. The advent of industrial food production and the manufacture of chemical and pharmaceutical products enabled the most rapid sustained population growth in human history.

By the mid-20th century, industrialized nations had adopted the principle of economic growth as their guiding star. And after the Great Depression of the 1920s, a new socio-economic system emerged to ensure this growth: consumption. Advertising encouraged more consumption and the rise of consumer credit enabled it, thereby creating more profits, jobs, investment returns, and tax revenues. Gross Domestic Product (GDP) became the metric for measuring the economy, with central banks steering it toward the ultimate, overarching goal that we still pursue today: growth.

Then, in the early 1980s, state-directed post-war capitalism was supplemented with the concept of market liberalization. This led to globalization, increased efficiency, and the privatization of formerly state-run services and functions. The financial sector was heavily deregulated, becoming the dominant force in the economy. This same 1980s thinking was revived following the financial crisis of 2007-2008 when market growth was spurred mainly through increased borrowing, as well as austerity measures in the public sector. The result is an ever-shrinking middle class, a (relative) flattening of economic growth rates, and growing inequality. Today, we find ourselves in an economic system where wealth is primarily generated from the fluctuating value of assets, and the real economy, based on production, consumption, and exchange, has taken a back seat.

Looking at the big picture, the last few centuries have brought us unprecedented material progress. Never before have so many people enjoyed prosperity, comfort, safety, and access to knowledge. Yet at the same time, the lingering effects of systemic economic exploitation have left hundreds of millions to live in poverty. It turns out that our impressive economic progress has made us more vulnerable and fragile, both socially and ecologically: From a social perspective, the fossil-fueled industry was predicated on social inequality, temporarily benefiting a few, while causing lasting hardship for many. And from an ecological viewpoint, burning fossil fuels has changed the global climate, thereby pushing the biosphere to the brink of collapse.

The dark side of contemporary finance and asset capitalism

To better understand how the current economic system is destabilizing itself, let's take a closer look at its various dysfunctions. Given the scope of this book, we'll forgo an in-depth analysis and just focus on the essentials. If you're already familiar with this topic, feel free to skip over the next few pages and into the next chapter.

We can roughly divide the problems of our current economic system into two main categories: 1. The incomplete and distorted portrayal of reality seen through the economic lens. 2. The trend toward unlimited accumulation of wealth, increasing acceleration, and economic hegemony. Let's now briefly examine both of these key problem areas.

1. Incomplete and distorted view of reality

Ecological distortion: Negative externalities

In neoclassical economic theory, prices are determined by supply and demand. But this simple reasoning overlooks some key issues, such as the fact that certain natural resources are available for *free*. What's more, the costs from long-term damage to the ecosystem are not factored into pricing, meaning that they don't actually steer behavior. And even though this is starting to gradually change – as seen in the debate on CO2 taxation, for example – we're still a long way from a truly holistic pricing approach.

Social distortion: Unpaid labor and exploitation

It's not just ecological costs that are excluded from the economic equation, but many social contributions as well. Some of the more blatant examples of this in today's finance capitalism are in the realms of care work and raising children. Capitalist societies depend on workers who trade their labor for wages, but the work of raising and educating these prospective employees is mostly borne by private individuals or relatively underpaid professional groups.[10]

Even more glaring are the historical injustices that fuelled the rise of capitalist societies in the Global North. Present-day capitalism is directly rooted in European colonial history and slavery. Without the exploitation of other countries and people (especially in the Global South), the capitalist social order could not have taken off as it did. Unfortunately, these historical debts have never been settled and continue to echo in structural racism and exploitation today.[11] To see this in practice, you need look no further than the continued colonial-style practices in the mining of rare earth elements, the "recycling" of the waste our affluence generates, or the working conditions of most of the textile industry.

Economic distortion: Debt-driven growth

Even the economic sphere acts irrationally, conveniently distorting and deliberately ignoring reality in order to continue its obsession with economic growth – no matter the source or cost.

This gives rise to the paradoxes mentioned before. As a metric, the gross domestic product is deeply flawed: It doesn't differentiate between climate-wrecking coal power plants and responsible renewable energy producers. It goes up when a car crashes into a tree and needs repairs. It's blind to people raising children or caring for relatives alongside their jobs.

Moreover, GDP doesn't care how growth is financed. As a result, in contemporary finance and asset capitalism, debt is a key driver of growth. And this is not only true in the financial sector but also in other sectors, where debt fuels growth by enabling investments and corporate acquisitions. This trend can be seen in the Janus Henderson Corporate Debt Index, indicating that global corporate net debt grew by over 30% between 2016 and 2023, with total debt hitting a staggering USD 305 trillion in Q1 2023.

This all means that much of our current economic growth is essentially borrowed. Borrowed from invisible unpaid labor, from future generations who will shoulder the cost of the ecological damage we wreak, and also from banks and investors making a killing by financing it all. The running theme is that short-term profits outweigh long-term obligations, and it is one that we'll revisit later in the book.

Institutional distortion: Public services vs. government support

In addition to its ecological and social repercussions, capitalism also has a bizarrely paradoxical relationship with the state. For the economy to freely develop, it needs various public goods and services that states and institutions provide. These include things like infrastructure, a money supply, and a legal system that protects property rights. IT also needs the state to intervene in systemic crises, for example when companies deemed too big to fail are bailed out.

Combine this with the unquenchable thirst for wealth inherent in capitalism, and we arrive at an interesting paradox: On one hand, companies rely on state services to foster trust in the market. But at the same time, especially in today's finance capitalism, many players go to extreme lengths to evade taxes and avoid contributing to these state services.

2. Unlimited accumulation of wealth, increasing acceleration, and economic hegemony

The constant growth imperative

As alluded to earlier, when considering potential changes to our economic system, the elephant in the room is *growth*. Again, we're faced with a paradox: From an ecological standpoint, unrestrained and indiscriminate growth is untenable. At the same time, our current social stability *depends* on growth. Without it, labor markets would crumble, unemployment would soar, and states' finances and social security systems would teeter on the brink of collapse.

But is unlimited economic growth even possible on a planet with finite resources? To date, we haven't managed to decouple economic growth from energy consumption (and thus from CO_2 emissions). And while the share of renewable energy is growing, it won't solve the problem at least in the medium term, because there's no way it can meet the soaring overall demand for energy.[12]

One possible solution would be to redefine growth and prosperity to include qualitative factors in addition to quantitative ones. However, especially on the global level, this will likely be a long and rocky road.

What is all this growth, anyway?

Our current capitalist system is predicated on growth. Without it, investors and financiers have no incentive to invest their capital – it would only lose value over time. And in the early days of the industrial-capitalist era, when natural resources seemed infinite and the ecological and social consequences more hidden, growth did initially benefit large swathes of society, especially in the Global North.

Since then, we've learned about the damage that indiscriminate quantitative growth can wreak, and this has led to ever louder calls for redefining what growth means. And the discussion has been extensive: you could probably fill entire libraries with volumes debating whether and how growth should be limited or redefined. Some key terms flung around include post-growth, degrowth, green growth, qualitative growth, and good growth.

Usually, economic growth is measured by GDP, meaning the statistically calculated aggregate value of all domestically produced goods and services. In the growth debate, GDP is often criticized for its narrow focus on consumption and its failure to reflect the social or ecological ramifications of the goods and services produced. It centers on material prosperity, with practically no regard for whether the overall well-being of living systems improves.

Proponents of green growth argue that our problems could be solved by decoupling economic growth from energy use and the resulting CO_2 emissions. Put simply, the idea is that the economy can continue to grow as long as we can produce the energy required without emitting CO_2. However, those in the degrowth movement are much more skeptical, arguing that emissions are far from the only unsolved problem with growth. Rather, it begets many other systemic issues, like excessive waste production and the unethical shifting of costs abroad. Not to mention the fact that building renewable energy sources is resource-intensive. This is why the degrowthers advocate for a shift away from our efficiency-centric economy to one that embraces the concept of sufficiency. They call for limiting global material and energy use to levels that enable a good life for all but within our planetary boundaries.[13]

As it stands, sustained growth is less of a theoretical problem than a practical one. If all goods and services produced brought positive social and ecological effects, the economy could theoretically continue to grow. Of course, there would still be physical constraints to consider, such as the availability and replenishment rate of resources, as well as the rate of land use and conversion of natural ecosystems. In practice, however, making this leap is beyond us, especially in the time we have left. According to a survey, only eleven out of 36 industrialized nations managed to decouple economic growth from CO_2 emissions in the period from 2013 to 2019.[14] Moreover, the decoupling is happening far too slowly. According to the study, it would take on average 220 years for the surveyed countries to cut their emissions by 95 percent – a goal which the Paris Climate Agreement requires reaching by 2050. What's more, by then these countries would have emitted 27 times more than agreed on in the treaty. In fact, to hit the 2050 goal, on average the decoupling would have to happen at ten times the current pace.

The transition between the "No More" and the "Not Yet," is where we find ourselves face to face with a paradox: we can't succeed without growth, and we can't succeed with it. This is part of the reason why regulatory efforts struggle to contain the adverse effects of growth. And for the moment, we need to admit that this paradox is unsolvable. Until the system is fundamentally reconfigured to enable a solution, the priority must be managing growth. This effort could take the shape of political frameworks such as globally enforced sustainability criteria, stricter regulation of the financial market, or changes to taxation principles.[15] But it could also mean giving certain organizations responsibility for assessing the big picture, determining what parts of the economy can still be safely allowed to grow and what parts need to be limited.

Growing financialization

Financialization means the increasingly important role that financial markets and financial instruments play in economic growth and decisions.

Financial institutions are crucial for a functioning economy because they enable investments and act as risk-takers. But since the massive deregulation of financial markets in the 1980s, we've seen a boom in the "productivization" of money, meaning that it is expected to be productive in its own right. The "invest money to make more money" logic of financial markets is reaching into more and more areas of the real economy.[16] When it comes to economic activity, money has shifted from being a means to an end to an end in itself, because it enables further growth.

The rising importance of financial markets and instruments spawns many problems: it drives economic growth that's essentially funded by debt, siphons off money that could benefit the real economy, encourages short-term thinking, hides climate risks in complex financial products, and exacerbates social inequality through widening wealth gaps.[17]

Growing inequality

This brings us to the fundamental problem at the heart of capitalism, namely that it's faster to grow an existing fortune through investing than it is to earn one through hard work. In other words, wealth attracts wealth, and over the past few decades, this dynamic has demonstrably led to an ever-widening gap between the rich and the poor. Social inequality and its disparate privileges have become more entrenched in society. And so far, for those born into less privilege, any state efforts to redistribute wealth have been a small consolation at best.

Lately, the debate over these disparities has grown more vocal, spurred on by the problematic knock-on effects of wealth. If we consider that the richest one percent of the population emits as much CO_2 as the poorest 66 percent combined, it's obvious that the lifestyles of the rich and super-rich take a heavy toll on our planet and society – and everyone bears the cost.

The link between capitalism and privilege

Privilege is a powerful indicator of how power is distributed in society, and one of the traits of capitalism is that it tends to *create and amplify* privilege. Those with access to wealth, education, healthcare, and other advantages are usually in a better position to shape their lives as they wish and benefit from the opportunities the system provides.

Of course, privileges don't just appear out of nowhere. They have deep roots in historical social structures like feudal systems, the legacy of colonialism, the outcomes of military conflicts, or our ingrained gender roles.

Privileges are a key issue affecting the opportunities and barriers we face in developing our economic system further. Continuing marginalization and discrimination mean that important perspectives for solving today's crises often go unheard. Instead of holding intersectional and inclusive discussions, they're often held in privileged circles. Instead of listening to those most affected by issues like climate change, solutions are crafted from a privileged "we know best" standpoint, by the very people interested in maintaining power. And surprise, surprise, the resulting solutions often recreate the same old patterns and biases[18] under a new guise.

Some of the most potent privileges today are the patriarchal structures that are deeply embedded in the capitalist system. The traditional division of labor between men and women, unequal inheritance laws, and the undervaluation of care work are all gender dynamics that structurally encourage a male-dominated society. Of course, we can't fully envision what the economy or world would look like with less patriarchal influences. But it's becoming increasingly clear that to overcome the current crises, we need to urgently amplify and empower non-male voices in society.[19]

The growing money supply and pseudo-quantification

From a systems theory perspective, in our economic system, money is a medium of communication – a neutral force, by itself. However, it becomes a problem if we ignore the negative social and ecological effects of how we use money. The problem is exacerbated as more money is put into circulation, which, unfortunately, is exactly what's happening – the bulk of the global money supply today is actually "book money," meaning it's created by issuing loans. This is one of the problems created by financialization.

Another challenge with money is that it caters to our natural human urge to simplify things and reduce complexity. On the one hand, this is very useful, because it means that across the globe, we're all happy to use the same simple language of money for pricing goods and services. Unfortunately, it also often lures us into the trap of pseudo-quantification even for the unquantifiable. For example, it's easy to calculate that Person A earns 2.7 times more than Person B, or that Person C has 3.8 times more money in the bank than Person D. But this doesn't mean that Person A is 2.7 times happier, or Person C 3.8 times more satisfied, than Person B. In fact, empirical evidence suggests that financial prosperity has only a *limited* influence on personal happiness and satisfaction.[20] Nevertheless, it's tempting to think otherwise and behave accordingly.

So the act of reducing real life to monetary units oversimplifies things and fails to capture our complex reality. And yet we constantly choose to look at ecological, social, and even our internal psychological issues through the narrow lens of the economy.

On the measurable and the immeasurable

It's been suggested that economic thinking is so dominant today because money enables *universal measurability* and *comparability* – two traits that our societal model swoons over.

There's nothing inherently wrong with quantifying and measuring things. The results help us to map the terrain of life, communicate, and track changes over time. However, problems do arise if we mistake these measurements and quantifications for reality. We need to remember that whenever we measure something or convert something into quantified units, we end up with a mere sliver of reality. After all, we live in complex systems influenced by countless interactions. And no matter how badly our linear cause-and-effect reasoning pines to convince us otherwise, it's impossible to fully quantify this complexity.[21]

Take a tree, for example. Determining its economic value would be a matter of measuring the market price of its timber. But this approach completely overlooks the tree's myriad other value-creating functions for humans and other life forms: it absorbs CO_2, regulates the temperature, plays a part in the water cycle, enhances soil quality, prevents erosion, offers a rich habitat for many organisms, and so on. How would we measure a tree's economic value, if we accounted for all of this added value, instead of seeing it as just uncut timber?

Life is made up of such complex relationships that we cannot hope to comprehend them all at once. Ulti-

> mately, this very elusiveness is what gives life its dynamic and ever-changing nature. Of course, this doesn't mean that in the Stellar Approach we would forgo measuring our own impact. Rather, we simply acknowledge that our measurements can only capture a sliver of a reality too vast to ever fully perceive.

Overproduction and waste

As mentioned before, there are two interesting dynamics at play in our economic system: On the one hand, we have the growth imperative and a flawed pricing mechanism. On the other, we have the heavy dependence of state finances on tax revenue and economic growth. This combination breeds a strange effect: striving for productivity and full employment becomes more important than what is actually produced. Keeping people employed is so good for social stability that, in the short term, the effect of negative externalities is largely ignored. It's as if we've collectively decided that as long as the economy grows, tax revenue flows, and state budgets stay balanced, we can worry about the bill later.

This kind of thinking has spun up a kind of perpetual motion machine, where for the sake of economic and social stability we "need" to keep producing. Unfortunately, the machine is largely indifferent to the societal or ecological benefits – or harms – that the produced goods bring about.

Sometimes keeping the national economy ticking even leads to absurdity: it may make economic sense to produce something useless and intended to be scrapped.[22] This ludicrous dynamic perhaps helps explain why, in 2020, the weight of human-made mass on Earth actually surpassed that of the total biomass.[23]

Short-sightedness

Economic performance is typically measured in short time frames: daily news on the ups and downs of stock markets, quarterly reports, annual financial statements, and overarching economic growth reviews on a monthly or yearly basis. These rhythms greatly influence the economy, and stock markets, and the algorithms that drive them react sharply to unexpected changes. As a result, economic activity tends to focus on the short term, meaning the next few months or, at most, the coming year.

As we've hopefully made abundantly clear already, this short-term focus is highly problematic. The short cycles of the economy are out of sync with the longer ones needed by, for example, our natural ecosystems to recover and regenerate.[24] As a result, we lose sight of the long-term ramifications of our actions, delay tackling urgent problems, and delude ourselves that all is well.

To really understand the damage that our short-term thinking has caused, a good thought exercise is to scale down the Earth's 4.6 billion-year history to 46 years. On this scale, humans have been around for about four hours. The Industrial Revolution, and with it the start of modern economic history, began just a minute ago. And in the past 30 seconds, we've devoured over 50% of the resources at our disposal, with some of them lost forever.

Clearly, it's imperative that we redesign our economic system to account for the long-term consequences of our actions.

Economic hegemony

One of the strengths of the capitalist system has always been adapting and absorbing new aspects of life into the realm of its economic logic of exploitation. Over the past few decades, the economic mindset has permeated many new areas, regardless of its suitability for them.

Today, it's not just businesses that operate on the principles of profitability and performance. We're also restructuring our education systems based on economic yardsticks and optimizing our healthcare systems for financial profit. Even our private lives aren't immune to economic principles: we monitor the quality of our sleep and gauge our self-worth by the number of likes we get on social media. We also feel pressure to use our time "meaningfully" – a criterion all too often defined based on some cost-benefit ratio.

Given how out of place economic thinking is in many areas, it's inevitable that goal conflicts will arise. At worst, the economic mindset might even run completely counter to the fundamental mission of specific subsystems (like in healthcare or education, for example), effectively leading their form and function to diverge.

The crumbling narrative of growth, progress and success

In summary: When compared to the span of human history, our current economic system is a relatively new development. The rapid industrialization and significant economic growth of the past century were driven by a fossil fuel frenzy that accelerated nearly all human activity, bringing with it an array of as-yet unresolved ecological issues. More recently, the astounding growth of the last few decades has been mainly driven by exponential profits fuelled by a deregulated financial system and our irresponsible and continued deferral of costs to the future. Since we who live on the planet today were born into this era, we view this acceleration as "normal." But zoom out just a little bit to the grand narrative of human history, and you'll see that it's a highly unusual anomaly.

There are also psychological and cultural aspects to our dependence on growth. For decades, economic growth has been synonymous with progress and success, a narrative promoted by advertisers, corporations, and politicians. As a result, many people consider a lack of growth to signal decline and failure.

The oft-touted narrative we hear is that future generations will always have it better. And for several decades, it's held true. But lately, this once-alluring promise of capitalism has begun to increasingly ring hollow, as our ever-rising standard of living is overshadowed by the hard-to-ignore threat of socio-ecological collapse. The consequences of our exuberant lifestyles are borne by our ecosystems, our health, and by coming generations deprived of a livable future. The metastasizing polycrisis underscores a fundamental truth: our survival hinges on the health of our planet. No planet, no people; no people, no economy. This hierarchy is inescapable and immutable.

No More: Is the System Broken?   49

Sustainability 1.0
Shareholder Value

Social and ecological considerations are seen as a means to an economic end.

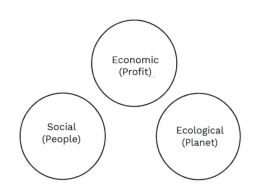

Sustainability 2.0
Stakeholder Value

All business activities are carried out with equal consideration for economic, ecological, and social goals.

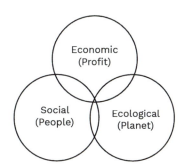

Sustainability 3.0
System Value

The goal is not only to avoid negative effects but to make a positive contribution.

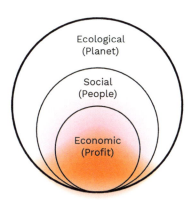

On endings and death

In today's economy, our mindset and behavior are dominated by themes of growth and new beginnings. Of course, we know that everything that begins must eventually come to an end. But good luck seeing that fact in the innovation-driven growth curves that only ever point up and to the right.

Is it a coincidence then that, along with the rise of the capitalist economic system, we've seen a gradual shift in attitudes towards death, especially in Western societies? Death has become a taboo subject for us, something to be pushed out of sight and mind. This attitude is reflected in our treatment of the elderly, in our desperation to prolong life and avoid aging, and in our considerable mental acrobatics to avoid acknowledging the truth of our mortality.

The connection between capitalism and our denial of death seems apparent. We know that nature, of which we are all a part, evolves in repeated cycles of growth and decay, of birth and death. However, in the realm of the economy, death is a much rarer occurrence. Sometimes organizations are kept alive even though they no longer serve any beneficial societal purpose. And ailing systems are propped up just to safeguard the narrative of progress and growth.

But imagine what an economy would look like if endings and death were seen as equally natural and necessary components as new beginnings and growth. To truly embrace a regenerative mindset, we need to not only reconcile our economy with the planet but also come to terms with our own mortality. It's a bigger topic that we'll expand on when we dive into the Stellar Principles of regenerative organizations.

In the title of this chapter, we asked if the system is broken. Well, is it?

The economic system is continuing to do an excellent job sustaining itself within the scope of the current rules of the game. The global economy is growing, and when any major systemic crisis strikes, states come to the rescue. So, instead of using the word "broken," it's perhaps more accurate to say that the system is up and running. In the context of the Three Horizons model, financial and asset capitalism clearly constitute the globally dominant system occupying Horizon 1 (H1). It's all *business-as-usual*, in other words.

At the same time, it's becoming increasingly hard to ignore the social and ecological threat posed by the system's flaws. We've long managed to defer paying the Pied Piper in this regard, but now he stands right behind our door, his knocking growing ever more insistent. Soon, splinters will fly. In other words, it's becoming harder and harder to hide the fact that the growth we see doesn't just bring technological and economic advancement, but is also driving rising social inequality, unsustainable demands for productivity, and ecocide on a global level.

In this chapter, we discussed how our current economic system, despite its many undeniable positives, is contributing to social and ecological destabilization. In the next chapter, we'll explore ways that the economic system could evolve to transcend these dysfunctional effects.

Reflection questions

- How am I doing in the current economic system? Where does it make me happy in my own life? Where does it make me unhappy?
- What privileges or comforts do I enjoy thanks to our economy that I would be reluctant to let go?
- Which of the downsides outlined in this chapter are evident around me? How do they impact me personally?
- When I consider both sides – the negative and the positive – what's the overall picture that forms in my head?

Not Yet: The Dawn of a Regenerative Economy

When we think about the future, the question "What would a desirable future be?" can be overshadowed by the inevitable follow-up: "And how do we get there?" So for a moment at least, let's disentangle these two important questions. Otherwise, we'll get bogged down in a swamp of "But we can't do that!" debates, conceptual path dependencies, and unmanageable complexity – all before we've even taken the first step! But if we instead start by openly conceiving a desirable future, that vision may be powerful enough to pull us toward it.

Fortunately, the Three Horizons model introduced earlier can help us to separate the what and how questions. There's the "viable future," or Horizon 3, which seems a long way off from where we stand today. Meanwhile, Horizon 2 represents the inevitable transition on the way there. In the next section, we'll tackle the question of how this transition could happen. But before that, let's take a closer look at the third horizon: what might an economy look like that transcends the dysfunctions of today's economic system?

To properly answer this question, we could dive down a well of complexity, considering it from political, economic, ethical, systemic, individual, psychological, or even spiritual perspectives.

Alternatively, we can opt for a far simpler starting point: *A beneficial and viable economic system cares for all humans on the planet and aligns with the immutable principles of life. It actively contributes to the health of the Earth and the organisms that inhabit it.*

A thought experiment: imagining a good future

Imagine, for a moment, a different kind of world: One in which the economy is based on rules that ensure it operates only within planetary boundaries. A world where companies genuinely care about the well-being of the planet and society at large, and this shows not only in their communication but also in the concrete and sincere actions they take. They limit what they extract from ecological and social systems to what they can give back. Many of them operate business models that actively contribute to the recovery of our battered ecosystems. Meanwhile, the global energy supply is completely based on renewable technologies.

Consumers are no longer forced to make a trade-off between a product being cheap and environmentally friendly. Instead, they can rest assured that almost all of the products and services on offer align with the well-being of life on this planet. Instead of endless spending, we focus more on the joys of life that cost nothing: human connection, learning, physical activity, love, conversation, contemplation, time spent in nature, and many others.

The legal framework has been adjusted worldwide so that business models that damage the planet or social cohesion in the long term are either unprofitable or consistently penalized. When we look back at the economy of the early 2000s, we wonder how we ever even thought that the old way of doing business was good for us as a society.

Everyone has contributed to this transformation, and we've succeeded in fundamentally changing the rules of the economy: Governments have modified the regulatory framework and introduced new effective steering mechanisms. Civil society has pushed for climate targets to be reached more quickly and for getting back on track with the Paris Climate Agreement. Companies have developed new business models, because the old ones weren't sustainable anymore, even from a purely economic standpoint.

Although the Earth is still warming due to the slow breakdown of atmospheric CO_2, we've succeeded in stopping deforestation, undertaken massive reforestation efforts, and reduced urban density, thereby helping us to somewhat cope with the higher average temperatures.

We benefit from a balanced interplay between global networking and decentralized supply systems. Meanwhile, companies themselves have also become increasingly decentralized and often smaller in size, leveraging digital tools to collaborate with each other. The resulting network of small companies has proved just as efficient as a big corporation, while also being more adaptive and flexible to external demands for change.

Technology still plays an important part in this world, but it's designed in a way that's mindful of its impact on people and our critical ecosystems. As a result, it contributes to our psycho-social well-being and the health of our natural systems.

The industrial and transportation sectors have not only been decarbonized but they've also been organized more intelligently thanks to digital technologies. As urban traffic congestion declines and nature reclaims more space, we all enjoy breathing cleaner air. Rural areas experience a renaissance thanks to decentralization and regionalization fostering new, smaller community hubs. As a result, regional cooperatives flourish.

We humans have the option to work less, as state revenue doesn't primarily depend on taxing consumption and work anymore. Consequently, people no longer measure their worth through their jobs and careers. This also eases the anxiety of certain roles being replaced by digital solutions and AI, allowing some so-called "bullshit jobs"[25] to disappear.

We've taken a critical look at privileges in order to right unfair disparities, and we make sure that decisions are made based on a broad range of perspectives. We've realized that diversity and inclusion make our societies more resilient and that by bringing together different viewpoints, we get better outcomes for all.

Does that sound like a utopia? Of course, it does. From where we stand today, this world is so distant it may as well be in another universe. In fact, in many ways, what we have today is the *exact opposite* of what was described.

Nevertheless, it's well worth asking yourself what a truly aspirational vision for our economy could look like. A vision where our battered planet and exhausted societies are regenerated. A vision where the harmonious coexistence of all life on Earth is paramount. A vision that leads to greater happiness and quality of life for all, which is something that today's economic metrics barely even capture.

From sustainability to regenerativity

The above vision for the future is often referred to as one of a "regenerative economy." This relatively new term has no universally agreed-upon definition yet, and real-world examples are few and far between. It's safe to assume that the concept will continue to change and evolve over the coming years.

In the Stellar Approach, we use the concept of the regenerative economy as a beacon to aim for. Of course, we won't get there overnight, but it's still worth taking a closer look at this potential future scenario. After all, we can only go full speed ahead when we know the right heading.

So, what does a "regenerative economy" actually mean? And how is regenerative economic activity different from sustainable economic activity? As we can see from the graph, the bulk of today's economy could be described as being in the "conventional" stage of development. And this makes perfect sense in the context of our current economic system: legal requirements are complied with, but there's little reason for anyone to go beyond that since it would just mean added short-term cost and less profit. However, as soon as we factor in social and ecological dependencies, our economic activity tends to evolve further along the graph toward regenerativity.

And in many sectors, there are already forces at work driving this kind of development. Many companies are going beyond mere legal requirements

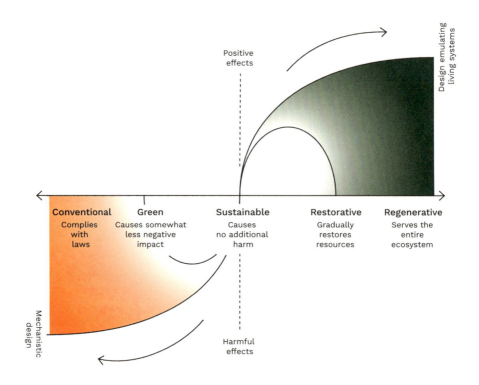

and weaving sustainability into every aspect of their strategy and operations. The reasons for this are varied:

- Decision-makers are grappling with the ethical dilemmas that arise when they consider the fate of future generations or that of their own children.
- Customers' needs and requirements are changing, and they expect more emphasis on sustainability.
- Employees' expectations are changing: they want a clear sense of purpose in their work and to make a real difference for the environment. This is especially true for younger generations.
- Investors are more focused on sustainability criteria, so companies falling short are finding it costly to raise capital.

- The economic costs of our inaction are becoming ever more visible and tangible. In other words, we find the costs of operating in a sustainable or generative way, long deferred, now waiting at our doorstep.
- New competitors are disrupting the market by offering sustainable solutions from the get-go.
- Last but not least, the regulatory landscape is also evolving, changing the rules of the game through new legal requirements.

In the traditional concept of sustainability, the goal is typically to avoid causing additional damage ("do no harm"). That's why sustainable practices focus on mitigating negative effects and reducing the ecological footprint. The end goal is to achieve climate neutrality, meaning net zero CO_2 emissions. Overall, sustainability strives for an equilibrium between economic, social, and ecological considerations, facilitated by a so-called "triple bottom line."

Where sustainability falls short

Sustainability is here to stay. As a topic, it's climbing higher on political and corporate agendas. And as awareness of the problems continues to spread, sustainability is growing increasingly prominent in public discourse too.

Unfortunately, though, many past efforts around sustainability have yet to yield actual outcomes, especially on the global level. What's more, because of the extensive damage we've wrought in the past few decades, merely avoiding more harm is no longer enough. Many ecosystems teeter so close to collapse that their swift restoration is imperative.

So far, sustainability alone has failed to restore a healthy balance between the economy, the planet, and society. To explain why, we want to highlight three key reasons that are particularly important in the context of the Stellar Approach. And all of them relate to our ability to think in terms of systems.

1. Sustainability seeks to mitigate or avoid harm **within the paradigm of today's economic system**. The thinking is that as long as growth is

green growth, the problem is solved. Unfortunately, this doesn't really tackle many of the fundamental issues we've discussed before, but rather just postpones them. As long as the global economic system is structured the way it is today, there will inevitably be hard-to-solve conflicts between profit and sustainability. Recognizing these dilemmas is the first necessary step toward genuine sustainable (or regenerative) change.

2. Sustainability tends to overlook the **multifaceted systemic relationships** between our current environmental and social challenges. Instead of examining the relationships between components, we focus on the individual components themselves. This means that even though we may have the best of intentions when trying to fix an individual problem, we can still inadvertently cause harm elsewhere because we do not and cannot see the big picture.

    For example, the climate catastrophe is often treated as a simple technical issue: "If the problem is that CO_2 emissions are too high, then we'll solve it through decarbonization." Now, while it's true that we need to decarbonize the economy, this approach ignores the interconnectedness between issues like the climate crisis, our consumer culture, global social injustices, the rebound effects of new technologies that diminish their impact, and the self-destabilizing character of our economic system. If we want to overcome the current polycrisis (or at least mitigate its effects), we need to understand that all these crises are closely interrelated. And this requires a systemic and intersectional perspective – one that recognizes, all at once, the various interfaces and connections between these crises.

    Moreover, the concept of sustainability often instrumentalizes nature.[26] The natural world is seen as something at our disposal: a vast reservoir we can draw resources from to produce goods. In this mindset, any excessive damage we cause can simply be compensated for somewhere else. Again, this overlooks the fact that the planet operates like a giant network – one that includes us humans. This means that systems can only substitute or compensate for each other to a limited extent. In other words, we need an approach that appreciates the mutual dependencies of nature, instead of instrumentalizing it. This could be considered a step forward in our approach, but in many ways it's actually us reverting to an understanding we once long held.

3. Last but not least, when **organizations tackle the issue of sustain-**

ability, they too tend to ignore systemic relationships: Sustainability work happens in isolation and siloes, instead of as an interdisciplinary effort. Centralized departments are set up to control the process, instead of embracing a decentralized co-creation effort. Procedural and technological innovation takes priority, leaving the necessary cultural innovation out of scope. We'll revisit these points in more detail when we discuss the transformation design of the Stellar Approach in the third chapter.

By contrast, restorative and regenerative economic practices broaden our horizons with a systemic perspective. They go beyond an instrumental view of nature and see the planet and life as a vast, self-regulating metabolic process, teeming with interaction between the individual parts. In a restorative economy, the focus is on gradually restoring essential ecosystems. This will be an urgent task for the coming decades if we want to ensure some kind of baseline minimum global quality of life. As the graph shows, the restorative phase also serves as a bridge to the regenerative stage of development on the far right of the graph. This stage initially focuses on what could best be described as "clean-up work," but this should eventually diminish as all economic activity centers on contributing positively to life on Earth (Net Positive).

A regenerative economy would still strive to develop and grow, of course, but this growth would look quite different – more akin to flourishing in the natural world. There would be a general understanding that, to enable this flourishing, one's own environments need to be positively developed too.

Planetary boundaries and the concept of a "safe and just space"

The defining trait of a regenerative economy is the fundamental understanding that we're embedded in and connected to various environments. This kind of economy reflects its myriad relationships with its environments and ensures that they stand in healthy balance for all.

Of course, the planet, with its multitude of ecosystems, constitutes the broadest of those environments. And in 2009, a group of scientists led by Johan Rockström from the Stockholm Resilience Center defined the planetary boundaries framework. It distinguishes between nine different planetary boundaries, each of which is vital to human survival: climate change, biosphere integrity, freshwater use, land use, biogeochemical flows, novel entities, air pollution, ocean acidification, and ozone depletion. The framework has been further refined since then, and in 2023, for the first time ever, all nine boundaries were successfully quantified. The results showed that, globally, already six out of nine had been crossed.[27]

To understand the gravity of this, you should know that these planetary boundaries are absolute, non-negotiable limits based on our best scientific knowledge.[28] Sustained breaches of these limits will destabilize vital systems for human survival. And this danger is exacerbated further by two other factors: First, there are tipping points in ecological subsystems, which, once crossed, can result in irreversible effects that can spiral out of control. Second, the sheer number of interactions between these subsystems greatly amplifies the non-linearity and unpredictability of any change.

The framework also defines a "safe operating space for humanity," meaning the maneuvering room we have. The boundaries have been defined in such a way that as long as we stay within them, based on our current understanding, it's unlikely we'll cross any tipping points. But beyond this safe space lies the "zone of uncertainty," where the risks become more unpredictable. And lest we forget: enacting any countermeasures would also take time.

Building on the concept of planetary boundaries, economist Kate Raworth proposes a definition for the regenerative economy with Doughnut Economics. In the Doughnut model, she supplements the planetary boundaries with the concept of the social foundation, derived from the UN's Sustainable Development Goals.

Not Yet: The Dawn of a Regenerative Economy   61

The idea is that whereas we need to stay below planetary boundaries, we must also stay above social boundaries.

The end result is a doughnut-shaped space that's ecologically safe and socially just – the "safe and just space."

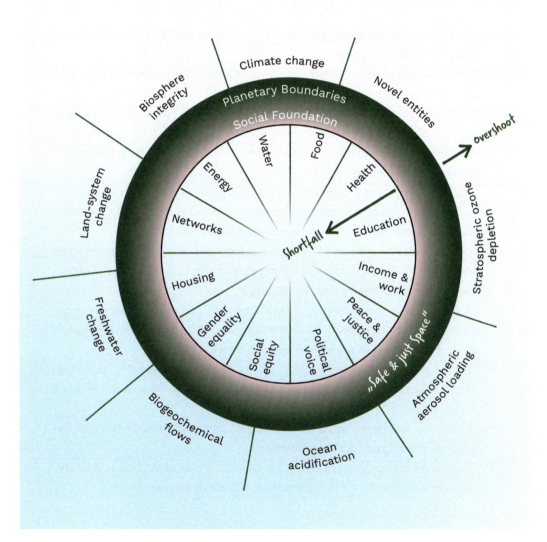

Key dimensions of a regenerative economy

By this point, you've probably got some idea of what a regenerative economy could look like. Let's complete this picture by summing up some of its key elements:

- The key message is that a regenerative economy sees itself as an **embedded part** of life and nature.
- From this perspective, humans are part of a network of relationships and **mutual dependencies**.
- **Resource use** happens within planetary boundaries, based on the carrying capacity of local ecosystems.
- **Progress** isn't measured by an unwavering rise in consumption but by our qualitative development and well-being.
- Economic activity is fundamentally **circular**. This is not just true of physical resources but also of intangibles like information and the opportunity to access things like education, healthcare and the like.
- **Natural, cultural, and social values** are seen as non-negotiable prerequisites for financial value creation. Financial capital is deployed to preserve these values and ensure their continuity.[29]
- There's a deep understanding of **systems** and the complex interrelationships that comprise them. There's no impulse to "control" these systems but rather to steward their development responsibly.
- Ecological and social responsibility are viewed **intersectionally**, as it's understood that a truly resilient world can only stand on a foundation of justice, equality, diversity, and inclusion.
- There's an emphasis on decentralized solutions tailored to the specific needs of **places and local communities.**
- There is a keen awareness of the **long-term effects** of economic activity. The relevant time frame is not quarters, but generations.

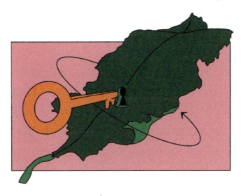

In many ways, a regenerative economy represents a more mature version of our current one. After all, isn't it naive, or even downright childish, to cling tooth and nail to prosperity and privilege, despite the blatant problems that today's economic activity creates? It's akin to a toddler demanding to build a snowman in the summer, oblivious and intransigent to the fact that there's no snow to be had.

To be clear, this doesn't mean we need to tear down the current economic system. Rather, in light of the consequences we're witnessing, we need to develop it in a mature and responsible way. This update process won't be linear, nor is there a magic formula that will cure all ills. What we do know, however, is that it will require a collaborative, co-creative mindset and including all relevant perspectives. The key question to ask is: how can we solve this together?

Imagining an economy that understands its role as a part of life – a small foray into our basic assumptions

Every major paradigm shift in history has come hand in hand with a change in mindset. This is no less true when it comes to seeing the economy as a part of life. To get there, we need to be willing to question our basic assumptions and zoom out to see the importance of our relationships with others. In our view there are two particularly important mental shifts when transitioning from degenerative to regenerative economic practices:

From linear thinking to systems thinking

Ever since philosophical rationalism emerged in the 17th century, our efforts to explain the world have largely centered around the themes of cognition, science, and classification.[30] This scientific approach has brought many benefits, including advances in natural sciences, mathematics, and astronomy, which in turn have helped us understand the complex, hidden connections in the natural world. However, this worldview often explains the world using linear cause-and-effect relationships: "If A, then B." And while this input/output model is useful in some cases, it also tends to oversimplify the complexity of life and downplay the plethora of interdependencies that comprise it.

The current polycrisis is exposing the shortcomings of this simple cause-and-effect thinking, as the crises are too intertwined to be solved with linear thinking. More than ever, we need the ability to solve problems from a systems perspective.

In a systemic view, the focus shifts from the individual components to the connections between them, reflecting the understanding that life's vitality stems from the relationships and their quality. Here, the aforementioned two-dimensional input/output reasoning unfolds into multi-dimensional thinking, where the fabric of life is weaved by networks of interdependent nodes. Of course, cause-and-effect dynamics won't disappear, but they should be complemented with an understanding of the vast mutual dependencies that they overlook.

Today though, the economy is still built on these linear if-then assumptions. Supply and demand, market action, and ultimately even the concept of "Homo economicus" are derived from this simplistic means-end rationality. As a result, other existing dependencies are deprioritized, because the simple model can't take into account multiple relationships at once.

But as our awareness of mutual dependencies grows, so does our ability to deal with simultaneity. While cause-and-effect relationships are always defined by a chronological before and after, this distinction isn't as clear in networks of mutual relationships. Hence, it's often said that in contrast to linear "either/or" thinking, complex environments require more of a "both/and" approach.

From exploitation to stewardship

Whereas the first paradigm shift broadens our spatial perspective, from a two-dimensional to a multidimensional one, the second relates to our temporal viewpoint. As mentioned earlier, it can be eye-opening to occasionally consider one's own life as part of the vast narrative of life itself.

As we zoom out in time, it's easy to see that we don't "own" the Earth. Nor do we even own our lives, at least not in the same sense as we own a pair of shoes. For a few decades, we get to play our part in this basically endless story of life, and then we must leave the stage. So it's easy to see that life, as a whole, is something far greater than any individual existence. With that in mind, our role is perhaps best described as that of a steward, caring for something more important than ourselves.

Observed through the narrow lens of a human lifespan, it's sometimes difficult to see this long-term view. In fact, our current social and economic systems encourage the exact opposite: We find ourselves surrounded by mechanisms delivering a constant stream of quick rewards. These can be financial, or also social, as is the case with the dopamine hit we get from online attention. In this kind of society, the ability to think beyond our own generation is not a given, unless we're willing to take responsibility. And yet at the same time, this kind of long-term thinking is more important than ever – the unfolding ecological crisis will increasingly necessitate measures that will mostly only be felt by future generations.

Are we in a crisis of consciousness?

The paradigm shifts described above bring us closer to the fundamental questions of life. When we speak of consciousness in the heading above, we mean the inner place from which we humans view the world. Regardless of whether we approach it via the lens of spirituality or quantum physics, we find ourselves in a realm where the explanatory models of empirical science fall short, necessitating alternative explanations.

When it comes to dealing with crises, our modern civilization is all about "doing something." We're like external observers who instinctively focus on measures to implement, technologies to innovate, or actions to undertake.

In doing so, we overlook the fact that we ourselves are these crises. Each day, every tangible action we take is preceded by an intangible thought or feeling in consciousness. In other words, we create reality from the inner perspective in which we experience it, meaning that the internal and external are in constant interplay.

Describing the regenerative economy, Satish Kumar writes: "... all good regenerative businesses are built on four pillars: ecological, social, spiritual and financial."[31] Likewise, Otto Scharmer identifies three key divides that need to be bridged for humanity to continue to develop here on Earth: the ecological divide, the social divide, and the spiritual divide.[32]

In our outward-focused world, it can easily feel like inner development is a waste of time. Yet, several studies on mindfulness practices and meditation have demonstrated that inner development helps us act with greater clarity, generosity, love, and compassion. It fosters a strong connection with ourselves, others, and the world, thereby enabling us to act from a place of connection.

Happily, the choice between external measures and internal development is not either/or. In fact, there's a strong case to be made that leading a life that's in balance and harmony with ourselves and all other living systems is only possible if we take our inner development seriously and make space for it. That's why, in the Stellar Approach, we don't solely focus on tangible, externally-directed methods, but also on our inner "equipment" for the journey. This work will happen at the levels of self-contact (I with myself), relational capacities (I with you), and field competencies (I with the world).[33]

Redefining success

It's clear that if we're serious about the principles of regenerative economic activity, we need to completely redefine organizational success. Currently, success is measured mostly via immediate economic profit, with barely any consideration for the impact on surrounding environmental systems. This holds especially true in the private sector, where a company is deemed profitable as long as it's in the black and delivers good shareholder returns. Unfortunately, the planet is not invited to the shareholder meetings.

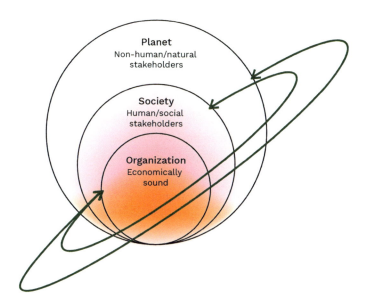

In a regenerative economy that understands itself as a part of life, the success of life as a whole supersedes mere economic success. This means that an otherwise profitable business model that damages vital ecosystems can no longer be considered successful. Rather, success requires "both/and" thinking: in addition to being economically sound, the company needs healthy relationships with the human and non-human stakeholders that surround it. Put simply, regenerative businesses earn money by solving more problems than they create.

Shaping the Regenerative Change

So how can we measure success in this holistic way? Let's take a quick tour of some potential methods.

Multi-Capital Accounting

In order to bridge the gap between today's economy and a regenerative one, a frequent proposal is to convert non-monetary forms of capital – such as natural capital, social capital, and cultural capital – into monetary units that can be included in financial calculations. Whether this is sensible or even feasible is a subject of debate, but, so far at least, there's no legal standard for including non-monetary forms of capital in an organization's profit and loss statement.

In recent years, several methods for holistic capital accounting have been developed under the umbrella term "multi-capital accounting." For example, the LIFTS model ("Limits of Foundations Towards Sustainability") is based on the doughnut framework. The "Triple Footprint Thesaurus" method proposes a new balance sheet that includes non-financial elements. The CARE model ("Comprehensive Accounting in Respect of Ecology") distinguishes between economic, ecological, and social capital and recommends adopting an integrated balance sheet. The "Common Good Balance Sheet" is another model aiming to quantify corporate success beyond mere financial metrics.[34]

Success criteria for regenerative business models: Some initial indicators

Organizations still struggle to operate in a fully regenerative way, in part because we're still in the process of defining what a regenerative business model could even look like. One meta-study analyzing various approaches to regenerative economic action proposed the following definition:

"... Organizations with regenerative business models focus on planetary health and societal wellbeing. They create and deliver value at multiple stakeholder levels—including nature, societies, customers, suppliers and partners, shareholders and investors, and employees—through activities promoting regenerative leadership, co-creative partnerships with nature, and justice and fairness. Capturing value through multi-capital accounting, they aim for a net positive impact across all stakeholder levels."[35]

Sounds pretty complicated, right? But this lengthy definition actually contains many helpful points for making the concept of regenerative economic activity more tangible:

1. The health of the planet and societal well-being are not just afterthoughts but rather the focus of the business model.
2. The emphasis isn't just on economic stakeholders – customers, suppliers, investors, and so forth – but on all stakeholders that the organization has a relationship with, whether human or non-human.
3. Regenerative leadership encourages and makes room for developing and testing regenerative approaches.
4. In regenerative business models, creating value also helps non-human nature flourish, making it a co-creative partnership of sorts.
5. To foster these co-creative partnerships with nature, owners and investors allocate a large chunk of their financial returns into non-monetary forms of capital and natural capital in particular.
6. Organizations with regenerative business models advocate for justice and fairness on many different strata, such as nature, society, employees, shareholders, and investors.

Absolute, context-sensitive metrics

Going forward, to truly gauge the impact of an endeavor, we'll need to understand whether we're increasing or decreasing the health of the overall system we find ourselves in. This requires defining context-sensitive metrics and absolute threshold values for them. So for example, when it comes to planetary boundaries, we know that consuming natural resources or introducing novel entities into ecosystems can only happen within a set budget that's determined by our best scientific knowledge. There's also growing support for the idea that social metrics too need specific threshold values, such as the local living wage.

ESGs, CSRD, ESRS – Regulatory steps toward a regenerative economy?

In any discussion around companies and the environment, sooner or later, ESGs are bound to come up. These environmental, social, and corporate governance concerns have quickly skyrocketed into public awareness, and they're already applied in many spaces: Investors use ESG ratings to evaluate their investments. Businesses define an ESG strategy to manage opportunities and risks related to sustainability. Consultancies and accounting firms support their clients in questions around ESG-related risks, compliance, and value growth. Wherever you turn, it's plain to see that ESGs are on a roll.

In fact, the three letters have also made their way into the regulatory lexicon. For example, as a part of the EU's Green Deal, many frameworks have been developed to encourage sustainable business. Some of them even show the first signs of a restorative or regenerative understanding of the economy. In this regard, two other ESG-related acronyms play an especially significant part: CSRD and ESRS.

The Corporate Sustainability Reporting Directive (CSRD) and the European Sustainability Reporting Standard (ESRS) regulate the nature and scope of sustainability reporting and non-financial reporting by companies in the EU. Importantly, the regulations incorporate the concept of "double materiality." This means companies need to assess both the actual and potential impact of their business activities on sustainability issues, as well as the impact of sustainability issues on their business model, strategy, and revenue. An issue is deemed material – thereby requiring it to be reported – if it impacts either area.

Encompassing over 1 000 data points that range from biodiversity to inclusion, these frameworks go well beyond portraying sustainability as a mere matter of CO_2 emissions and decarbonization. What's more, the directives explicitly mention restorative and even reparative aspects.[36] Thus, we can say that current EU legislation includes elements of a regenerative understanding that will likely become mandatory in the future.

But do these regulations actually promote a regenerative economy? A vocal choir of critics isn't convinced: ESG criteria have been denounced as being too open to interpretation, making it too easy to market a product as sustainable and engage in greenwashing. And there are also other concerns regarding the laxness of the EU standards: For example, initially only companies with 500 employees or more need to adhere to EU reporting regulations. Moreover, indirect emissions in the value chain (also known as Scope 3 emissions) can be ignored until 2028. And finally, disclosing the materiality or immateriality of certain climate-related aspects is voluntary for now. As yet, it's unclear whether these regulations will be tightened and when.

It's also unclear whether regulations for more comprehensive measurement and reporting will actually move us toward regenerativity. What is clear is that none of the approaches presented above have yet succeeded in integrating sustainability considerations into the standard tools of corporate accounting. Whether mandatory or not, companies are currently introducing new calculations and reports *alongside* their balance sheets or income statements. This means that there's no single framework for addressing conflicts between profit and sustainability, necessitating that different accounting and reporting mechanisms be weighed against each other.[37]

The regenerative narrative: Do we need new heroes?

The question of how we measure success isn't just a technical question. The answer influences what kind of narratives we embrace as a society. What success stories do we tell ourselves in today's economy, versus a regenerative one? Who will be the new heroes and what will their tales be? Will we laud the 100x growth stories, regardless of the towering environmental cost? Or will we rather tell stories of individuals and business models that were dedicated to the welfare of all life on this planet?

A regenerative understanding of the economy is a good step toward overcoming the ecological and social dysfunctions of today's economic system. Of course, from where we stand now (H1), a regenerative economy (H3) seems like a distant utopia. And a vague one at that – no one knows exactly what this future economy will look like. But it's already clear that if we want a viable and resilient society, we can't keep postponing our response to the big challenge. We need to learn how to transform our current economic practices so they don't drive massive social inequality and disastrous ecological damage. Moreover, we need to understand *who* can contribute to this change and *where*.

In this chapter, we've explored the prevailing understanding of what a regenerative economy constitutes and envisioned what a future-proof update to today's economic system could look like.

Knowing the pitfalls of the *business-as-usual* approach and keeping a vision of *business-as-the-world-needs* in mind, we'll move on to the next chapter, which addresses the transition – the second horizon.

Reflection questions

- How would I personally be able to tell that if the economy operated in harmony with all of Earth's living systems? What would be different from today?
- What signals do I see around me that suggest a shift toward a regenerative economy is occurring?
- How could I promote a regenerative direction in the context of my work, using my own circle of influence?

74 Shaping the Regenerative Change

The Transition: Changing the Rules While We Are Playing the Game

In 1972, the Club of Rome published the book, "Limits to Growth." In it, they warned of the ecological and social dangers posed by our economic activities. And while not all of their predictions have held perfectly true, the overall basic prognosis they made is hauntingly close to what has come to pass since then.

In their 2022[38] follow-up "Earth for All," the authors again draw on a wealth of empirical data to model different development scenarios, just as they did before. But this time, their analysis is fueled by far more computational power than was available in the 1970s. Out of the (theoretically infinite) array of possible future scenarios they find, they choose two for closer comparison: the first is called "Too Little, Too Late," and the second "Giant Leap."

As the name suggests, in the "Too Little, Too Late" scenario, efforts are made to tackle the current challenges, but they're not ambitious enough. Humanity does not find a path of resilient coexistence with the rest of nature. As a result, irreversible ecological tipping points are crossed and social inequality rises, leading to growing social instability across the globe. Markets become more volatile and fragile, ultimately hurting the economy too – all because we failed to act in a timely and decisive manner.

But in the second, "Giant Leap" scenario, sweeping collective changes are made for the benefit of society and the economy. To do so, the authors identify five turnarounds that humanity must adopt, each supported by three sets of specific actions. Only one of the five turnarounds directly addresses ecological concerns (energy), whereas the other four pertain to social issues (poverty, inequality, empowerment, food). This underscores once again the intertwined nature of the ecological and social challenges we face.

Overall, the "Giant Leap" scenario leads to the stabilization of our planetary ecosystems, the transformation of our economic and social systems in a regenerative and distributive direction, and enhanced global welfare. The authors have also calculated the total cost of all these proposed measures, arriving at an estimate of 2 to 4 percent of the global Gross Domestic Product. A formidable sum, without a doubt, but absolutely doable.

So, why don't we just implement their plan? As you can imagine, there are various reasons for why many people aren't on board: They choose to ignore the state of the world, see the threat as mere media manipulation, or continue to hope that some technological solution will come to the rescue. They might also feel overwhelmed by it all or just blinded by their own short-term self-interest. Moreover, geopolitical power is usually closely tied to economic interests, which is why governments around the world seem unable or unwilling to act in concert on the topic. And then there are also the myriad inner psychological barriers that stand in our way.

Last but not least, there are also systemic forces that block our way. We'll now explore these in more detail, as they form an important basis for the transformation design of the Stellar Approach.

The systems theory perspective

Systems theory differentiates between organic, psychic, and social systems, and their modes of operation. Organizations and the economic system are classified as social systems, whereas we humans belong to both the organic (body) and psychic (consciousness) systems. Regardless of their type, all systems are fundamentally driven to sustain and replicate themselves. This can be clearly seen in the way our economic system excels at self-preservation – so much so that it greatly exacerbates problems in surrounding systems, as previously noted.

According to systems theory, a system's ability to self-preserve is limited by the environments it interacts with – a process known as co-evolutionary development. In other words, if a system continues to replicate itself despite harming the environments it depends on, it is bound to eventually reach a limit where it can no longer self-replicate. In organic systems (such as plants and cells), the surrounding environment will often correct the problem by halting the unchecked spread of a single system. In social systems, things are more complicated – the mechanism for correction is perhaps best described as "voluntary self-restraint."[39]

This is the point of tension where the crises currently plaguing us are spawned. Yes, the economy seems to function well enough within its own systemic logic. But it completely fails to recognize its interdependencies with other relevant environments or act in co-evolutionary harmony with them. Put simply: it's not helping all systems to flourish together. And its focus on self-preservation is only amplified by the close ties between the economic system and surrounding systems such as the political sphere.

In the last few chapters, we've often referred to the Three Horizons model. In it, the first horizon, (H1 or *business-as-usual*) begins to shift as it outlives its usefulness. Through systems theory, we can now get a more granular view of this: Today's dominant horizon H1 continues to be highly useful in the frame of reference of the economic system. But as soon as we consider the environments that are essential for the survival of the economic system, it becomes anything but useful.

If we want an economy that acts in a co-evolutionary fashion, it requires changes. New rules to foster voluntary self-restraint and benefit the environments that people, organizations, and the economy are embedded in. We also need to be much more competent in managing interdependencies – a skill that could (somewhat awkwardly) be termed "interdependence competence."

Unfortunately, we can't just call a timeout, come up with a new societal and economic design, and then resume play under the new set of rules. No, we're called upon to carry out this urgently needed overhaul *in the heat of action*. In other words, we need to change the rules while we are playing the game.

So how will these new rules come about? Living systems don't change in a linear fashion and definitely not overnight – it's just not possible to simply leap from one stable state to another. Societal change occurs in a complex web of coexistence and interaction, shaped by communications, currents, impulses, and conflicts. For a long time, we won't be able to predict which new design will prevail – at least not until new agreements emerge that are reflected in social systems and subsystems. And we won't know where the change comes from: Sometimes, it's the political and legal systems that lead the way, for example by adjusting the legal framework, followed by social norms or individual attitudes. And sometimes it's the other way around. Either way, one thing is certain: unless we try, nothing will change.

Working on the system and in the system

At the beginning of this book, we distinguished between working *on* the economic system and working *in* the economic system. Both are needed: We need people in political roles who can change the regulatory framework, developing and shaping the incentive structures and other measures that steer behavior. Here, politicians have the rather unenviable task of having to change the framework of the economy without accidentally choking it in the process and thereby jeopardizing social stability.

At the same time, we need change *in* the system. Here, all stakeholders are called upon to create change in their own circle of influence, whether in companies, associations, trade unions, civil society, or among fellow citizens. Businesses play an especially important part here because, as economic subsystems of their own, they can directly shape the reality of the economy and drive innovation. Companies need to acknowledge the importance of their interdependencies and take responsibility not only for themselves but also for the vital systems around them. They must understand that voluntary self-restraint is necessary to enable the neighboring systems – and in turn themselves – to survive. Only then can the economic system begin to develop new patterns from within.

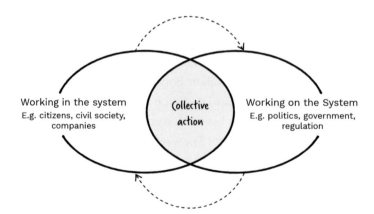

Incidentally, we find ourselves in a remarkable situation where even some key economic stakeholders are imploring politicians to change the regulatory framework swiftly and decisively. In fact, at COP27, over a hundred CEOs and senior executives published an open letter to global political leaders, pledging their commitment to work together to accelerate the transition to net zero. This plea makes perfect sense if you think about it: As long as the competition continues to operate under the old rules, anyone following the new ones will be at a disadvantage. Hence the demand for a uniform set of binding rules to guarantee a level playing field, so corporate leaders can confidently plan for the future.

What this means for organizations: Navigating the paradox

Again, we come to a paradox, this time one faced by individual organizations and companies. Like any other system, organizations need to do whatever they can to survive in their environments. However, we now find ourselves at a juncture where the demands of the economic environment are increasingly at odds with the needs of social and ecological environments. We know that regenerative change is necessary because the long-term survival of business models, markets, and even future generations depends on it. Yet, in the short term, too much regenerative change could also be detrimental to a business, because it won't yet be rewarded by investors, stock markets, or financiers, not to mention the added risk of social upheaval.

So, can organizations reconcile these requirements? As usual when it comes to a complex change process, it won't happen all at once, but rather step by step. The regenerative transformation can only succeed if it has one foot in the "No More" – meaning the older H1 systems destined for eventual obsolescence – and another in the "Not Yet" – meaning the new H3 systems that are still to emerge. **What we need now is a clear sense of direction, a step-by-step approach, and the ability to learn and adapt as we go.** This approach is sometimes called "radical incrementalism," which entails painting a grand vision and then moving toward it step by step.

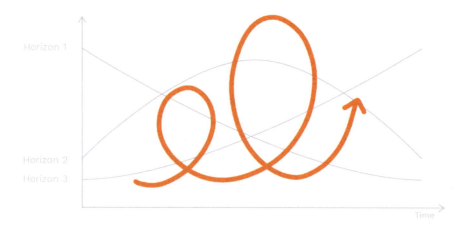

A Clear Direction and A Steady Pace

In the Stellar Approach, we use the **Stellar Principles** to determine the direction of the journey. We'll introduce these in the next chapter. Moreover, we'll provide a framework for the transformation process, which will shape the journey along each step of the way and ensure we stay on the right path. The further we travel, the more we stretch the limits of the system toward Horizon 3, even without ever fully leaving Horizon 1 behind. We'll dive into the details of this **transformation design** in the next chapter.

But why change anything when my current business model is so lucrative? (Also known as: "But how on earth can I explain this to my shareholders?")

Right now, the regenerative vision of the future sounds like it requires a drastic reshuffling of priorities. We've prioritized economic growth and profit for so many decades that the new paradigm might seem counterintuitive: "Why should I make a change when I'm prospering financially now, especially when I might be the only one who makes the leap?"

So, let's now take a look at some counter-arguments to this viewpoint, stemming from economic, existential, and moral perspectives. How much weight they carry depends on the timeframe you consider. The list is neither exhaustive nor universal, so please feel free to pick out the arguments that resonate most with you.

- **Common sense:** We know that our current economic activities are gradually undermining the very foundation of life. They've driven our world to such a fragile and volatile cliff edge that the risk of falling off has become an existential one – for companies and for humanity itself. And while we have proved that we can defy the fundamental principles of life for a few decades, ultimately, our choices will catch up with us. Both we and, above all, future generations, will bear the costs we've deferred over the past 150 years of industrial history. We know from science what our current path leads to, and this alone should be enough to make us change our course.
- **The resilience of our business models:** While the survival of humanity may not yet be a concern in the medium term, the survival of markets and business models certainly should be. If we fail to reconcile the economy with the planet and co-develop our vital environments, the repercussions will soon be severe. As society and the economy become increasingly vulnerable, many business practices as we know them today will no longer work. In a 2-degree world, the value-creation opportunities and markets will shift so drastically that they'll render the majority of today's business

models nonviable. Thus, regenerative economic activity actually aligns the organization toward new medium-term value drivers, thereby strengthening the resilience of both itself and its stakeholders.
- **Staying ahead of the curve:** The legislative landscape is constantly evolving, already including some requirements that go beyond mere harm prevention. Provisions like the principle of dual materiality and the focus on restoring damaged ecosystems send a clear message of the direction we're headed in. And even though legislative processes can be lengthy, this trend is likely to continue. That's why for organizations, the best course of action is to proactively develop relevant competencies and foster a culture that welcomes and smooths the way for regenerative solutions. This enables the organization to get ahead of the emerging legal requirements, instead of chasing them.
- **New ecosystems and market opportunities:** From an economic innovation standpoint, proactive action is better than mere defensive reaction. The regenerative transformation won't just change how the economy operates, but it will also open up new spaces for business models – the kind that prioritize planetary health and societal well-being alongside financial value creation. Such models will become increasingly prominent and celebrated as the dysfunctions of existing ones become more apparent.

  In a sense, a regenerative approach to business is just a radical take on user orientation. The concept of human-centered design is already widely used today, and the regenerative view on this could be termed "beyond-human-centered design," "planet-centered design," or "life-centered design." The only difference to run-of-the-mill human-centered design lies in systemic thinking and a greater emphasis on long-term orientation. Solutions that meet current user needs but become part of the problem five, ten, or twenty years from now, will ultimately turn against the users – and, by extension, against the solution provider's business model.
- **Managing cost risk:** Conventional economic activity is also increasingly hurting the cost side of business: The mounting costs of socio-ecological crises are no longer falling solely on society but also reverberating back to companies. The risks of unsustainable business models are growing

increasingly hard to predict, as the costs associated with emissions and other negative impacts rise. And although the cost of raising capital is still relatively insensitive to the distinction between sustainable and unsustainable businesses, the first shifts in valuation standards are already visible. Furthermore, the recruitment costs for new staff will also grow if companies can't point to a convincing plan for addressing the challenges of the coming decades.

- **Changing customer needs:** As customers increasingly feel the impact of today's economic activities, they become insistent and critical in their demands for change. Companies that want to continue to sell their products and services in the future will face new generations of customers – customers who see and feel the effects of irresponsible business in their daily lives and therefore closely scrutinize corporate responsibility.
- **The moral compass:** Last but not least, there's the moral aspect. At the end of the day, we're dealing with moral obligations, not just towards all life today but also in the future. Even if our own generation won't have to suffer the worst effects of the polycrisis, we have a clear moral imperative to leave a habitable planet for future generations. Trillions of future people will have to live with the consequences of our decisions today.

From an economic standpoint, embracing regenerativity is a bet on the future, and we predict that companies starting early will be the ones to reap the biggest economic rewards. It's a smart move that secures their right to exist in the long term and makes their business models more resilient, even if it initially feels like an additional investment.

In the big picture, it's also a bet on our own continued survival on this planet. And ultimately, it's the only chance we have. While we can't change the past, we can still shape the future. So, we have to ask ourselves: looking back on today, how do we want to feel about the things we can still influence?

What about our feelings?

So far, we've focused on change occurring in social systems, like the economy and individual organizations. But change on this level also requires change in psychological systems – in our inner mental life.[40]

To succeed in the regenerative transformation we'll need our heads, hands, and hearts, meaning rational thought, decisive action, and an awareness of our own feelings: How do we feel when, day after day, we're confronted with the ongoing destruction of our world? With news of flooded cities, vast regions on fire, and people and animals dying? And where is the space for us to talk about our fears? The space to grieve what we've lost? These are important questions because, often, accepting our own feelings is the first prerequisite for change.

Moreover, as individuals, we need to be willing to develop our own "inner equipment" for the journey. This includes our attitudes, values, and beliefs, as well as considerable self-awareness. We also need the ability to relate to others and feel empathy toward beings both human and non-human. You'll recall that we touched upon this inner world earlier as we explored the grand questions of consciousness (see page 66).

Psychologists and trauma experts have long studied the connection between destructive environmental behavior and unresolved developmental traumas and deficiencies.[41] It's clear that to enable this journey to a regenerative world, we must be willing to confront and integrate the "shadow aspects" of our own minds.

The Inner Development Goals map out the key individual development dimensions needed to drive a sustainable or regenerative transformation. Even better, this framework offers concrete tools for people to strengthen these abilities.[42]

In the Stellar Approach, we ensure that in addition to team and organizational dynamics, we leave ample space for emotions and personal development. In fact, we dedicate time to this topic at the end of each learning module.

From "More of the same" to "More of the other"

By now, it should hopefully be clear that many of the crises we face today are related to the economic development of the last two centuries. We've discussed how financial and asset capitalism is destabilizing both our social cohesion and our planet as a whole. The fact that we're gradually eroding the necessities of life is not a random coincidence but a logical and traceable outcome of the current system.

To change this, we're called upon to redesign the system and its subsystems. And since we can't solve the polycrisis with the same mindset that created it, we'll need a whole new approach. Organizations would be well-advised to start their regenerative journey now, even if it feels overwhelming. The sooner they do so, the sooner they'll start to not only contribute to solving our problems but also enhance their own future resilience. Of course, inevitable goal conflicts will crop up as new behavioral patterns collide with the limits of the old system. Ultimately, the companies and organizations that start the journey today will be in the best position to succeed tomorrow.

Well done, you've now completed the theoretical portion of the book! In the next chapters and sections, we'll explore how the Stellar Approach can help shape the great transformation endeavor.

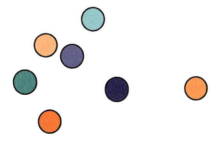

Shaping the Regenerative Change

Reflection questions

- How can I use my own circle of influence to contribute to regenerative change?
- What kind of cooperation or support would I need, and from whom?
- How could I involve these people in the process?
- What goal conflicts might arise in the process, and with whom could I resolve them?

The key takeaways from this chapter

Our current economic system is acting in an increasingly self-sabotaging way. Everything that doesn't fit into its logic of economic exploitation tends to be deprioritized, and as a result, the very basis for life is being eroded.

But happily, there's a way to reach a healthy long-term balance between the economy and the social and ecological systems around it. This *regenerative* approach places utmost importance on the process of life, encompassing not just humans but *all* life on Earth.

To successfully transition from a degenerative to a regenerative economy, we need to work on many fronts: We need interventions on the political level, of course. But we also need change within the system, meaning on the level of companies, non-governmental organizations, and civil society. And last but not least, we also need to work on the level of our own inner psychology.

In the coming years, organizations will face a paradox: while still operating as part of the economic system, they need to stretch the limits of that system to secure their own long-term survival.

How Organizations Can Contribute to Regenerative Change

We've covered a lot of ground so far, and we hope that you've given yourself the time to let everything sink in properly. Sometimes weighty topics need a while to settle. Now, the time has come to continue our journey. Are you ready?

In this chapter and throughout the rest of the book, we'll be exploring the question of how organizations can contribute to regenerative change in a concrete way.

In the previous chapter, we identified two key ingredients that organizations need for a regenerative transformation: a clear sense of direction and a well-defined **process** that doesn't disrupt everything all at once, working one step at a time instead.

In this chapter, we'll explain how the Stellar Approach combines these elements to help teams and organizations follow the regenerative development path. Of the two elements, let's focus on *direction* first.

90 How Organizations Can Contribute to Regenerative Change

The Stellar Principles – Our Guiding Stars

We like to think of regenerative development as a journey, and journeys need a clear starting direction. Say you're walking across a desert to find an oasis. You'd probably want to have some idea of which direction to head in, right?

The same is true for organizational change. In fact, knowing the direction becomes all the more important when it's not just individuals embarking on the journey, but entire groups.

When introducing the Stellar Approach to organizations, we typically need to engage with large groups when trying to give them a sense of direction. Unfortunately, we don't usually have time for a detailed explanation of all the different facets of regenerativity. This is where the Stellar Principles come in.

You can think of the Stellar Principles as the design principles for a regenerative organization: **guiding stars** that teams can follow on the Stellar Approach transformation journey. The more these **four principles** are integrated into the daily work of the teams, the more regenerative their actions will become.

In the previous chapter, we described in detail the main elements of regenerative economic activity. The Stellar Principles draw on those as well as on the core theme of regenerativity: the fact that this planet and all its inhabitants, including us humans, are part of a living system. Hence, all our actions, including our economic activity, should make sense in this larger frame of reference. **A regenerative economy sees itself as an integral part of life, operating in harmony with life's non-negotiable basic principles.** So in a way, you could say that the Stellar Principles are derived from the basic principles of life itself.

They can be used as regenerative design principles across the entire organization. And when we design an organization based on them, we ensure that it becomes more regenerative, one step at a time, and thereby does its part to change the economic system from within.

Of course, "life" is a pretty complex phenomenon that defies any attempt to summarize it into a few catchy principles. So, while we acknowledge that our attempt is simplistic and abridged, we use it anyway, because it helps us to navigate in complexity.[1] And as stated before in the Check-in, we can live with a little simplifying, as long as we do so consciously and acknowledge the complexity behind the veil.

We believe that these four key principles are not only broad enough to capture much of the "texture" of life, but they're also directly applicable to organizations and the economy:

Design Principles of Life	Application in the Economy	Stellar Principles
Interdependence	Stakeholder orientation	Embedded
Diversity as a resilience factor	Diversity and inclusion	Diverse
Cycles and constant renewal	Resource use	Circular
Infinite process	Long-term perspective	Long-term

Principle: Embedded

We structure interdependencies with other stakeholders – both human and non-human – so that our positive impact outweighs any potential negative impact.

One of the characteristics of living systems is that value-creating relationships between participants are mutually beneficial. Due to this principle, the entire planet operates like a vast metabolic process: A bee sips nectar from a flower, carries pollen away to pollinate other plants, and creates new life in the process. Squirrels spread seeds dropped by trees in the autumn. Fungi serve not only as a communication medium between plants but also hasten the organic decomposition process. The list could go on for as long as life itself.[2]

And the principles governing the planet govern us humans too. We're inherently social creatures who can only thrive together with each other, not in conflict with each other. This doesn't just apply to our relationship with other people but also to the natural resources that we need to survive. It's crucial, then, to remember that we're not alone in this world but live in a network of interdependencies. Thus, helping our environments thrive is not an act of altruism per se but something we must do for our own survival.

In the context of regenerative economic activity, interdependence means that we need to look beyond ourselves. We need to make a conscious effort to consider all our stakeholders and cultivate healthy, high-quality relationships with them. And this encompasses both human and non-human stakeholders, all of whom are impacted by our economic actions.

For each Stellar Principle, we'll share two examples to illustrate how they might look in practice. Please note that these aren't fully regenerative organizations, as so far they are few and far between. So consider these examples as inspiration for initial ideas on how regenerative principles can be translated into the real world of business.

How Organizations Can Contribute to Regenerative Change

Windcloud runs data centers powered by renewable energy and uses the excess heat for a secondary venture, an algae farm.

Digital infrastructure is a significant factor in the global energy and climate equation, with digital devices accounting for up to 12 percent of global electricity demand and rising. Data centers, a particularly energy-intense part of this infrastructure, require power 24/7, every day of the year. The Nordfriesland-based company Windcloud has developed sustainable and CO_2-neutral data centers powered exclusively by local renewable energy, mainly wind power. This way, Windcloud has access to a reliable supply of renewable energy. Moreover, the data centers are set up in old military installations, and the heat they produce is put to use in an algae farm. The algae sequesters CO_2 as it grows, and once harvested, serves as raw material in the food, pharmaceutical, and cosmetics industries. This novel approach makes Windcloud's business model both more sustainable and more profitable.

The Carl Zeiss Foundation invests in the systems surrounding its two companies, Zeiss and Schott.

The Carl Zeiss Foundation is the sole shareholder in the companies Carl Zeiss AG and Schott AG. Its two main responsibilities are to safeguard the future of these two companies and to promote science. The foundation's statutes prohibit the sale of shares in these companies, and dividends are either reinvested or allocated towards advancing the fields of mathematics, computer science, natural sciences, and technology. The support is directed to areas where the foundation and the two companies are located. In this way, the foundation assures the continued independent existence of Zeiss and Schott, while also driving social engagement and supporting key stakeholders in surrounding systems.

Principle: Diverse

To make our organization more resilient, we promote inclusivity and harness the power of diversity in our actions.

Life depends on diversity: it increases the resilience of a system and thus helps ensure its survival. Just consider what happens without diversity. For example, the monocultures that dominate industrial farming practices create a cascade of problems: many species disappear from the ecosystem, nutrients leach from the soil, and pathogens emerge that sicken plants, animals and, increasingly, humans. Last but not least, pest infestations proliferate, necessitating the use of insecticides that again harm other organisms.

Diversity and inclusion are also essential elements for the regenerative transformation to succeed. If social groups are systematically underrepresented in the discussion, their innovative impulses cannot be used. And so, instead of finding genuine social innovations, we end up with solutions that perpetuate the same old dysfunctional dynamics. As climate activist Elsa Mengistu points out, combating the climate crisis requires an intersectional approach: "If you want to do environmental work, you also have to do anti-racist work. Otherwise, your environmentalism is only geared towards 30 percent of the population."[3]

Also in business, diversity is an important factor: Supply chains reliant on a few big players are more fragile than those with an array of smaller suppliers. And companies that are unable to embrace the needs of a diverse society will fade into obscurity.

So, what does diversity mean in the context of regenerative economic activity? It means considering social perspectives in decision-making, always being aware of groups that may be marginalized by the organization's actions, and understanding that diverse perspectives are essential for the organization's resilience.

Wildling makes minimalist barefoot shoes and embraces diversity in its products, materials, and views.

Wildling has been producing comfortable minimalist shoes from natural materials like wool and hemp in Portugal since 2015. The company embraces diversity on many levels: First, diversity is an integral part of its corporate culture – society is diverse, and Wildling aims to reflect this. Moreover, the company is committed to the idea of learning together as a diverse group. Second, diversity plays a big part in Wildling's products too: They make all their shoes unisex because gender should not dictate what kind of shoes are comfortable. So, with Wildling, not only do you avoid narrow shoes, but also narrow gender categories. Third, the company also promotes diversity – namely biodiversity – through its chosen product materials. It uses wool from endangered sheep breeds grazing on pastures rather than those fed monoculture crops. In this way, Wildling actively contributes to the health and resilience of its local ecosystems.

Tony's Chocolonely has made it its mission to sell 100% slave-free chocolate.

A Dutch journalist founded Tony's Chocolonely in 2005 after the use of modern slavery in the cocoa supply chain was discovered. Following extensive awareness-raising about the conditions on cocoa farms in West Africa, the company turned its attention to its own supply chain. Using its 5 sourcing principles (Traceable Beans, A Higher Price, Strong Farmers, The Long Term, Better Productivity and Quality), Tony's wants to lift cocoa farmers out of poverty and end child labor. To achieve this, the company has established a transparent supply chain based on direct partnerships. It signs five-year contracts with farmers and pays extra premiums to ensure a living wage for them. The sourcing principles have proved effective: compared to other cooperatives, cases of child labor in Tony's are ten times lower, and the average income of farmers double. What's more, Tony's goes a step further with the Open Chain initiative, inviting competitors to join them on the path to slave-free chocolate.

Principle: Circular

In all our products and services, one cycle feeds into the next, and our responsibility encompasses their entire lifespan. We recognize that true flourishing requires all things to have both a beginning and an end.

The fundamental nature of life is circular and cyclical. It is defined by constant creation and passing away – the birth and death that punctuate the process of life. Even our own life, unfolding right now as we read this book, will eventually come to an end. But the torch of the larger life process will be carried on by the many generations that follow us.

The principle of circularity perhaps best illustrates why today's economy is so fundamentally at odds with our environmental systems and the planet itself. Life follows the shape of a closed loop, whereas today's economy follows the shape of an endlessly rising curve. If we wish to create a sustainable and livable world, we need to somehow reconcile these two fundamental shapes.

Growth also defines nature, of course. But unlike economic growth, natural growth happens on the principle that the old must pass away to provide fertile ground for the new. This is the central difference between growing and *flourishing*. In the latter, decay is an inherent part.

Life's cyclicality also means it has a rhythm to it: the cycles of day and night, wake and sleep, growth and decay. And even our daily work depends on a rhythm of toil and rest. We can't always be at our peak performance; rather, productive times need to be complemented with rest. Regeneration is a necessity that can no longer be postponed.

For a regenerative organization, the principle of circularity is relevant on many levels. Key questions that arise from it include: How can we concretely close loops in our business model? How do we manage our resources in line with the fundamental principles of renewal and regeneration? And how can we apply those same principles to managing the energy that each employee contributes to the company?

Concular specializes in circular construction, preserving today's resources for future generations.

The company's origins trace back to Restado, Europe's largest online marketplace for used building materials. Wishing to amplify their positive impact, the founders decided to expand the business model to include a digital ecosystem for circular construction. Thus was born Concular, a company that uses digital and collaborative means to close material loops in construction sector projects. Basically, it uses a digital database to record the materials used in new and existing buildings, thereby enabling future building owners to reuse them. Moreover, Concular can help in circular conversions and demolitions of properties, transferring the recovered materials to be used in new projects. Finally, Concular supports new construction undertakings in managing material cycles, making life cycle assessments, and choosing sustainable or circular materials. In these ways, Concular's services provide ecological and economic benefits for all stakeholders, actively reducing emissions and waste, and preserving valuable resources for future generations.

Renault is transforming its largest French factory into a circular ecosystem – the first of its kind in the European automotive industry.

Since 2021, Renault has been transforming its oldest and largest factory in Flins, France, into an industrial ecosystem. This "Refactory" is a bet on the circular economy, spanning 232 hectares and aiming to employ over 3 000 people by 2030. The goal is to produce vehicles in a cleaner, more sustainable way, and to extend the time that the materials used remain in circulation. The Refactory operates with four activity centers (Re-trofit, Re-energy, Re-cycle, and Re-start), refurbishing used vehicles and repurposing materials to be fed back into the value chain. Renault plans to refurbish more than 45 000 used vehicles annually. Even manufacturing robots from car factories are given a new life here, and car batteries are repurposed as energy storage devices. Moreover, the Refactory includes an Open Innovation Hub, aimed at bringing together a variety of stakeholders to further strengthen their expertise and spur research in the circular economy.

Principle: Long-Term

We consider the long-term effects of our economic activities.

All individual living entities will sooner or later pass away, but the cycle of life itself has no foreseeable end. Perhaps someday, trillions of years from now, the universe will collapse back on itself into a single point of infinite mass. But even then the question remains: is that really the end of life?

As discussed in the previous chapter, our current economic system is relatively indifferent to its long-term effects – a dynamic only reinforced by the growing prominence of the financial markets and financialization. We also noted that the rhythms of the economic system are only partially compatible with those of our environmental systems. This is particularly unfortunate, as the natural ecosystems we depend on need time to regenerate and recover – something we've egregiously overlooked in recent decades.

A regenerative organization aims to remedy this by adopting a markedly different perspective, thinking not in terms of quarters, but generations. It asks questions like: What impact will our current economic actions have on future generations? How can we ensure our actions today are such that future generations, too, will see our success as something to celebrate?

The Generation Forest plants and manages permanent mixed forests, ensuring their long-term value.	This cooperative acquires largely deforested areas in Panama and grows near-natural mixed permanent forests on them. In this way, they combat climate change as the growing trees capture carbon dioxide and also help bring back wildlife and enhance biodiversity. These efforts are funded through cooperative shares: each member must finance at least 500 square meters of forest. Members can also expect to see an eventual return on their investment,	as the forest will be thinned when the trees are ready for harvesting. The tropical timber is valuable, and the sale proceeds will be distributed to the members. The investment is not for the short-sighted though, as it can take roughly 25 years before the first proceeds are distributed. However, by then forest will have true long-lasting value because as a functioning ecosystem, wood can be harvested from it for many years to come.
Reckhaus is transforming itself innovatively, going from insect exterminator to insect conservator.	Since the 1950s, Reckhaus' business has been the production of insecticides. But this all changed in 2012 when two conceptual artists asked the owner about the value of a fly. This simple question prompted him to reflect on the relationship between humans and animals, sparking a profound transformation of the business that continues to this day. Because their products are all about eradicating insects indoors, the company works to ensure that insect diversity is preserved elsewhere. The "Insect Respect" seal developed by Reckhaus indicates that the company uses part	of the revenues to establish compensatory habitats to protect insects. Other companies also adopted the seal, thereby expanding the reach of the initiative. Moreover, by printing warning labels and guides, Reckhaus also tells people how to prevent insects from coming into their homes in the first place. And most recently, the company launched the first-ever live trap for insects. And this also makes business sense: in the big picture, it's clear that Reckhaus is also working to preserve its own business – in a world without insects, an insecticide manufacturer would be obsolete.

The Stellar Principles allow us to map out the direction of the regenerative journey. They help pin down the foundational principles for designing organizations that are regenerative and resilient in the long run.

But the question remains: how can we actually get started and set out in this direction?

We'll need a framework to guide us and, of course, some concrete methods would come in handy too. So in the next chapter, we'll explore the framework, meaning the fundamental transformation design of the Stellar Approach. Then, in Part 2 of the book, we'll dive deep into the methods and practical implementation side of things.

Reflection questions

- When I look at my own organization and my work through the lens of the Stellar Principles, what stands out to me?
- What artifacts can I observe that seem connected to these principles?
- Where does my organization align with these principles, and where does it clash?
- And on a personal level: where does my behavior align with these principles, and where does it clash?

The Stellar Approach Transformation Design

In most organizations today, the question isn't *if* they should become more sustainable, but *how* they can do so. They've probably developed strategies for sustainability or decarbonization, devised implementation plans, and even zeroed in on some next actions to implement. And this is all fine. But in our experience, organizations embarking on this journey often run into roughly the same obstacles, and these can usually be traced back to the transformation design.

As we've seen in previous chapters, sustainability is already a highly complex subject in its own right. But the *transformation toward sustainability* adds a whole new layer of complexity: not only do substantively different solutions need to be developed, but entire systems need to be reconsidered – be they organizations, business models, or the economy as a whole.

In this chapter, we'll describe the three organizational challenges that we consistently see cropping up in our work to support transformations. First, we'll briefly explain how the Stellar Approach addresses these challenges in its fundamental design. Then, in the second part of the book, we'll delve deeper into the practical implementation.

1. Challenge: Large organizations often struggle to change due to their sheer size.

It's a Herculean task for a company with tens of thousands of employees to become sustainable, let alone regenerative. Every aspect of the company – leadership, business models, collaboration modes, supply chains, customer relationships, and so forth – needs to be scrutinized from a sustainability perspective.

To tackle this challenge, most large organizations turn to centralization. Sustainability management and corporate social responsibility departments are set up to coordinate and supervise sustainability efforts, usually in consultation with top management. And using central roles to guide sustainability activities can make sense, but the challenge is that the lion's share of other departments and units also need to get onboard and manifest this in their daily work.

Unfortunately, micromanagement and centralized command-and-control functions are unlikely to achieve the sought-after regenerative change. What we need is the collective impact of the thousands of individual decisions made every day throughout the organization. Done right, sustainable and regenerative development mean that *every* employee contributes within their respective areas of responsibility.

The situation is comparable to the evolution of digitalization. In the early days, central departments typically took the lead, until it became apparent that digitalization impacts every corner of the organization. The same goes for sustainability and regenerativity: sustainable and regenerative organizations require these habits to be adopted *throughout* the organization.

Solution: Unlocking the innovation potential of the entire organization at the Team level

This need for comprehensive action throughout the organization is precisely why the Stellar Approach is, at its heart, a development program for teams. It enables each team to progressively make their day-to-day work more regenerative, no matter what their specific field. Even in a regenerative economy, a marketing team will still work with marketing, albeit probably with different objectives and content. And production teams will continue to produce, though likely both the product and their production processes will look very different.

The Stellar Approach helps teams update their approach to providing their services. Degenerative aspects are gradually identified and reduced, while the regenerative ones are developed and reinforced. Thus, the Stellar Approach isn't really a training program per se, as it doesn't just teach new concepts and tools. Rather, it takes services that are already provided in an organization and helps develop them further. We collaborate with teams on their areas of responsibility, helping them to gradually make their work more regenerative.

Of course, in any organization, there's also a wide range of systemic factors that individual teams have limited control over: How does the company leadership behave? Does the company as a whole have a clear strategic intent and

well-defined ambition? How does the company's governance reflect sustainability and regenerativity? What conditions must be met for behaviors to change?[4]

But despite these systemic factors, there are compelling reasons for starting the transformation gradually with individual teams:

- Each team has its own playing field, so to speak: its own area of responsibility to begin its regenerative transformation in. The Stellar Approach relies on the power of one's **own circle of influence**, and this fosters both effectiveness and self-efficacy. Feelings of powerlessness – "There's nothing we can do anyway" – give way to clarity on how each and every one of us can contribute in ways big and small – "Let's get started."
- An organization can be seen as a constant stream of operative **decisions** made within its structures, and they occur predominantly at the team level. As these decisions gradually become more sustainable and regenerative, likewise the overall organization will become more sustainable and regenerative.

- As we've said many times before, transformation processes are **not linear**. Thus, it would be a fallacy to think that we can grasp the grand scheme of things beforehand. A helpful analogy is that of a mosaic: we start by placing individual pieces where they belong, but the big picture can only emerge later. In the same way, when we work with subsystems, meaning teams, we also change the overarching system, meaning the organization.[5]
- By working with individual teams, we strengthen the **co-intelligence** of the organization. Instead of tackling this massive transformation through central units or disconnected silos, we foster a shared language across teams and a decentralized competency for solving problems.
- Last but not least, this approach mirrors the **natural processes** that we too are a part of. In living organisms, change can begin at a cellular level and still gradually come to steer the development of the entire creature. Similarly, in a regenerative transformation, even profound change can begin on the team level.

2. Challenge: There's too much talk and too little action.

In many organizations, sustainability is seen mainly as a matter of strategy and reporting. A lot of time is invested into developing intricate strategies and roadmaps, some even extending decades into the future. Of course, by the time those plans become relevant, the future will have changed several times already. But even that aside, the question remains how exactly these goals can be achieved. Too often, there's a gaping divide between the theory of the strategic roadmap and its practical implementation.

What's more, there are literally thousands of employees who are kept busy by governance and reporting projects, and the new EU directive on sustainability reporting will no doubt only bog them down further. They collect data, create taxonomies, design systems for classification and rating, and define more or less meaningful measurement criteria. At worst, all this effort makes organizations see sustainability as a pure reporting question: "Our ESG reporting systems are up and running, so we must be sustainable now. Cheers!"

Of course, there's nothing wrong with strategic planning or good reporting practices. But the problem is that in many organizations, there seems to be a wide chasm between the amount of time spent on strategic discussion versus the actual observable real-world impact.

A successful regenerative change requires that we all collectively agree on a direction to go in and boldly take action on all levels to get there. This is far from easy. In fact, it's such a daunting challenge that it can be easy to feel disoriented or powerless. That's why it's all the more important to, first of all, break this task down into manageable individual components. And second of all, establish a process that creates clarity around our shared goals and drives a steady rate of progress while also enabling us to adapt as we make our way together. And third, foster a culture that encourages and nurtures regenerative solutions throughout the organization.

Solution: A step-by-step path to regenerative economic activity

The above considerations are reflected in the iterative, action-focused nature of the Stellar Approach. Completing the Stellar Journey enables teams to learn regenerative skills and establish new habits. Moreover, it helps them develop their own inner equipment for the journey, meaning things like attitudes, values, beliefs, and relational competencies. You could say it equips their heads, hands, and hearts for regenerative action. In the next part of the book, we'll delve into the Stellar Practices and Stellar Virtues that enable this.

It's important to know that the Stellar Approach is not like a set of IKEA assembly instructions that you can mindlessly follow to completion. The complexity and interconnectedness of our society make that impossible for many reasons: No one today can accurately predict what regenerative economic activity will look like in a given sector in the future.[6] At the same time, development never follows a straight line in complex environments, meaning planning horizons must be kept short. Nor is development ever really "finished." Rather, it flows like a river, sometimes slowly, sometimes quickly, and always changing its shape.

This also means that the Stellar Journey is never really over. Its modules outline a path of regenerative transformation that has no predefined endpoint, and which is reshaped as new learnings emerge along the way. It encourages teams to take action – to design and implement prototypes, conduct experiments, and facilitate systematic learning and improvement – all in order to keep moving forward, one step at a time. You can think of the Stellar Approach as a training regime for our regenerative muscles. And the more we make it into a habit, the better we get at overcoming new challenges and incrementally developing regenerative solutions.

3. Challenge: Our current sustainability efforts don't even come close to addressing the challenges we face. And we know this.
There's an ever-clearer gap between what the world needs and what can be monetized. The nigh-exclusive focus on short-term returns and growth that characterizes business-as-usual is no longer compatible with the external world. In fact, many companies grapple with the constant conflicts of interest and cognitive dissonances that stem from these two hard-to-reconcile truths: 1) Shareholders insist on maximal returns. 2) The transformation toward sus-

tainability or regenerativity requires investments, which will temporarily impact returns. As a result, CEOs struggle to satisfy an ever-widening group of stakeholders.

There are stormy times ahead: the economy and the financial system will be shaken, with ripple effects disrupting markets, supply chains, and business models everywhere. Unfortunately, most organizations and their leaders are poorly prepared to weather this storm. Our current business management models are outdated, meaning academic research based on them is also increasingly unhelpful. Meanwhile, few are willing to express doubts about the dominant paradigm or the stability of the current system, for fear of the reception such opinions will get. Similarly, systemic conflicts between objectives are rarely brought up or discussed in organizations, meaning they remain unresolved.

If we in an organization wish to develop our economic activities in a regenerative direction, we need a broad and *advanced* understanding of economic, ecological, and social interrelationships. Moreover, we need a culture of innovation that continually evaluates and adjusts business models to make them regenerative. And we need spaces where potential conflicts of interest can be brought to light, because only then can they be addressed.

Solution: Integrating conflicting goals

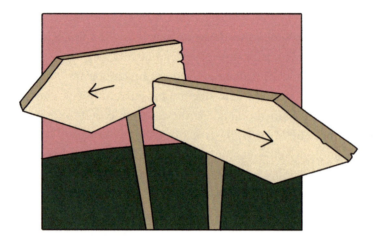

In the Stellar Approach, we align on a shared understanding of the direction to head in and adopt a conscious approach to addressing goal conflicts. We follow the Stellar Principles as guiding stars that lead us from *business-as-usual* to *business-as-the-world-needs*. And while the Stellar Approach helps us plot the rough course, the specific implementation is deliberately left open.

Naturally, this path is dotted with conflicts of interest with leaders, other parts of the organization, the top management, the owners, and the economic system itself, to name a few. But in the Stellar process, we don't see these as unwanted problems to be swept under the rug, but rather as valuable insights to fuel the further development of the organization and the economic system itself. Only by openly discussing these conflicts of interest can we make informed and conscious decisions about what to do with them. This is why in the Stellar process, we ensure that conflicts of interest are brought to light so that relevant stakeholders can address them.

Hopefully, this chapter has given you an understanding of the basic workings of the Stellar Approach and of how organizations can use it in their regenerative transformation. Together with the theoretical foundation presented before, you should now have everything you need to start the Stellar Journey and learn its methods. In Part 2 we take the first steps.

The Stellar Approach Transformation Design

Reflection questions

- What small steps immediately come to my mind for making my own team's work and impact more regenerative?
- Where do I see the limits of my own circle of influence? Whom could I involve to help expand them?
- In my own work, what would help me embark on a regenerative development path?

The key takeaways from this chapter

Organizations looking to embark on a regenerative transformation path need clarity on the chosen direction and a transformation design that supports incremental progress.

In the Stellar Approach, the direction is given by the Stellar Principles. Derived from the key design principles of life, the Stellar Principles embrace the basic idea that the regenerative economy sees itself as a part of life.

The four Stellar Principles are:
1. **embedded**
2. **diverse**
3. **circular**
4. **long-term**

The transformation design of the Stellar Approach supports decentralized, step-by-step change. On the Stellar Journey, regenerative knowledge will be shared, regenerative habits strengthened, and room made for personal growth. In this way, gradually, teams can grow their competence in finding regenerative solutions. Meanwhile, the goal conflicts that inevitably arise are made visible, which means they can be addressed in the open.

The Stellar Approach lights the way but is agnostic regarding the details of implementation. In the end, every organization needs to map out its own regenerative journey, and the Stellar Approach can help with that

Part 2

The Stellar Approach

The Stellar Approach

Welcome to Part 2 of the book, where we get practical. The content is divided into three chapters that explore how the Stellar Approach actually drives regenerative change in organizations:

In **Chapter 1**, we prepare for the Stellar Journey by introducing its methodological foundation, including the **Stellar Practices** and **Stellar Virtues.** We'll also take a peek at the **three workshop modules** that tie together the elements of the Stellar Approach. Finally, we'll present three key tools that enable us to follow, **step by step, the path of regenerative development.**

Chapter 2 takes us right to the heart of the Stellar Approach: the **team-based change curriculum**. Here, we'll take an in-depth look at each of the three modules of the Stellar Journey while also describing our methodological approach.

Chapter 3 zooms out and examines how the Stellar Journeys of individual teams can be embedded into a **broader transformation architecture.** (Spoiler: it's by introducing additional key workstreams for a successful regenerative change.)

Preparing for the Stellar Journey

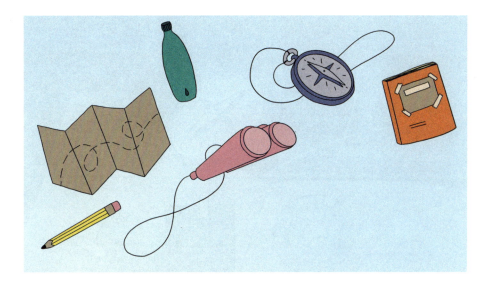

By now, you're already familiar with the first element of the Stellar Journey: the Stellar Principles. They define the kind of economic activity that would support life. They serve as guiding stars, lighting the right direction for the regenerative transformation and the desired destination we wish to reach.

Of course, seen from today, that destination may seem beyond reach. And that's perfectly alright. The goal isn't to fully adopt all the principles overnight but to make our way one step at a time.

At the same time, the Stellar Principles are still fairly abstract. To really bring them to life, we have to translate them into concrete actions. This is where the Stellar Practices come in.

118 The Stellar Approach

Packing the Equipment for Our Journey: The Stellar Practices

You can think of the Stellar Practices as the *equipment* needed for turning the Stellar Principles into tangible actions and solid team habits.

We've identified seven Stellar Practices needed for regenerative transformation. Each of them gradually guides the organization's actions to better align with the Stellar Principles. The practices aim to convey **knowledge**, establish **habits**, and develop our **inner equipment**, meaning our attitudes, values, relational competencies, and so forth.

The Stellar Approach works best when it's used regularly. It's a bit like fitness training, where working out a little but often is better than doing so intensely but rarely. Hence, it's not meant to be used only as a team development tool, but as a default anchor for mindset and conduct that steers day-to-day work. That's why everything in the Stellar Approach is crafted in a way that helps teams find their own rhythm with the Stellar Practices.

Next, we'll share a quick overview of the seven Stellar Practices of regenerative organizations. Even though we list each practice separately here, please remember that they are deeply interwoven and mutually complementing. Hence, we recommend that you always keep the context of the entire set in mind.

Stellar Practice 1: Understanding Interconnectedness

The first Stellar Practice helps team members broaden their perspectives. They understand their systemic connections to their environments and learn how to place their economic activities in a larger ecological and social context. To help them get there, we use well-established concepts from sustainable and regenerative economics. Moreover, we ensure that, along the way, we develop a shared understanding of the methods used.

Stellar Practice 2: Using Our Own Circle of Influence

Building on the expanded understanding from the first Stellar Practice, the team now takes a closer look at their own circle of influence. They map out their relationships with stakeholders, both human and non-human, including natural ecosystems. The team then develops potential actions to increase their positive impact on stakeholders, while minimizing the negative impact.

Stellar Practice 3: Setting a Shared Intention

Now, armed with an understanding of the context and some concrete design ideas to boot, the team can articulate a shared intention for its regenerative journey. To be effective, regenerative work needs a mutually agreed direction and a clear view of how one's own work ties into the big picture. This is why, in the third Stellar Practice, the team defines a shared intention for how, specifically, they will contribute to making the organization incrementally more regenerative.

The Stellar Practices 121

Stellar Practice 4:
Designing Circular Processes

In the fourth and fifth Stellar Practices, we turn our attention to the step-by-step implementation of the above. With the fourth practice, the team strengthens its competency in circular thinking and action. They practice this skill when cooperating within the team (iterative work) but also in the context of the production and service processes that they're responsible for (circular economic activity).

Stellar Practice 5:
Making Regenerative Decisions

The fifth Stellar Practice enhances the team's ability to consider regenerative perspectives in its decisions. The team learns to work in regenerative roles and to systematically apply these roles in its decision-making.

Stellar Practice 6:
Making Progress Visible

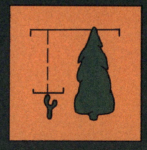

With the sixth Stellar Practice, the team learns to define meaningful indicators of their progress on the regenerative path. The team also gains the confidence to share its story and successes with other parts of the organization.

Stellar Practice 7:
Staying Effective

The seventh and final Stellar Practice focuses on the self-efficacy of team members. Regenerative teams deliberately set aside time to care for their own resilience and relational capabilities. What's more, they don't shy away from or suppress their emotions, but rather see them as valuable data for their continued development. Team members support each other as partners on this path.

To recap, here's a brief overview of all seven Stellar Practices and their intended target states:

Stellar Practice 1	**Understanding Interconnectedness**	Team members are able to place their actions and impact within a broader ecological and social context.
Stellar Practice 2	**Using Our Own Circle of Influence**	Team members are aware of their interdependencies with the human and non-human stakeholders in their circle of influence. They integrate this broader perspective into the actions they take.
Stellar Practice 3	**Setting a Shared Intention**	The team is aware of its regenerative contribution and aligns its work to support it.
Stellar Practice 4	**Designing Circular Processes**	The team is able to design processes that are iterative and circular.
Stellar Practice 5	**Making Regenerative Decisions**	Decisions are made in a way that progressively increases the team's positive impact on human and non-human stakeholders.
Stellar Practice 6	**Making Progress Visible**	The team is able to measure its regenerative impact and knows how to communicate it to others.
Stellar Practice 7	**Staying Effective**	Team members learn how to stay effective and make time for regeneration.

124 The Stellar Approach

Inner Fitness Training: The Stellar Virtues

Beyond the principles and practices, the Stellar Virtues constitute the final element needed for the Stellar Journey.

The Stellar Virtues are the *inner anchors* that foster our resilience throughout the transformation process. We see these three virtues as particularly important in a regenerative transformation:[1]

Stellar Virtue 1: Courage

It takes courage to make something new. As paradigms shift, new ideas can sometimes seem so radically different from what we're used to that it's easy to dismiss them. They're called naive or idealistic, or even ignored altogether. This happens all the time – we've probably all seen sincere improvement suggestions get derided as unrealistic, ignorant, or even cynical. Yet, it's important to be able to boldly share one's views and invite others to discuss them constructively. That's why the first Stellar Virtue strengthens the inner bravery of individual team members and the team as a whole.

Stellar Virtue 2: Creative Joy

Discussions around sustainability are often imbued with a certain gloominess. The enormity of the task at hand, the potential negative lifestyle changes ahead, and the looming threat of having to sacrifice comforts can all contribute to a feeling of overwhelm: "C'mon! Really, we have to deal with this too now?!"

But we can flip this perspective: Regenerative economic activity brings our behavior into harmony with our environments, finding balance with them and enabling them to flourish. In this way, we can make our shared existence on this planet more resilient and help to secure its future. The second Stellar Virtue invites us to find joy in developing systems together as a team and using our own circle of influence to create solutions that serve the greater good.

Stellar Virtue 3: Perseverance

The regenerative transformation isn't a sprint but a marathon. Along the way, there'll be tailwinds to help push us along but also headwinds that hold us back. So, to stay the course, we need not only a toolkit of handy methods to use but also the inner perseverance to keep going. What we need is a kind of "flexible consistency": "Flexible" because the transformation process isn't linear and there'll always be new information to consider before the next step. And "consistency" because we mustn't lose sight of the overall direction of the transformation, no matter how many steps we take.

The third Stellar Virtue cultivates this inner ability to stay focused on the distant horizon while also attending to the next steps on the path.

When implementing the Stellar Approach, we begin by focusing on these three virtues. But we also encourage teams to add other internal abilities that they themselves consider useful on their regenerative journey. Moreover, we propose that the teams engage in an ongoing dialog regarding the virtues, as this helps team members to continually reflect on them and support each other.

The Stellar Path: Context, Direction, and Impact

Module 2: Direction

Stellar Practices:
4. Designing Circular Processes
5. Making Regenerative Decisions

Stellar Virtue: Creative Joy

Well done! Having learned the Stellar Principles, Practices, and Virtues, you now already know the most important elements of the Stellar Approach.

- The **Stellar Principles** are the guiding stars for the Stellar Journey, illuminating the regenerative direction to follow.
- The **Stellar Practices** constitute the equipment that teams need for the journey, and they turn the direction into action.
- The **Stellar Virtues** cultivate inner strength, providing anchors to bolster resilience on the regenerative path.

So how can we integrate these elements into something that teams can use?

Simple: we've grouped the components into **three workshop modules** that teams complete: **Context**, **Direction**, and **Impact**. These modules form the foundation of the team-based change curriculum that we'll describe in more detail in the second chapter (see from page 140 onwards).

Module 1: Context

Here, the team understands the network of interdependent relationships it's embedded in. It also learns how it can use its own circle of influence to contribute to regenerative transformation. Finally, it sets a clear intention for the regenerative journey. Throughout this module, the Stellar Practices 1 through 3 and the Stellar Virtue "Courage," play an important part.

Module 2: Direction

Now, with clarity regarding the team's shared intention and the latitude they have for shaping their own work, we get to implementation. Over the course of the module, the team will find it increasingly natural to operate in iterations and cycles. Moreover, they'll begin to incorporate regenerative perspectives into their decision-making. This workshop module maps to Stellar Practices 4 and 5, and the Stellar Virtue of Creative Joy.

Module 3: Impact

In the last module, the team adopts new metrics to gauge its progress in the chosen direction. It feels confident in continually assessing its progress and adjusting its next steps as needed. The team also learns how to stay effective so that it doesn't run out of steam on the regenerative journey. This final workshop module draws on Stellar Practices 6 and 7, and the Stellar Virtue of "Perseverance."

The workshop modules are designed for **individual teams**. And by "team," we mean a smallish group of four to twelve people working toward a common goal, providing some kind of service together. Of course, in a larger transformation, there's nothing to stop multiple teams from taking the journey simultaneously. We'll explore how this looks in more detail in Chapter 3, "The Big Picture: The Stellar Approach as a Part of the Regenerative Transformation."

To make the journey easier, the Stellar Approach uses a **teaching approach** where the three workshop modules – Context, Direction, and Impact – build on each other. Moreover, experienced Stellar trainers support the team as they complete the modules for the first time. The goal is that by the end of this guided journey, the team will be well-equipped and trained to continue on the regenerative path independently.

The contents of the three modules can be divided into learning units of varying lengths, depending on the team's needs. For some teams, full-day workshops may work best, whereas others might prefer shorter, more frequent sessions. But regardless of the exact split, **at least six full days** are needed to cover all three modules.

In this book, we present each of the three modules as a **two-day workshop**, spaced roughly four to six weeks apart (see from page 144 onwards). In addition, there's also a kick-off session, as well as 90-minute pit stops between the modules. These sessions are meant to support teams in implementation questions where needed and also to provide space for deep dives and individual reflection.

132   The Stellar Approach

How We'll Make Our Way: Even the Longest Odysseys Begin with Small Steps

As said before, regenerative development happens one small step at a time. If we wait to take some giant and flawless leap – so meticulously planned that it accounts for all eventualities and catapults us straight into a regenerative future – we'll be waiting forever.

Taking small steps helps us to gradually build new behaviors and habits, leading ultimately to a new reality. The starting point should be wherever we feel we can be effective right away – we'll adapt our next steps as we learn.

The task ahead of us is very complex, which is why, in the Stellar Approach, we try to break it down into small, manageable steps. To do this, we rely on three key concepts: **working with tensions**, **operating in sprints**, and **dealing with goal conflicts in a transparent way**.

So, before we dive into the three workshop modules and the various accompanying methods in the next chapter, we'd like to briefly introduce these complexity-reducing elements. They're a prominent part of our working modus and will be applied repeatedly throughout the modules.

Let's start with the concept of working with tensions. The basic idea of tension-based work is straightforward: whenever people work together toward common goals, tensions will inevitably arise. Even though they're usually understood as something negative, our definition is broader than that: tensions aren't just problems or conflicts, but any gaps between what is (the current state) and what could be (potential future states).

The idea is that by identifying and processing these tensions in an orderly way, the team can contribute to the gradual development of the organization as a whole. This is why we sometimes describe tensions as "fuel for the organization's development."[2]

On the Stellar Journey, whenever a team member senses a tension, we store it in a **tension stash**. This stash can be a digital whiteboard, a large poster with Post-its on it, or whatever format works for the team. The main thing is that it's accessible throughout the journey because, at the latest at the end of each module, the tensions will be "harvested" and processed into next steps.

Some key things to keep in mind when **dealing with tensions**:

- Ask: **"What do you need?"** It's not enough to just throw out a tension to the group and expect someone else to solve it. Rather, the person expressing the tension must own it and be responsible for solving it. This doesn't mean that the owner needs to personally take every step in solving it, but it is their responsibility to clarify what they need to resolve the tension. Hence, when processing a tension in the team, we ask: "What do you need?" And we only consider a tension resolved when the owner says "I have what I need (for now)." While this may sound like a simple process, it usually feels awkward at first and takes some practice to get the hang of. But in our experience, it's well worth it and ultimately leads to more clarity and solution orientation.
- Adopt a mindset of **"Is this safe enough to try?"** We've already alluded to this kind of thinking earlier in the book: In complex environments, it's not about finding the *perfect* solution, but about taking the next step that's safe

enough to try. If and when new tensions arise, they get processed and integrated into ever-better solutions. No solution can be permanent anyway, because life itself also continues to evolve.

At the end of each workshop module, we empty the tension stash, employing three methods for **dealing with the tensions:**

1. Most tensions can be **resolved directly**. This is the case if, for example, the person holding the tension just wants to share information, or they need something from another team member who can provide it right away. It might be as simple as the two agreeing on the next step to be able to move forward with their work. As soon as the tension holder has what they need, the tension is – for now at least – resolved and removed from the tension stash.
2. Some tensions might need to be **processed through projects** if resolving them requires multiple steps. This is where **sprints** come in, and we use them to process these more complicated tensions between workshop modules. Working in sprints allows us to complete some projects during the three-month Stellar Journey, thereby already making the team's actions incrementally more regenerative.

Tensions of this second category are transferred into a **sprint backlog**, where they get broken down into small, meaningful steps. The backlog allows us to organize and make visible everything that needs attention: the team's to-dos, work packages, and responsibilities.

At the end of each workshop module, we plan a sprint that lasts until the next module. This means that, depending on how the workshops are scheduled, each sprint lasts roughly four to six weeks, starting with a sprint planning meeting. Here, the team pulls all the to-dos from the backlog that it aims to tackle during the sprint. Anything that can't be addressed in the sprint stays in the backlog and gets carried over to the next workshop module for further processing.

3. Finally, there are also tensions stemming from **goal conflicts**. Whenever a team begins its regenerative journey, goal conflicts are sure to crop up. After all, the journey is all about establishing new patterns and behaviors that push the boundaries of conventional economic activity – friction is bound to ensue! Some typical goal conflicts we see include:
   - "We want to implement this sustainable solution, but it would cost too much (in the short term) and break our budget."
   - "We want to build a regenerative business model but refuse to prioritize building the knowledge and ecosystem connections we need."
   - "We'd like to make our buildings regenerative, but that would mean giving up two percentage points of profit this year."
   - "Our team would like to adopt a CO_2-neutral travel policy, but this would require changing the company-wide policy, which the HR team refuses to do for cost reasons."
   - "Our organization's growth demands conflict with the limits of our ecosystems."

We see even goal conflicts like these primarily as tensions to be dealt with by identifying the next steps for resolving them. However, sometimes it's not possible to define the immediate next step in the workshop module, because the inherent dilemmas and paradoxes can't be resolved on the spot.

Goal conflicts that can't be resolved right away are organized into the **Goal Conflict Navigator**.[3] This tool gives us a conceptual framework for differentiating between four levels of goal conflicts:

1. Goal conflicts between individuals or roles within the team
2. Goal conflicts within the organization, but outside of the team
   - Goal conflicts with other organizational units
   - Goal conflicts with the management or leadership level
   - Goal conflicts with the owners
3. Goal conflicts outside of the organization
4. Goal conflicts at the level of the economic system.

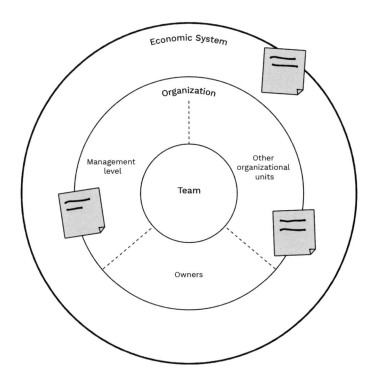

In our experience, it's important to document even the most seemingly intractable goal conflicts, as this frees us up to stop thinking about them and keep moving. Some of them might not even be solvable by us but require collaborating or forming alliances with other stakeholders. Especially when it comes to fundamental systemic paradoxes, like the demands for growth clashing with our ecosystems, we need to accept that solutions can and will only emerge further down the path. But as long as we remain aware of these dilemmas, we don't need to let them stand in our way.

Just like the tension stash, we'll keep the Goal Conflict Navigator updated and visible throughout the Stellar Journey. And in each workshop, we'll regularly check if any new potential steps have come to light that could help us deal with the conflicts.

What about bigger projects?

The goal of the Stellar Approach is to enhance teams' competence in finding sustainable and regenerative solutions to the challenges they face. And this is something that should happen across the entire organization, not just in individual specialized departments. To truly become more sustainable or regenerative, the organization needs widespread proficiency in these skills and a shared language for daily decisions big and small.

That said, projects will inevitably arise that go beyond what's possible during the Stellar Journey. They may demand more time or expertise than is available, for example. Those who already work with the topic of sustainability probably know what we're talking about. Consider, for instance, a project for redesigning a production process to be less resource-intensive – it's clearly not feasible in just 2–4 weeks but requires a more in-depth approach.

In the Stellar process, these in-depth projects are usually made into sprint projects, similar to projects that stem from tensions, only longer. And although their timeline tends to exceed the three-month team development process with the workshop modules, that doesn't mean they're left unaddressed. Rather, the sprint projects are kicked off during the three months with iterative project roadmaps that the team can keep implementing after the Stellar process.

The key takeaways from this chapter

The Stellar Practices enable teams to hone their regenerative skills and build regenerative habits. They help the team to unlock new solution spaces and move toward regenerative sustainability, one step at a time.

The seven Stellar practices are:
1. **Understanding Interconnectedness**
2. **Using Our Own Circle of Influence**
3. **Setting a Shared Intention**
4. **Designing Circular Processes**
5. **Making Regenerative Decisions**
6. **Making Progress Visible**
7. **Staying Effective**

The Stellar Journey brings all the elements of the Stellar Approach together: The four Stellar Principles are the guiding stars, providing a direction to follow. The seven Stellar Practices give teams the equipment they need to make their way. And finally, the Stellar Virtues – Courage, Creative joy, and Perseverance – cultivate the inner strength needed for the journey, both in individuals and the team as a whole.

The journey is organized into three workshop modules: Context, Direction, and Impact. These modules build on one another and help the team integrate the Stellar elements into its daily work.

It takes about twelve weeks to cover all the content of the Stellar Journey, and at least six full days should be devoted to the workshop modules.

On the Stellar Journey, regenerative development happens in small steps. To support this incremental approach, we work with tensions and sprints and strive to make potential goal conflicts transparent.

140 The Stellar Approach

The Stellar Journey: Modules and Methods

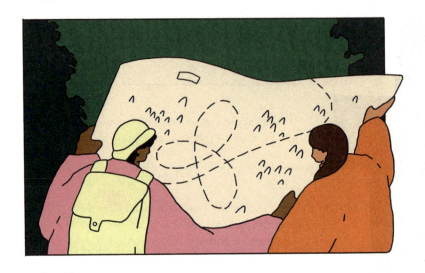

In this chapter, we'll follow the course of the Stellar Journey. Each of the sub-chapters will guide us through one of the three workshop modules: Context, Direction, and Impact. We'll explain the methods used in each module and offer practical tips for applying the Stellar Approach in your own team or for guiding other teams.

The goal of this book is to enable you to use the Stellar Approach on your own. No matter whether you're a leader or team member, after reading the book, you should have a clear idea of how to start the Stellar Journey in your own team.

If you're a facilitator, the teaching approach in this book should help you guide other teams on their regenerative journeys. We also offer sample agendas for all three of the workshop modules, which tie together the overall narrative of the Stellar Journey.

Of course, at the same time, no book can fully replace in-person training and professional development. Nor can anyone become an experienced workshop facilitator just by reading books.

If you do decide to start your own Stellar Journey, there are a few critical necessities to keep an eye on. For example, you should ensure that all participants can attend the workshops from beginning to end. What's more, you need to clarify who the facilitator is, why people are there, and what the goal of the journey is. To help you get the preparations right, you'll find a comprehensive checklist for workshops in the appendix.

Before we continue, we want to point out something important about our teaching approach: the Stellar Approach is focused on the *behavior* of teams. Using the Stellar Principles, Practices, and Virtues, we aim to broaden the team's perspective and focus on finding something doable in the next step. The goal of the journey is to establish regenerative behaviors in the team, develop a new mindset through action, and in this way, to incrementally make the entire organization more regenerative.

At the same time, we need to consider the *conditions* of the journey. After all, a sweeping regenerative transformation can only succeed if any systemic dependencies are identified and addressed. We'll ask questions like: When do we need to escalate and involve the management level above us? Where do conflicts arise between what behavior is incentivized and where we wish to go? How does regenerative action impact our economic performance indicators, like revenue or profitability? How will we deal with conflicting goals? In our experience, change in behaviors and conditions often resembles a swinging pendulum: new behaviors increase the need to change the conditions, and new conditions in turn foster new behaviors.[1]

And what about *"culture,"* often extolled as a magical cure for all woes? Clearly, company culture is important in transformation efforts, because it can either help or hinder progress. But it can't be directly influenced – in systems theory terms, it's an "undecidable decision premise"[2] that makes certain kinds of organizational behavior more or less likely. This is why attempts to develop culture by imposing top-down values and visions tend to fail. Culture emerges from the thousands of daily interactions in an organization, which is why it can't be controlled. Therefore, we believe a more promising approach is to shape behavior and conditions instead. When we propose new ways of doing things and demonstrate their impact, like magic, attitudes and culture begin to evolve too.

Other aspects that tend to change along the way are the language we use and the internal map we navigate with.

From a systems theory perspective, organizations consist of communication, and anything that's not communicated, doesn't really exist. That's why it's so crucial to find a common vocabulary for what we want to talk about and where we want to go. People must be able to discuss new concepts so that everyone understands them in the same way. This facilitates communication, which helps to set that shared direction.

Now, with this theoretical preamble out of the way, we're ready to dive into the curriculum and take a closer look at the workshop modules and their corresponding methods.

Module 1: Context

The first step on the path to a regenerative economy involves gaining a broad understanding of the context in which people, organizations, and the economy are embedded. We simply must understand these systemic dependencies if we mean to shape our development in a regenerative way. And not just understand them in abstract terms, but grasp very specifically how they relate to our own organization and team.

Module 1 focuses on the Stellar Virtue of courage, and the first three of the seven Stellar Practices:

1. **Understanding Interconnectedness:** Where do we stand in the world? How would we categorize our organization and team in the grand scheme of things? Where do we have latitude to do as we see fit?
2. **Using Our Own Circle of Influence:** How can we incrementally make our playing field more regenerative? How can we address impulses for change that lie outside our circle of influence?
3. **Setting a Shared Intention:** In our circle of influence, what regenerative contribution will we make? What will serve as our compass, providing a direction to align ourselves with?

We consider Module 1 successfully completed if we've achieved these goals with the team:

- [ ] The team understands what the Stellar Approach is and the elements it's made up of.
- [ ] The team has a basic understanding of the different levels of sustainability.
- [ ] The team is familiar with the concept of regenerativity and the common frameworks around it.
- [ ] The team is able to apply the concept of regenerativity to its own organization and has identified some initial action areas.
- [ ] The team has defined the scope for action in its circle of influence and formulated the contribution it wants to make to regenerative change.
- [ ] The team members have learned some basic techniques for consciously managing their inner resources.
- [ ] The team can raise tensions and goal conflicts, as well as develop next steps for resolving them.
- [ ] The team has created an initial sprint backlog with clear goals for the next six weeks, which it can start working on immediately after the module.

Stellar Practice 1: Understanding Interconnectedness

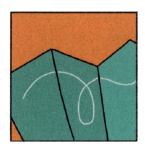

Where do we stand in the world? How would we categorize our organization and team in the grand scheme of things? Where do we have latitude to do as we see fit?

We've laced up our boots, and it's time to start the Stellar Journey. As always, we like to take a moment first to mentally "arrive" and find our shared focus together with the team. Therefore, we begin with a check-in, presenting the agenda for the workshop and taking time to clarify any intentions, hopes, and wishes that team members might have for the journey. Afterwards, we give a brief introduction on the topic at hand:

- We lay down the basic framework for the content of the workshop: we underscore the need for transformation, present the various levels of sustainability, and share a first peek at the concept of regenerative economic activity (see page 56).
- We present the four Stellar Principles as the guiding stars that will accompany us through all three modules (see page 90).
- We introduce the elements that enable step-by-step progress on our journey: tension-based work, sprint work, and the transparent handling of goal conflicts (see page 132).

After this simple orientation, we dive into the concrete methods related to the Stellar Practice of "Understanding Interconnectedness." As you'll recall, this practice is all about the team gaining a broader understanding of the networks it's embedded in.

In conventional economic activity, teams or organizations typically don't care about what goes on beyond their own market. They focus on customers, suppliers, and potential competitors. Other external environments only matter if they directly affect the market, for example via regulations.

But lately, due to the growing efforts around sustainability and stricter reporting responsibilities, many organizations are starting to care more about social and environmental systems. Sadly though, these concerns often fall by the wayside in the chaos of everyday business.

In the first part of the book, we saw how the only way to enable ubiquitous healthy development in the long run is to co-develop our vital social and ecological environments together with us. Hence, the team needs to ask itself some tough questions: What surrounding systems are we, as a team, part of? What systems do our activities impact and how? Which human and non-human stakeholders or entities are we already mindful of, and which have we overlooked so far?

The first Stellar Practice gives the team a shared starting point and baseline knowledge that can be built on later. Depending on the team's prior experience with sustainability, we can make our way through this practice more or less quickly.

Concepts to make the complexity of it all somewhat more manageable

It can be pretty challenging to capture all the interdependent relationships that a team is embedded in. That's why, to help us do so, we rely on some basic concepts related to sustainable and regenerative economic activity.

Of course, it's hard to make a definitive list of *the key* concepts, since they are constantly evolving through new research, and new models can emerge too. But we believe that the following "buffet" of concepts does a pretty good job of covering everything that we build on in the Stellar Approach:

- The UN's Sustainable Development Goals
- Scope 1–3
- Science Based Targets (for Nature)
- Ecosystem services
- Doughnut Economics and Planetary Boundaries

- Infinite Games
- Biomimicry
- Permaculture
- Inner Development Goals

In the appendix of this book, you'll find "concept cards" for each of these, replete with brief descriptions. They also include an explanation of who typically needs the concept, how it can help with regenerative development, and what key questions it should spark for the team.

Understanding the concept of a sustainable and regenerative economy

The concept cards come into play very early on in the Stellar team process. In the kick-off session that we run before even commencing Module 1, we hand them out to team members and ask that they review them. Then, in Module 1, they can explain the concepts to each other and highlight how they are significant for the team. This happens in three simple steps:[3]

1 | CHOOSING THE CONCEPTS
The team chooses 3–5 concepts that are especially relevant for them.

2 | TRANSLATING THE CONCEPTS TO THE CONTEXT OF THE TEAM
The chosen concepts are discussed in small groups, using questions like:
- How does this concept relate to our daily work?
- What can we do about it, and what must we do about it?
- What questions do they impel us to ask ourselves?
- Which aspects of the Stellar Principles do we see reflected in this concept?

The most important findings are jotted down somewhere, for example on a flipchart or whiteboard.

3 | PRESENTING THE RESULTS AND COLLECTING TENSIONS
The small groups share their findings with each other. Any tensions that arose during the discussion are captured in the tension stash.

Module 1: Context   149

 The team understands how key concepts in sustainability and regenerativity relate to its own work.

 60 minutes

 Concept cards, whiteboard or flipchart, pens

Experiencing the safe and just space of the regenerative economy

Next, we dive deeper into the concept of a "safe and just space" as described by Kate Raworth in the doughnut model.[4] Understanding this space is so fundamental to regenerative economic activity that we conduct an exercise to allow the team to physically experience what it feels like.[5]

1 | UNDERSTANDING THE DOUGHNUT MODEL
We give a brief introduction to the doughnut model. Here, the focus is on understanding how the planetary boundaries and social foundations carve out a space in the shape of a doughnut. A detailed understanding of each individual dimension isn't necessary yet.

2 | THE OUTER BOUNDARY
To symbolize the planetary boundaries, team members lay a rope on the floor in the shape of a circle. Then, we explain what it means:
"This rope represents the maximum strain we can safely put on the planet. If we cross beyond the rope, we exceed the planetary boundaries. Within the rope, we're in a safe space for humanity."

Next, cards with the names of the nine planetary boundaries are laid on the outside of the circle and briefly presented. Any comprehension questions can be clarified at this point. The team members are then invited to first stand in the circle and then outside the circle, paying attention to any sensations they experience in their body as they do.

150   The Stellar Approach

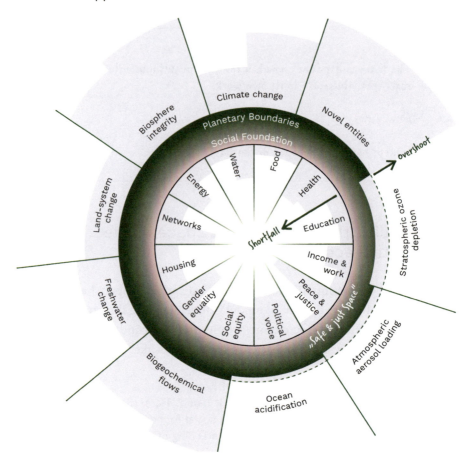

3 | THE INNER BOUNDARY

Just as in step 2, a rope is laid down: *"This rope represents the social foundation, meaning the things we need to lead a good life."* Once again, cards with the names of the various dimensions are set down on the floor and any comprehension questions clarified.

Once all the inner boundaries have been presented, we then take a look at the empirical data on where the world currently stands in relation to these limits.[6]

4 | STEPPING INTO THE DOUGHNUT

The team members are invited to move around the different spaces of the doughnut. They're asked to remain silent, pay close attention to their physical sensations, and take their time with each space.

5 | THREE ROUNDS OF REFLECTION IN PAIRS

The team members are asked to stop in front of a colleague and answer three questions. Each person has two minutes to share their thoughts with the other person, who is asked to listen carefully. Then the roles are switched for another two minutes. The questions to answer are:

1. When you connect with the outer edge of the doughnut, meaning the planetary boundaries: what place in nature do you cherish dearly and hope to never lose?
2. When you connect with the inner edge of the doughnut, meaning the basic requirements for a good life: share something that has enabled you to be here today – something that others may not be lucky enough to have.
3. When you connect with the space in the doughnut, meaning the "safe and just space": share some way that you could contribute to moving humanity into that space.

Once each pair is done, they again walk silently and find a new partner. After three rounds of reflection of about four minutes each, the exercise is over.

6 | REFLECTING AS A GROUP

The team members share their experiences with the group:
- What made you happy/annoyed/surprised about the perceptions that others shared with you?
- Did you notice any connections or overlaps between what you shared and what you heard?
- What are your current thoughts and feelings about the spaces inside and around the doughnut?

7 | COLLECTING TENSIONS

Any tensions that arose can be collected either now or after the next exercise.

The team understands the concept of the "safe and just space" and can experience it on an emotional level.

 45–60 minutes

 Cards for the planetary boundaries and the social foundations, two long bits of rope or cable.

Applying the doughnut to ourselves

Now that all team members have understood and experienced the doughnut, we apply the model to the team itself:

1 | MAPPING
Here, we can reuse the cards with the planetary boundaries and social foundations from the previous exercise. With the help of two questions, they're positioned in a simple matrix:
- Which planetary boundaries or social foundations are relevant for our work and how?
- Where are we already taking responsibility with our activities? Where are we only getting started with this?

2 | EXCHANGE
We examine the social foundations and the planetary boundaries, one after the other, and discuss what connection we as an organization or as a team have to them. We also look at what we're already doing and where we might have latitude to do more. Depending on the size of the group, this exchange can take place between the whole team or in small groups.

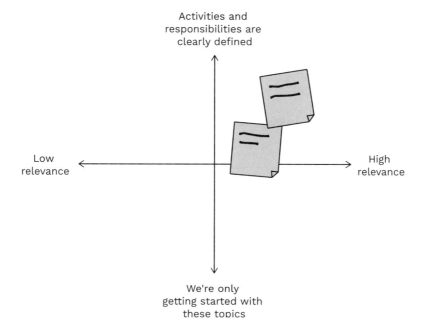

3 | REFLECTION
Next, we take the time to answer the following questions together as a team:
- What have we as an organization or team learned about the safe and just space? What stands out to us?
- Where do we see discrepancies between where we are and where we want to be? Where do we see the need to take action as a team? What would we like to change?

4 | COLLECTING TENSIONS
To end on, any tensions that arose are collected and stored in the tension stash.

5 | LONG-TERM PERSPECTIVE
Finally, we use a simple question to shift our perspective to the long-term view: "What would our grandchildren say about what we've just talked about?" Here, the focus is on intuitive answers – whatever comes to mind first.

> The team sees itself through the lens of the safe and just space.
>
> 45–60 minutes
>
> Cards for the planetary boundaries and the social foundations, a whiteboard.

Diversity and inclusion as elements of the regenerative transformation

Thanks to the previous exercises, the team should now have a broader understanding of the ecological and social dependencies it's embedded in. Moreover, it's starting to see its own economic activity in this context too. Next, we go a step further by examining how structural social effects can have a positive or negative effect on the regenerative transformation.

The polycrisis is a tangle of several crises, which means that isolated interventions will always be insufficient. To effectively tackle the ecological issues we face, we also need to address challenges in structural social dynamics. And to get this right, we need to include different perspectives: an intersectional and inclusive approach is the only way to ensure that all relevant voices are heard and hence, that the solutions work for all those affected. Understanding different perspectives is also the only way to lift people out of ignorance. The Stellar principle "diverse" is meant to reflect these issues.

Module 1: Context   155

Recognizing our privileges

If we want to incorporate different perspectives into our work, we need an inclusive environment that explicitly values and makes room for diversity. In other words, inclusion is a prerequisite for diversity to bloom. To help the team grasp this dynamic, we like to run an exercise on structural privileges.[7]

1 | INDIVIDUAL REFLECTION
Using the wheel of privilege below, each team member maps out their own privileges. If they find some dimensions difficult to evaluate or would rather keep them private, they can omit them.

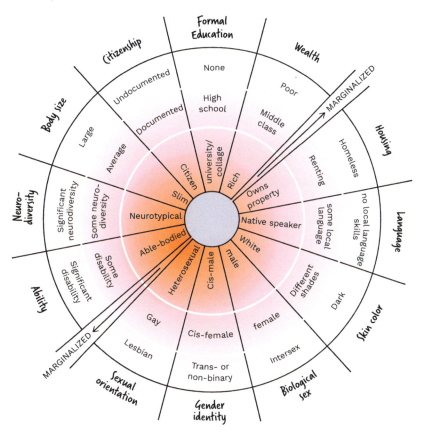

2 | PAIR DISCUSSION
Team members form pairs with someone they trust and share their perspectives regarding the following question:
- How can we use our own privileges in a targeted way to enable broader participation for everyone?

Each pair then jointly reflects on what perspectives are missing from the team and how they would benefit the team's work. They then consider the following questions:
- What do we need in order to integrate these missing perspectives into our decision-making?
- How can we shape our decision-making process so that people who can bring these perspectives will feel valued and effective?

3 | SUMMARY
The team comes together to summarize the key findings from the pairs.
- What have we learned, both as individuals and as a team?
- Do we need to take action somewhere? Is there something we want to do differently than before?

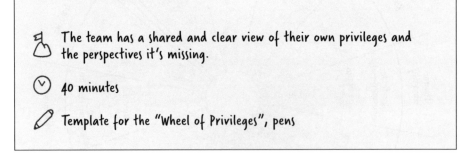

The team has a shared and clear view of their own privileges and the perspectives it's missing.

40 minutes

Template for the "Wheel of Privileges", pens

For many teams, this is the first time that they openly speak about privilege, and we believe that the resulting increased awareness of structural privilege already makes this time well spent. And of course, if any need for action is identified, it's captured in the tension stash as usual.

In Module 2, we'll look more closely at the question of how to incorporate missing voices when we discuss regenerative roles (see page 197).

Stellar Practice 2: Using Our Own Circle of Influence

How can we incrementally make our playing field more regenerative? How can we address impulses for change that lie outside our circle of influence?

The health of a regenerative economy depends on the quality of relationships between all parts of the system. Regenerative organizations know this and therefore invest to improve this quality. That's why, with the second Stellar Practice, the team takes a closer look at the system of relationships it's embedded in. It also begins to explore the latitude it has to independently move in a more regenerative direction.

Here, it's crucial to keep an eye on how decisions made elsewhere – either in or outside of the organization – affect the team's own circle of influence, and vice versa. Teams that work regeneratively know their own circle of influence and use it to drive the regenerative transformation forward. They also understand where their circle ends and what to do with the ideas that lie on its fringes.

The first concept we use to guide us in this Stellar practice is the "Circle of Influence" model, which was created by Stephen Covey, author of the all-time bestseller "The 7 Habits of Highly Effective People." You may remember it from our earlier discussion on goal conflicts and the reasons for moving in small steps. In this simple model, Covey distinguishes between three different circles:

- **Circle of Control:** Encompasses all the things we can decide on our own and directly control with our actions.
- **Circle of Influence:** Contains things that we can't directly decide ourselves but which we can influence to an extent.
- **Circle of Concern:** Here, we find all the issues that concern us but which we can't influence.

The Stellar Approach

In the Stellar Approach, we use this model for two main purposes:

1. To make team decisions faster and more manageable. Here, the following questions are helpful: What can we decide on our own? Where do we need other decision-makers from within or even outside of the organization? How can we feed our views into decision-making processes beyond our team? Where do goal conflicts arise that we can't immediately resolve?
2. To help the team overcome feelings of powerlessness and take action in their own circle of influence. The challenges around sustainability and re-generativity lie in such a tangled web of systemic and global dynamics that it's easy to forget that there *is* room to act in. By using this model, we refocus on the things we can change in our circle of influence. This bolsters the team's self-efficacy and, ideally, also inspires the broader organization.

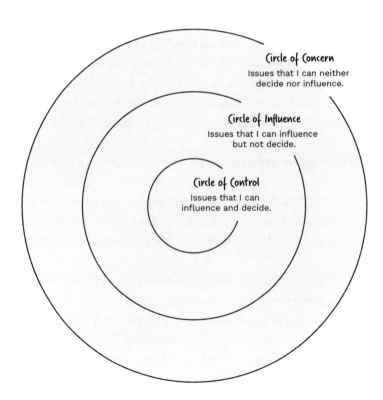

Keeping these two purposes in mind, we can examine the team's service provision process more closely. To structure the system of relationships that the team operates in and to spot opportunities for improvement, we employ the *Regenerative Business Canvas (RBC)*. This is a tool that draws on some of the fundamental models of circular economics.

The Regenerative Business Canvas distinguishes between the four phases of a linear value chain and describes four ways of closing loops in it. To make it easier to understand, we'll use an illustrative and admittedly non-exhaustive example to showcase how it can be applied to a business.

- **Resource inputs:** What do we need in order to provide our services? This can include financial resources, people's time and expertise, materials, energy, and technology. Where do we source them from and what context are they in turn embedded in?
  As a fictional, simplified **example**, *consider a small hole-in-the-wall restaurant specializing in french fries: Fry-Day. To provide their service, Fry-Day needs lots*

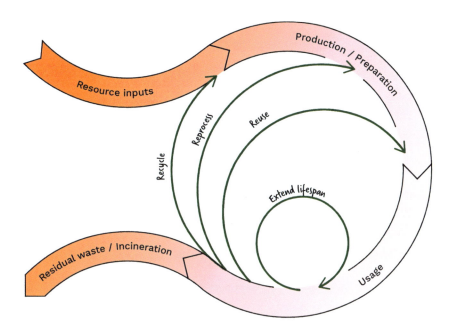

of resources. Walk into their storeroom, and you'll see plastic bags of potatoes from various countries, little satchels of ketchup, disposable forks, and so on – all bought from a food service wholesaler. For their energy needs, their local power company is happy to sell them electricity generated from a conventional mix of energy sources. And of course, the restaurant also needs water, as well as the time and energy of the people working there.

- **Production/Preparation:** Who's involved in or affected by the production of our products and/or services?
  In the case of Fry-Day, a freelancer prints and distributes promotional flyers, and the restaurateur cooks the french fries.
- **Usage:** Who or what is impacted by the use of our products or services?
  Fry-Day's happy customers come to mind first, of course. But also their families are indirectly affected, because the customers may have altered their lunch plans. Or the neighborhood as a whole may be affected, if the smell of frying oil spreads widely enough.
- **Residual waste/Incineration:** What elements or materials are left over from our product or service that can't be used for anything anymore?
  At Fry-Day, this includes waste like the flyers, napkins, and disposable bowls and forks, which can't be reused in any way. The same is true for leftover food and the packaging for the ingredients, like say the plastic bags that the potatoes come in.
- **Four loops** to reduce resource consumption and waste:[8]
  - How can we prolong the lifespan of the product or service we provide? How can we boost the average usage rate of our products so that fewer need to be produced?
  - Once used, can the product be passed on and reused?
  - What parts of the product can be reprocessed and fed back into the loop?
  - What raw materials can be recycled and reused?

  At Fry-Day, the spent cooking oil is sold to another company to be (partially) processed into biodiesel.

Applying the Regenerative Business Canvas: How can we improve our relationships with our stakeholders?

On a practical level, we apply the RBC in a six-step exercise. It helps us to get an overview of the team's stakeholders and their influence, as well as to identify some initial opportunities for action.[9] Depending on the size of the team, we work either with the whole team or in small groups. It's worth noting that even teams that aren't directly involved in production processes can use the exercise because it helps them develop a better understanding of their environmental systems. As a result, they might, say, reexamine an upstream product that they themselves use to provide their service.

1 | DEPICTING THE CURRENT STATE OF THE SERVICE PROVISION PROCESS.
The team outlines the lifecycle of their service via the RBC. Key steps in the process are marked on Post-its and matched to the four phases, as described above. Here, the focus is solely on the status quo – how things actually are.

2 | MAPPING STAKEHOLDERS
The team identifies all the stakeholders in its service provision process and maps them to the phases of the RBC. This includes not just human stakeholders but non-human ones too: local water system, animals, and so forth. Indirect stakeholders should also be included, meaning employees' families, supply chain participants, and natural systems in the areas where the raw materials are produced. For many teams, this step alone could easily take days and go very deep into various environmental systems, but this would rapidly get very complex. Hence, at this stage, we spend only 10–15 minutes on this topic and work with what we've found in that time window. There's always the option to dive deeper later on.

3 | ASSESSING THE IMPACT ON STAKEHOLDERS
The team evaluates the impact of its service provision on each stakeholder. It examines the social and environmental effects separately and uses a simple scale from -2 ("very harmful") to +2 ("very beneficial").

Here, it makes sense to start with the stakeholders where the assessment is easiest to make, be that quantitatively or qualitatively. If it turns out that better data is needed to make a more granular evaluation, then tensions may well arise in the course of the exercise. As usual, these are captured in the tension stash.

4 | GRADING THE REQUIRED ACTIONS
The team flags the Post-its where they see the most urgent need for action, thereby generating a heat map. In addition, the team also marks any Post-Its where there are quick wins to be had.

5 | CAPTURING NEXT STEPS
Finally, the team captures any to-dos and next steps. At this point, individual tasks might also be put directly into the sprint backlog because they'll be tackled in the first sprint between module 1 and module 2.

6 | COLLECTING TENSIONS
As usual, tensions are collected and stored in the tension stash.

 The team has an overview of all the human and non-human stakeholders involved in its service provision and has identified some initial opportunities for action.

 60 minutes

 Regenerative Business Canvas template, Post-its, pens*

---

* You can download the template here: thedive.link/en/rbc

Stellar Practice 3: Setting a Shared Intention

In our circle of influence, what regenerative contribution will we make? What will serve as our compass, providing a direction to align ourselves with?

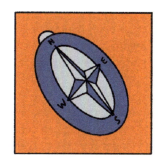

By now, the team should have a broad understanding of the systemic dependencies its activities are embedded in (Stellar Practice 1). What's more, it has closely examined the stakeholder relationships in its circle of influence and found the first potential areas for change (Stellar Practice 2).

As a result, team members now understand the context well enough to define their shared intention: what will their specific contribution be to making the organization incrementally more regenerative?

This last step in Module 1 is vital because teams work best when they have a shared direction to strive in. This is why defining the regenerative contribution explicitly is so important. The key questions that guide the team in this discussion are:

- If our organization were regenerative, what would our team be needed for?
- Using its own circle of influence, how can our team contribute to making the organization more regenerative?

Our team's contribution to making our organization more regenerative

The team articulates and aligns on their specific contribution. In other words, they integrate the perspectives of all team members and define a motivating direction that they can all rally behind. To arrive at this, they use the two-step integration tournament.

The Stellar Approach

1 | FILLING IN THE CONTRIBUTION CANVAS INDIVIDUALLY

Each team member takes the time to individually reflect on a few guiding statements to help them craft their own contribution. They fill in each of the four initial statements, using sentences, keywords, or even metaphors, as they see fit.

- In our team, I see significant potential for more sustainability or regenerativity in these areas: …
- In our organization, I see a necessity for regenerative change in these areas: …
- We as a team can contribute to the regenerative shift in the product and service landscape of our organization by …
- This is something I'd like to change immediately: …

Using the answers as inspiration, each team member can now fill in the final blank with one sentence, which is a prototype of their contribution:

- In a regenerative organization, our team is needed because …

Please note: Here the focus is solely on formulating contribution prototypes that are "safe enough to try." The exact wording can of course be further reworked and refined along the Stellar Journey as needed.

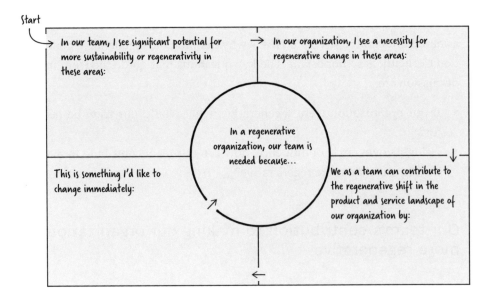

2 | INTEGRATION PLAYOFFS

The main gist here is that the playoffs take place as integration rounds. In each round, participants form pairs that jointly formulate a new contribution, using their individual versions as a basis. Since the result is a prototype that will be worked on later, it doesn't need to be perfect, as long as both parties are happy with it. As a last step, each pair decides who of them will act as their representative in the next integration round.

In the next round, whoever was chosen pairs up with the representative from another pair, and they repeat the process. This time, they use the contributions they defined in the last round as a basis for a joint version. Once they're both happy with the outcome, they again decide who will represent them in the next round.

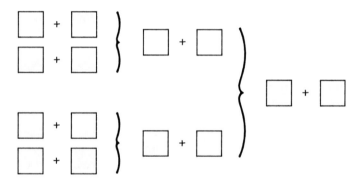

In the final round of the playoffs, the last two contributions are integrated by the two remaining representatives. Once their work is done, they present the outcome to the team, who review it together. If the team voices any safety concerns[10] or urgent change requests, these are considered and, where possible, resolved through modifying the wording of the contribution.

Again, we can't emphasize enough that the contribution is *not* set in stone. It's enough that the team feels comfortable with the prototype, and it's safe enough to try for now. Should any new tensions arise later, they can always be integrated, and the contribution refined. And of course, the tournament can be completely redone if the team changes in some fundamental way.

166 The Stellar Approach

> The regenerative contribution of the team is articulated in a single sentence, integrating the individual perspectives of all team members.
>
> 60–75 minutes
>
> "Our Contribution" template, Post-its, pens

We'll continue working with the contribution in Module 2, where we'll derive **concrete milestones** for making it (Stellar Practice 4) as well as define the **roles and responsibilities necessary to do so** (Stellar Practice 5).

Purpose, vision, strategy, goals, contribution – How are they all related?

Purpose, strategy, vision … The myriad of different strategic elements and terms can sometimes seem confusing enough as it is, even without the regenerative perspective thrown into the mix. So, let's see if we can clarify things a bit, shall we?

By viewing things through a regenerative lens, we see that we have stakeholders beyond our organization and the market we operate in. And even though our relationships with them are vital for our survival, we often overlook them. By zooming out, we can complement our existing strategic elements with a regenerative contribution.

As the Stellar Journey continues, we might find that tensions emerge between the team's regenerative contribution and the vision, strategy, or purpose of the team or organization. Nevertheless, we recommend that teams don't rush to change these elements, but rather try and see first whether tensions do in fact arise.[11]

Module 1: Context 167

Moving items from the tensions stash to the backlog of the first sprint

At the end of Module 1, we take all the tensions in the tension stash and add a next step to each. In practice, this means examining the tensions one by one and determining what the tension holder needs for it to be resolved.

Often, this just means clarifying a question or gathering opinions from the group, which only takes a few minutes.

But other kinds of tensions may spawn tasks or work packages that need to be processed further. These are fed into the sprint planning for the first sprint, which will take place during the roughly 4 to 6 weeks between the first and second modules.

To help choose the tasks and work packages to be processed in the first sprint, each item gets prioritized according to effort, benefit, importance, and/or the energy available to complete them. Responsibility for the chosen tasks and work packages are assigned to individuals, and the tasks are visualized on a simple Kanban board with four columns: "Backlog," "To Do," "In Progress," and "Done."

Goal conflicts that can't be resolved right away are put into the Goal Conflict Navigator so that we don't lose sight of them and can continue working on them later.

Once Module 1 is over, the team then begins, in small steps, to tackle the tasks from the sprint planning. Right away, this allows them to experience

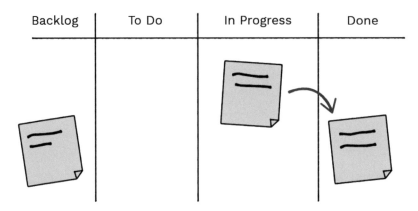

firsthand the power of self-efficacy and gives them a reason to celebrate their progress. Usually, here, the mood is already elated, and we call for some applause and hearty cheers to rouse it further.[12]

Inner Work in Module 1

At this point, the team has worked through the full contents of Stellar Practices 1 through 3. They've reflected on and discussed regenerativity, coming to grips with what it means in practice. To complement this "external" work, at the end of each day, we turn our focus inwards.

Strictly speaking, the following exercises and rituals belong to the seventh Stellar Practice, "Staying Effective." But because inner work is so important throughout the Stellar Journey, we engage in it at the end of all three modules.

These methods aim to develop relationship skills, reinforce resilience, and enhance one's ability to deal with dilemmas and ambiguities. And in Module 1, their main focus is on our **personal feelings** and **resilience**.

Thoughts create feelings: Harnessing emotions in transformation processes

It's a fundamental truth that change always evokes feelings. Sometimes, the dominant ones might be worry or fear: What will this transformation mean for my role? Can we even manage a transformation when our day-to-day work is so stressful already?

Anger can also crop up, for example, if projects move too slowly, communication is lacking, or seemingly unsolvable goal conflicts block the way. Other feelings, such as helplessness, overwhelm, excitement, and enthusiasm, can also arise. Throughout this journey, it's very likely that we'll need to deal with an entire whirlwind of emotions.

In many workplaces, people avoid discussing their feelings. This is problematic because whether we like it or not, emotions greatly influence what we do. And if we don't dedicate time to consciously observe and understand them, it obscures their influence: Fear can still paralyze us. Unrecognized anger can lead to rash decisions. Overwhelm can cause us to withdraw into our shells.

Our feelings are powerful guides, and if there's ever a time when guidance is indispensable, it's during times of change. That's why it's so important that we learn to consciously acknowledge and accept our emotions, with kindness. By doing so, we see that even emotions like anger can be harnessed as a source of tremendous energy. As long as we see the anger as a signal that something needs to change, we can then channel that energy to bring about that change.

This is why, in the Stellar Journey, we deliberately make room for feelings. For some, this might feel strange at first, but doing so enables us to act responsibly, instead of being steered by our unconscious feelings.

What does this look like in practice? In each Stellar Module, we engage in two rituals: **"Virtue Coach"** and **"Pause and Nurture Hope."** Next, we take a look at the Virtual Coach ritual, and in Module 2, we'll focus on nurturing hope (see page 211).

A Courage work-out with the Virtue Coach

The first Stellar Virtue is courage, and it is indispensable on the regenerative development path: We need courage to advocate for change, especially when it would be more comfortable and convenient to leave things as they are. We need it to bravely let go of the old, even when we don't yet fully understand the new. We need it to explore our feelings — both pleasant and unpleasant — and integrate them into the change process in a healthy way. We need it to learn to be vulnerable as a team. And finally, we need courage to recognize traits in ourselves that we'd rather deny, for example, sometimes being too judgmental of others.

Though the exact questions differ between virtues, the Virtue Trainer ritual follows the same format in each module:

1 | PAIR INTERVIEWS
Team members form pairs and conduct short interviews with each other. To do this, they find a place where they won't be disturbed – this could well be outdoors so they get a bit of fresh air. First, Person A interviews Person B and takes notes of their responses. Then, they switch roles. The interview questions they pose are:
- How courageous do you feel at the moment, on a scale of 1 to 10?
- Think back to a moment in the past when you felt very courageous. Describe that situation.
- What made you feel courageous then? What helps you feel courageous in general?
- What mental image, sound, or gesture do you currently associate with your courage?

2 | ANCHORING THE VIRTUE IN THE TEAM
After the interviews, the team forms a standing circle. All the team members take turns to show the physical gesture, describe the image, or make the sound that they associate with their courage. People can ask questions about the meaning behind these, but they don't necessarily need to be answered.

Finally, the team celebrates their collective courage with a volley of cheers and hurrahs.

 The team members become aware of their personal resources around this virtue and find a tangible way to make these resources more accessible.

 30 minutes

 Guiding questions for the Courage Virtue Trainer exercise, paper or Post-its, pens

Resilience in Module 1

Major transitions are always demanding, and even more so when it's a regenerative transformation. That's why we equip the team with methods and techniques to help keep up its strength and deal with the inevitable dilemmas and ambiguities it will meet. In other words, we teach the team to *manage its own resilience*.

Resilience is the inner strength or power to overcome exceptional challenges. We need it to navigate through the constant changes we face in these times and to become stronger as we do. In the Stellar Approach, we also use the concept of "Personal Regeneration." Just as it is with nature, cultivating our resilience requires nourishment and ample time to recharge.

Of course, resilience isn't some static trait but an ability that can be strengthened like any other. One way is to actively nurture your well-being. Another is to protect yourself from resilience-degrading risk factors by understanding your personal risk factors and things that help you cope with difficulties.[13]

Ensuring there's plenty of water under the keel

To explain the concept of resilience in simple terms, we can use the analogy of a boat in shallow water. The water level represents our inner balance and, by extension, our ability to handle any challenges that may arise.

When we're stressed and exhausted, the water level is low, making even small obstacles potentially difficult to get over. But when we're in a good balance, and the water level is high, we can navigate even large rocks with calm and confidence.

Module 1: Context 173

Next, we put the boat analogy to use in a reflection exercise with the team:

1 | INDIVIDUAL REFLECTION
Each team member takes the time to consider the following questions through the lens of the boat analogy, taking notes along the way:
- What conditions or activities generally raise my personal water level?
- What conditions or activities generally lower my personal water level?
- What conditions or activities raise the team's water level?

2 | SHARING HIGHLIGHTS
The team comes together to share the key findings from step 1.

3 | AGREEING ON MICRO HABITS
The team commits to at least one small change in their day-to-day work that helps them maintain balance and raise the team's overall water level. These so-called *micro habits* are much easier to put into practice than sweeping changes.

For example, the team might agree to start weekly meetings with a "water level check." Or they could introduce a new break at work when everyone takes a shared walk to clear their heads. Or they might start a habit of always taking a moment to pause and clarify their intentions before starting a conversation. The main thing is that the habit should feel doable. Ideally, it should even spark a bit of excitement.

The team documents the commitments it deems safe enough to try and trials them before the next module.

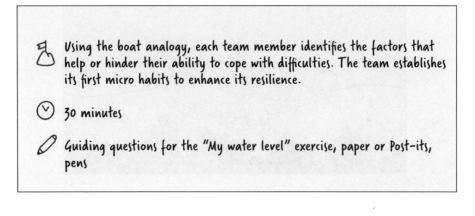

With these final inner work exercises, we bring the first Stellar Module, "Context," to a close. Ideally, we'll now have accomplished and can check off the goals we set for ourselves at the beginning of the module.

- ☑ The team understands what the Stellar Approach is and the elements it's made up of.
- ☑ The team has a basic understanding of the different levels of sustainability.
- ☑ The team is familiar with the concept of regenerativity and the common frameworks around it.
- ☑ The team is able to apply the concept of regenerativity to its own organization and has identified some initial action areas.
- ☑ The team has defined the scope for action in its circle of influence and formulated the contribution it wants to make to regenerative change.
- ☑ The team members have learned some basic techniques for consciously managing their inner resources.
- ☑ The team can raise tensions and goal conflicts, as well as develop next steps for resolving them.
- ☑ The team has created an initial sprint backlog with clear goals for the next six weeks, which it can start working on immediately after the module.

Workshop Agenda Module 1
Day 1

9:00 — **Welcome and check-in**

Goals and intentions for the journey
Introduction to regenerative economic activity and the Stellar Principles
Working with tensions, sprints, and goal conflicts

10:45 — **Break**

Basics of sustainability and regenerativity
Sharing outcomes together

12:30 — **Lunch break**

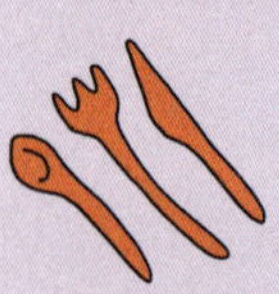

Exploring the safe and just space of the doughnut
Going deeper into the Stellar Principles

14:45 — **Break**

Privileges within the team
Processing tensions
Virtue Coach: Courage

17:30 — **Wrap-up, check-out**

Example

Module 1: Context   **177**

Workshop Agenda Module 1
Day 2

9:00	👋	**Check-in**
		Introduction to the Regenerative Business Canvas
		The Regenerative Business Canvas for our team
11:15	☕	**Break**
		Working individually with the Contribution Canvas
		Contribution playoffs
13:00	🍴	**Lunch break**
		Energizer exercise
		Sprint planning and Sprint 1 kick-off
15:30	☕	**Break**
		Introduction to resilience: the boat analogy
		Processing tensions
		Pause and Nurture Hope
		(see instructions in Module 2)
17:30	👋	**Wrap-up, check-out**

Example

Module 2: Direction

It's time to get our hands dirty. In Module 2, we take the insights gleaned from the journey so far and anchor them into the team's daily work. We also further develop the team's ability to take regenerative action.

Usually, at this point, several weeks will have passed since the completion of Module 1. During this time, the team has had the chance to apply its learnings and work on the tasks from the sprint backlog.

Module 2 builds on these first practical experiences and provides a clear methodological framework for regenerative action. In it, we draw on the Stellar Virtue of Creative Joy and the fourth and fifth Stellar Practices:

4. **Designing Circular Processes:** How can we make our way towards a regenerative future, step by step? How can we embrace a circular mindset when designing our processes?
5. **Making Regenerative Decisions:** How can we make decisions in such a way that their positive impact on our stakeholders – both human and non-human – outweighs any potential negative impact?

To start Module 2, we briefly recap what happened in Module 1 and also hold a retro meeting to review the results of the first sprint. We also explain that Module 2 will divide its time between Stellar Practices 4 and 5, and that we consider it to have been a success if, together with the team, we've hit these goals:

- [ ] The team has a clear vision of how exactly they'll make their regenerative contribution over the next three to five years.
- [ ] Team members know how to use tensions to develop processes in an iterative way.
- [ ] The team has applied circular thinking to its own circle of influence and identified initial steps to close loops.
- [ ] The team has created roles necessary for its regenerative development journey.
- [ ] The team has learned to incorporate regenerative perspectives into its decision-making.
- [ ] The team knows how to use regenerative routines in its meetings and has revised its existing meetings accordingly.
- [ ] The team becomes even more confident in managing its internal resources.
- [ ] The team's sprint backlog has been updated, with clear to-dos defined for the next four to six weeks.

Stellar Practice 4: Designing Circular Processes

How can we make our way towards a regenerative future, step by step? How can we embrace a circular mindset when designing our processes?

The basic cycle and rhythm of life is made up of growth and decay. Plant and animal life ebbs and flows with environmental factors like temperature, air pressure, and seasons. Even the cells in our bodies are constantly in the process of breaking down and being replaced. And of course, our social systems aren't static either – they're constantly being reshaped by what's communicated in them. Any sense of temporary stability can only ever exist as a bubble in a sea of flux, destined to pop. This is a fundamental fact of life.

Unfortunately, our organizational and economic processes are only partially compatible with it: Our day-to-day work is dominated by cause-and-effect thinking, linear process planning, and a command-and-control mindset. Today's linear economic model, also known as "take-make-waste," necessitates resource use at a level far beyond natural regeneration times, making it wholly unsustainable. The past two decades have clearly shown that this model has reached its limits.

A regenerative team, on the other hand, operates in harmony with life's fundamental penchant for change and development. Using the fourth Stellar Practice, the team can train itself to embrace a mindset of continuous development that will serve as a bedrock for the way they design their processes and work together:

- We help the team work better together by teaching **iterative and agile methods and process logics**. You may recall that we presented examples of these when discussing tensions and sprints.
- We also aim to shape the team's economic activity, meaning its production and/or service processes. We familiarize them with the **basic principles**

of circular economic activity and make some first strides toward closing loops.

Iterative work and a long-term orientation

Embracing an iterative and agile way of working raises an interesting tension: On the one hand, we know that life isn't linear and can't be controlled with any precision and that, in complex environments, the only thing we can do is take the next step forward.

But on the other hand, we learned in Part 1 that our current economic system sorely needs to consider its long-term effects more, meaning a time scale of generations rather than quarters. This is what the Stellar Principle "Long-Term" is all about.

So, we can't predict or control the long term but simultaneously need to keep it in mind. How is that supposed to work?

One possible solution is something we described in Part 1 as "radical incrementalism": aiming high and moving step by step, adapting along the way as needed. This thinking is mirrored in the Stellar Approach, where we set long-term goals or visions and then take incremental steps toward them, adjusting the vision en route as needed.

Looking forward to success (in five to ten years)

The combination of long-term orientation and step-by-step implementation sets the stage for Module 2. The team already defined its regenerative contribution in Module 1, and now it's time to hammer out the details: what will this contribution actually look like over the next five to ten years? In the exercise below, we'll articulate a future vision to strive for and retrace our steps back to the present that we have influence over.

1 | WARM-UP

Before the actual exercise, we take a moment to acknowledge and accept that our own finite lives are embedded in the larger process of life on Earth. For this purpose, we use either a moment of collective reflection or an exercise based on physical awareness.

One excellent exercise for this is called "Human Layers," one of the many inspiring content pieces offered by the "Long Time Academy."[14] It's basically a mental voyage through time, where we spend a few minutes traveling 90 years back in time, and then 90 years into the future. Thus, we cover a span of 180 years, during which the world has changed in unimaginable ways and will continue to change in unimaginable ways.

2 | INDIVIDUAL REFLECTION

Next, the team defines a future point in time that they will focus on, for example, five years from now.[15] Each team member then takes the time to consider this future moment individually, by answering guiding questions about it. This is not a utopia or dystopia, but a future where the team has been successful in its efforts to improve the way things are. The basic thinking is: "Our contribution had an impact – many difficulties have been overcome, and we found it possible to change some key rules." Here are the questions each team member answers:

- Compared to today, what, specifically, is different in the year X?
- How is this change evident in our team or organization?
- And how do people outside of the team notice that this change has occurred?
- What have we stopped doing? What have we started?
- In concrete terms, this is what our work and our contribution will look like in the year X ... (using bullet points or sentences, whatever works)

3 | LISTENING WALK IN PAIRS

Team members form pairs and take a short walk together outdoors, ideally in nature. As they do, they share their visions for the future.

First, Person A takes 5 minutes to talk about their vision for the future, while Person simply listens in silence. Then, both of them continue walking in silence for 5 minutes. Then they switch roles, with Person B talking about their vision for 5 minutes, while Person A just listens. This is followed by another 5 minutes of silent walking together, after which they use the last 5 minutes of the walk to discuss what they heard and make their way back to the workshop.

Back in the group, the pair notes down some concrete examples of how the fruits of their work are evident in their visions. There's no need to try to be exhaustive — three to five examples should suffice.

 The team has envisioned how their regenerative contribution will be evident in the future.

 60 minutes

 "Our Team in X Years" template, pens

Pathways to the future

Next, we take the individual visions for the future and the concrete examples, and we feed them into a *backcasting* exercise. It's a useful way of creating stories and narratives about a desired future state, as well as mapping out concrete pathways to get there. You can think of it as the opposite of forecasting: instead of extrapolating from today's experiences and assigning probabilities to different scenarios, backcasting starts with the desirable future and traces how it could come about. The underlying mindsets are basically: "Here comes the future, and I should be reacting!" versus "What kind of future do I want and how can I contribute to making it happen?"

1 | BACKCASTING IN SMALL GROUPS
In this exercise, we work in small groups of 4–5 people. First, each group takes a few minutes to go through the concrete examples that came out of their Listening Walks. They select two or three and place them into a circle on the right side of the backcasting template.

The Stellar Approach

Then, they go backward from there, answering the following questions and populating the template as they go:
- For this goal to have been achieved, what needs to have happened before?
- What steps have helped enable this outcome?
- How must the organization have developed to make this outcome possible?

In this way, the team is combining analytical reasoning and creativity to look ahead to the coming years. Things get particularly interesting when we also consider hard-to-predict developments in surrounding systems: What will the impact of artificial intelligence be? How will the political landscape evolve? What trends are shaping the value structure of society, now and tomorrow? What black swan events could help our cause?

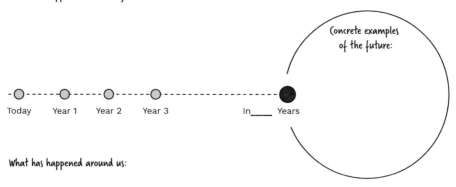

2 | DEFINING GOALS FOR THE FIRST YEAR

Next, the small groups turn their focus to the first year in the template. What overarching milestones, such as sustainability targets, important events, or regular strategy meetings, are relevant during this time? What interim goals can we hit in a year, and what steps do they require when?

3 | SYNTHESIS AND COLLECTING TENSIONS
In the final step, the small groups present their results to one another, with each group answering the following questions:
- What are 2–5 important development threads that we've found and wish to pursue?
- What 2–3 potential next steps have we identified?

Once all groups have had their turn to present, all the threads are placed in a shared backcasting template, while also looking out for and jotting down possible synergies between the different threads.

To end the exercise, we collect tensions and put them in the tension stash.

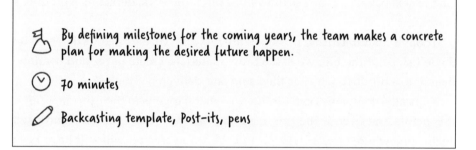

By defining milestones for the coming years, the team makes a concrete plan for making the desired future happen.

70 minutes

Backcasting template, Post-its, pens

The first steps toward circular economic activity

The team should now have an idea of how it can combine a long-term direction with a step-by-step approach. What's more, they continue to practice working iteratively and incrementally via tensions, sprints, and navigating goal conflicts – all basic infrastructure in the Stellar modules and beyond.

In the next step, we'll apply the principles of circular economic activity to the services the team provides – in other words, the production and/or service processes that the team is responsible for.

If we want to create an economy that respects our planetary boundaries and has a regenerative relationship with our natural systems, we need *circular* rather than linear processes. But this is easier said than done. Ready-made, proven answers or solutions are hard to come by in most cases. Often, we need to choose between several less-than-ideal options. Just consider this conundrum: In an area with scarce water, should we still wash dirty reusable packaging materials? Or should we ship the materials somewhere with more water? Or should we, in this case, opt for disposable packaging made from renewable materials?

It's not an easy choice, and the answer always depends.

The circular economy 101

On the next page, you can see the Value Hill framework, depicting a product's lifespan.

Today's manufacturing processes are typically very simple, as depicted on the left slope of the hill: we extract raw materials, create parts, and combine them into a product, which is then sold and delivered. That's it.

Typically, companies can't influence what happens to their products after this point. And even if the raw materials are eventually recycled and used again somewhere else, a large part of the value created will still have been lost and a lot of energy wasted. So it would be far more sensible to reuse the products.

At the same time, we know that the lifespan of many products – from paper bags to power drills – is very short. So in general, the goal should be to keep products as high up on the hill as possible for as long as possible. This would significantly reduce the amount of energy and raw materials used.

The most efficient way to achieve this is to change processes to avoid having to produce some products (**refuse**). A simple example would be using ceramic dishware to make disposable plates obsolete.

Products should be made in a resource-efficient manner, aiming for excellent quality and a long service life (**reduce**). Then, once bought, products should be used as much and for as long as possible. For example, power drills are rarely used, so ten people in a building could share one instead of each buying their own. As long as they maintain it well, this would mean a 90

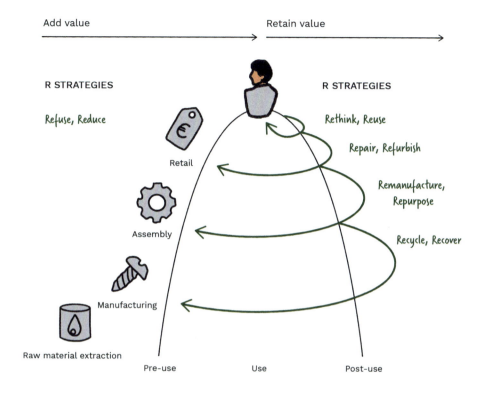

percent reduction in raw material consumption, as estimated by Adam Riese **(rethink, reuse).**

If the drill eventually breaks down, it should ideally be both feasible and significantly cheaper to fix it than buy a new one. And once the drill isn't needed anymore, it can be refurbished and sold to someone who does need it **(refurbish)**. And once that's no longer possible either, the parts of the drill can be disassembled and used for other products **(remanufacture, repurpose).**

In all of these dimensions, many of today's products fall well short. But the good news is that this means there's plenty of room to ideate how to close loops!

Closing loops: Embedding circular thinking into the day-to-day

Circular thinking entails looking for ways to close loops while also bearing in mind various interdependencies. This kind of thinking often opens up new solution possibilities and can be a significant lever for improvement: after all, roughly 80 percent of a product's ecological footprint is determined by the design of the product, the business, and the relevant processes.

While this might sound simple, closing loops is sometimes very complex. That said, a little can go a long way: even though in the Stellar Approach we only offer an initial introduction to circular design, typically the team comes up with a bounty of ideas for making its processes more circular. What's more, they often find simple ways to take small steps that already have a positive impact. If the team wants to dive deeper, we define separate sprint projects for this. But the starting point is always this next exercise, which serves to kick off the process of business model innovation:

1 | COLLECTING IDEAS

To start, the team picks a product from their own area of responsibility. For production teams, this could be something tangible, whereas for service teams, it might be an upstream product or process that they need to provide their service. Sometimes, it makes sense to take the business model previously examined through the Regenerative Business Canvas, and to develop it further through this exercise (see page 161).

Working in small groups, team members gather ideas for how to keep the product on top of the value hill for longer. To enable this, we provide R-cards depicting various R-strategies. Each small group draws one or two cards from the deck and runs a brainstorming session around them. At this point, they don't need to worry about implementation or try to come up with the perfect idea – quantity beats quality. From the list of initial ideas that results, each small group then picks two to explore in more detail by asking: "What would this accomplish, and what would it require?"

Module 2: Direction   **189**

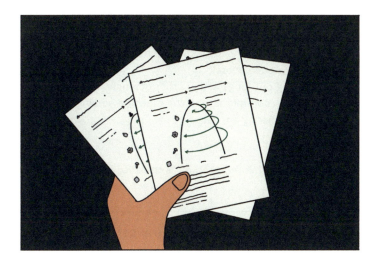

Card 1 – Make the product redundant (refuse)
The most regenerative solution is always to modify processes so that some products aren't even needed anymore.
> Example: Reusable coffee cups render disposable cups redundant.

Brainstorming questions:
- How can we still provide the function of our product without having to manufacture it anymore?
- What impact would this have on our current business model?

Card 2 – Resource efficiency (reduce)
More efficient manufacturing processes and longer product lifespans conserve energy and raw materials.
> Examples: Improving the energy efficiency of a soft-serve ice cream machine or an industrial washing machine.

Brainstorming questions:
- How can we manufacture our product more resource-efficiently?
- How can we improve the quality and lifespan of the product?
- How can we reduce its resource consumption during use?

Card 3 – Intensify use (rethink)

Each product is used for as long as possible and as much as possible so that fewer products need to be produced overall.

> Examples: Renting out long-lasting products instead of selling ones that wear out quickly. A communal washing machine serving all the residents in a building. Car-sharing services.

Brainstorming question:
- How can we ensure that our product is used for longer, more often, and by more users?

Card 4 – Passing on products after use (reuse)

Once a product has been used, the user returns it so that it can be sold or passed on for reuse.

> Examples: Second-hand stores and flea markets. Supermarkets donating expired but edible food to charities. Bottle deposits. Second-hand bookstores.

Brainstorming questions:
- How can we ensure that our product isn't discarded after use but returned back to us?
- What would we need to change in our product to make it reusable?
- What distribution channels could we use to sell it as a pre-owned product?

Card 5 – Repair and maintenance (repair)

A product's lifespan can be extended through repair and maintenance, and this becomes increasingly important the more the product is used (see Card 3).

> Examples: Appliances with readily available spare parts that can be replaced with standard tools. An outdoor clothing company offering unlimited free repairs for its products.

Brainstorming questions:
- What kind of maintenance would prolong the usability of our product?
- How can we encourage users to take good care of our product?
- How can we ensure that our product can be easily repaired?

Card 6 – Refurbish

Once a product isn't needed anymore, it's returned, refurbished, and resold to be used again and again.

> Examples: A marketplace for refurbished mobile phones. A guarantee that software updates will still support older devices.

Brainstorming questions:
- What aspects of our product limit its potential for long-term use?
- How can we ensure that our product can be refurbished at reasonable effort and cost?
- What can we do to ensure that our products are returned to us?

Card 7 – Reusing parts (remanufacture, repurpose)

Once a product doesn't work anymore, its parts are used in other products. To enable this, users need to return the product.

> Examples: Repurposing old car batteries into energy storage systems. Making mobile phone handlebar mounts out of scrap bicycle inner tubes.

Brainstorming questions:
- What product parts can we reuse for the same purpose, for example in a newer model?
- What product parts can we reuse for another purpose, for example in a different product?

Card 8 – Recycling raw materials (recycle)

Once a product reaches the end of its lifespan, its materials can be reclaimed and reused. The value of the product itself is lost, and only the value of the materials is preserved. A prerequisite for recycling is that the user returns the product.

> Examples: Recycling paper and glass. Resmelting aluminum, which incidentally requires only around 5% of the energy needed for primary production.

Brainstorming questions:
- What composite materials in our product can we design to be recyclable?
- What raw materials in our product can be replaced with renewable and/or compostable materials?
- How can we recover our products after use?

Sometimes, the different questions on the cards can prompt similar ideas, which might hint at some obvious solutions or low-hanging fruits. Cards that clearly don't apply to the context at hand can be discarded. All ideas, whether small and pragmatic or ambitious and visionary, are collected on Post-Its and put on a whiteboard. Each small group then picks two to three ideas to work on further by asking the following questions:
- Here's what the ideal interaction with our customers should look like …
- This is what the idea means for our business model …
- Here are the experts, partners, and colleagues whom we need for the next steps …
- For this idea, we also need …

2 | SYNTHESIS
The small groups present their findings to each other and answer any questions that come up. As they do this, the team looks for connections between ideas and assesses their effectiveness.

Once this is done, they discuss the following questions:
- Which ideas do we want to explore further?
- What information do we need to do so?
- What first steps can we take to advance this idea?
- What economic effects do we need to keep in mind?

As usual, any tensions that emerge from this exercise are captured in the tension stash. If necessary, larger projects can be put directly into the sprint backlog.

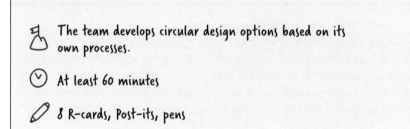

The team develops circular design options based on its own processes.

At least 60 minutes

8 R-cards, Post-its, pens

Stellar Practice 5: Making Regenerative Decisions

How can we make decisions in such a way that their positive impact on our stakeholders – both human and non-human – outweighs any potential negative impact?

The previous Stellar Practice taught the team how to design circular processes. This is true both in their day-to-day work together, where tension-based work has become the norm, and also in the production and service processes that they are responsible for.

Now, the fifth Stellar Practice adds another important skill for regenerative action: it teaches the team to be aware of how it *makes decisions* and what perspectives influence said decisions.

To this end, we'll work with **roles** and introduce new **decision-making processes**. At the end of the practice, we'll also take a quick look at **meetings**, as this is the forum where most team decisions are typically made and a frequent source of frustration in organizations.

Using roles and clear accountabilities to achieve goals more easily

Roles are a core component of many approaches related to agility or responsiveness in organizations.[16] In the Stellar Approach, we use roles to clearly designate regenerative accountabilities as well as to bring to light perspectives that are often underrepresented in organizational decisions.

The main point of roles is that they are distinct from the people filling them. Thus, each team member can hold many roles, enabling greater flexibility. It's also important to document roles clearly in a place where the entire team can easily see them.

Each role needs a few key components:
- A name, like "Project Manager."
- A purpose: Why does the role exist? What is its contribution to the

> overall contribution of the team or organization?
> - Accountabilities, meaning recurring tasks. Two or three are enough to get started since roles are flexible and can be adjusted as needed. Above, a recurring task means a responsibility that has no predefined end point, but which will come up repeatedly until otherwise decided. This is in contrast to responsibilities which have a clear "definition of done" that enables them to be checked off permanently. These non-recurring tasks or task packages aren't considered components of roles, at least not by us.

Defining Regenerative Roles

We're now in a position to take the team's contribution from Module 1 and translate it into concrete accountabilities. In our experience, roles are a useful concept for this, because they're so flexible – an important trait considering that the path we traced via backcasting is very likely to change along the way.

Please note: Teams that already work with roles will probably find this exercise relatively easy. Teams that have never encountered role-based work before might benefit from a short introductory session to the concept.

1 | IDEATING ACTIVITIES
The team splits into small groups or pairs and then, with the contribution and backcasting from Module 1 in hand, lists out the activities needed to take the first steps identified in the backcasting. As they do so, they group related activities into clusters and give each cluster a temporary name. As with the previous exercise around the contribution, the goal should not be to make the clusters perfect or complete, but rather to just get them to a point where they're safe enough to try.

2 | DISTINGUISHING BETWEEN RECURRING AND NON-RECURRING ACTIVITIES
Next, each small group sorts the activity clusters into recurring and non-recurring cluster groups. The non-recurring clusters are put into either the tension stash or, in the case of larger projects, the sprint backlog, to be prioritized at the end of Module 2. Meanwhile, the recurring activity clusters will form the basis for the regenerative roles.

3 | MAKING ROLES EXPLICIT

The recurring activity clusters are now divided among the small groups, who define roles for each of the clusters. They start with the purpose of the role, based on the shortest possible answer to the following questions:
- Why are these activities necessary?
- Why do we need a role that performs these activities?

The end result should be a purpose that describes a state where the role is perfectly fulfilled, for example: "Quarter after quarter, our supply chain becomes increasingly sustainable."

Next, the role is given a name that sounds good, describes it accurately, and empowers the person holding it.

Then, accountabilities are defined for each role. One to three are enough at this stage, and they can be supplemented or adapted later on.

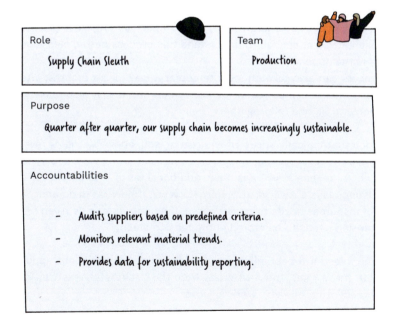

4 | FINALIZING ROLES TOGETHER

The small groups present their findings to each other and adapt the roles if needed. Again, the guiding mantra should be "Is this safe enough to try?"

At the latest here, it's good to take a little break and get some fresh air into the room.

5 | DISTRIBUTING ROLES

It's now time to fill the newly created roles. This can be done using one of the methods below, depending on the team's governance system:

1. **Assigning roles:** The team leader considers who would be suitable for each role and fills them accordingly. For this to work, it's usually important to involve the prospective role holders in these decisions and listen to their feedback.
2. **"Grabbing" roles:** Team members simply pick the roles that they feel naturally suited for, based on their background and motivation. If no one objects due to safety concerns, this can be a very quick way of filling the roles.
3. **An integrative election process:** People are elected to fill roles. The integrative election process is a little bit different from the anonymous simple majority election that most people know from, for example, electing class presidents or representatives at school. To understand this process better, please see the glossary in the appendix.

Team members can also take on roles temporarily, say for six months, after which the role assignments can be reconsidered. Sometimes, it may also make sense for several people to fill one role together.

One question that typically arises when creating and, above all, *filling* regenerative roles is where the resources for these roles will come from. Here, it's important to note that not all regenerative roles mean additional tasks – sometimes it's enough to give existing tasks a regenerative spin. However, if new tasks do arise, then the question of resources needs to be answered. If no answer can be given right away, then the tension needs to be stored in the tension stash.

Once all the roles have been filled, it's time for some rambunctious applause and cheers! With these roles, the next steps from the backcasting exercise have now been anchored into the team's work together.

Module 2: Direction 197

 The activities derived from the team's contribution and the backcasting exercise are turned into roles.

 120 minutes (depending on the number of roles)

 Role templates, Post-its, pens

The standard Stellar roles help keep the medium and long-term effects in mind

Roles are a useful way of clarifying the division of regenerative accountabilities in a team. But more than that, roles can also help reflect indirect and long-term effects in decision-making processes.

As we saw in Part 1, living systems can start to hurt their own self-preservation if they fail to co-develop their surrounding systems. And in our short-sighted, degenerative economic system, surrounding systems tend to be ignored because they have no immediate impact on business models.

In contrast, taking surrounding systems into account is part and parcel of a regenerative mindset. It's normal to ask, for example: "What would the planet have to say about this decision?" And if you think about it, this should really be standard practice across all organizations, because the Earth is our only home, and its health does de facto also underlie long-term business success.

That's why, in the Stellar Approach, we anchor three standard roles into the team, each representing a regenerative viewpoint[17]:

- The Earth
- Future generations
- Marginalized stakeholders

These perspectives are drawn directly from the Stellar Principles:

- Earth (and its ecosystems) combine the principles "Embedded" and "Circular."
- Future generations represent the principle "Long-term."
- Marginalized stakeholders stem from the principle "Diverse."

Before the team makes a decision, these roles share their perspectives on it. One concrete way to facilitate this is by setting up three empty chairs around the meeting room table. The role-holders can then temporarily sit on these and share their viewpoints, thus mentally separating themselves from their other roles, which might also have a say in the decision. The goal of all of this is to increase the chances that the team's and organization's actions become more regenerative and structurally just.

Filling the standard regenerative roles

Next, we present the three standard roles to the team and discuss how the team can actively incorporate one or more of them into its decision-making processes. Of course, it's always possible to modify the standard roles, it's just important to know that the more concrete the description of the role, the better it can contribute to decision-making.

1 | CONNECTING WITH THE STANDARD ROLES INDIVIDUALLY
Once the roles have been presented, team members take a few minutes to imagine themselves in the roles.

2 | MAKING THE STANDARD ROLES CONCRETE
The team splits into three small groups, each one tailoring one of the roles to the team's context. They do this by asking: "Which of the Earth's systems, which voices from future generations, and which marginalized stakeholders are most affected by our actions and can contribute to our decision-making?"

Earth

Purpose:

The perspective of our home planet gets significant consideration in our decisions.

Accountabilities:

- Deliberately keeps their distance from current team processes to be able to observe them from an external viewpoint.
- Connects with the perspective and needs of the Earth — a 4.6-billion year-old planet that has been thrown off balance in the past 200 years. (To make this more concrete, this should be further specified to mean parts of the Earth that are especially relevant to the team's context, for example: "The local water system," "The minerals used in our products," and "The forest next to our factory.")
- Actively brings this perspective into decision-making processes.

Future generations

Purpose:

The perspective of future generations gets significant consideration in our decisions.

Accountabilities:

- Deliberately keeps their distance from current team processes to be able to observe them from an external viewpoint.
- Connects with the perspective and needs of the seventh generation from today, 200 years down the line. (This should made tangible in the team's own context, for example: "Those continuing this company's work in the year 2200").
- Actively brings this perspective into decision-making processes.

Marginalized stakeholders

Purpose:

The perspective of marginalized stakeholders gets significant consideration in our decisions.

Accountabilities:

- Deliberately keeps their distance from current team processes to be able to observe them from an external viewpoint.
- Connects with the perspective and needs of voiceless stakeholders, for example in the supply chain (This should made tangible in the team's own context, for example: "The coal industry workers in this country").
- Actively brings this perspective into decision-making processes.

The Stellar Approach

3 | FILLING THE STANDARD ROLES

After the small groups present the revised standard roles to each other, the team picks one or more that are relevant for them and safe enough to try. These are then filled (see page 196).

Since these regenerative standard roles are often unfamiliar territory for the team, they might opt to only fill them temporarily, say for the next six months. Alternatively, the team can decide to fill these only during the Stellar modules. In any case, at the end of the Stellar Journey, we'll determine the future of these roles together with the team.

 The standard regenerative roles are anchored in the team.

 45–60 minutes

 Role descriptions for the standard regenerative roles.

Becoming more regenerative, decision by decision

Thanks to the regenerative roles – including the standard ones – the team is now much more likely to widen its gaze beyond its own survival and start behaving mindfully toward its surrounding systems.

However, these roles can really only have an impact when decisions are made. This is why decisions are the second major component of the fifth Stellar Practice. In fact, you could say that they are *the only* essential component for making regenerativity a tangible part of the team's work. From a systems theory perspective, the smallest unit of an organization is a decision, or more precisely, communication about a decision. Therefore, if we can gradually shape our decisions to make regenerative outcomes more likely, the entire team and organization will also become more regenerative.

Decisions, decisions, decisions ...

So how can we shape decisions to be more regenerative?

First and foremost, the team needs to know how to distinguish between different modes of decision-making and consciously apply them where appropriate.

1 | COLLECTING CURRENT WAYS OF MAKING DECISIONS
The team brainstorms and lists the various decision-making modes it's familiar with, starting with specific examples from their everyday work. Building on this initial list, we then introduce additional modes through discussion cards. These can be briefly clarified if necessary.

202 The Stellar Approach

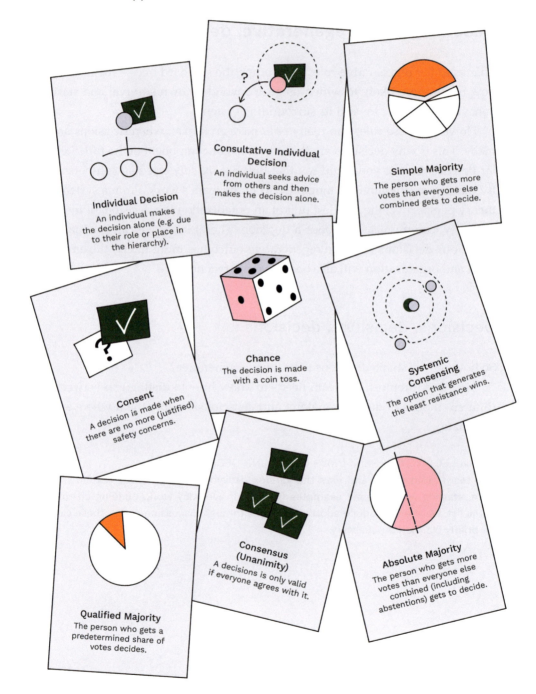

Module 2: Direction   203

2 | REFLECTING ON THE REGENERATIVE ROLES – INCLUDING THE STANDARD ONES – VIS-À-VIS DECISIONS

Participants take turns drawing decision cards and then discuss what it would mean for the regenerative roles in the team if decisions were made with the mode in question.

3 | BIG PICTURE AND RESONANCE

The team reiterates their most important findings. Here, they should realize that there is no one right way of making decisions – depending on the situation, different modes may work better than others.

As a final point, the team discusses whether they want to use a different decision-making mode for some decisions going forward. Any tensions that crop up are stored in the tension stash.

 The team learns about different ways of making decisions and knows how to make an informed choice from among them.

 30 minutes

 "Types of decisions" cards

One of the decision-making modes covered is especially relevant in regenerative economic activity: consent. That's why we'll dive a little bit deeper to understand it better. Just to be clear, this is *not* the same thing as consensus, which is probably the better-known of the two.

Consensus decisions, where all team members need to agree on something, often take a *long* time to reach, robbing the team of momentum. On the other hand, if a single individual like a leader makes all the decisions, this is of course much faster but runs the risk of missing important perspectives. Consent hits the sweet spot by integrating many perspectives while still enabling relatively fast decisions and, therefore, progress.

On the path to regenerative economic activity, decisions are often complicated by goal conflicts and ambiguity. The consent process can help navigate these obstacles by systematically making space for different voices and incorporating regenerative roles into decision-making. Especially when it comes to far-reaching decisions, it's well worth the time investment.

Unlike consensus, the consent process isn't focused on getting everyone to agree, but rather on no one objecting. Consider the following example: One team member senses a tension. Let's call them the tension-holder. They present this tension to the team, along with a proposal for how to resolve it. All the other team members can then ask clarifying questions to better understand the proposal and also share their initial reaction to it. Based on these reactions, the tension-holder can amend the proposal, after which the team is asked if they have any objections to the proposal due to safety concerns. If valid concerns are voiced, they get integrated into the proposal, until something safe enough to try is found. If new tensions emerge later, then further proposals can be made to resolve them. In the next exercise, we'll explain each step of this process in more detail.

Integrating regenerative arguments into decisions (the rIDM process)

To make consent-based decisions, we use *Integrative Decision Making* or IDM, a method rooted in Holacracy. We've adapted it somewhat for the Stellar Approach, so for the sake of clarity, we'll call our version *regenerative Integrative Decision Making* or rIDM. It requires a facilitator and someone to act as a scribe, documenting the proposal along with any modifications that are made to it.

1 | DESCRIBING THE TENSION
The tension-holder explains what the tension is and, specifically, what the problem is that needs to be solved.

2 | MAKING A PROPOSAL
The tension-holder presents a concrete proposal for how to resolve the tension. The solution doesn't need to be perfect or very detailed. Rather, they outline the rough idea in writing for everyone to see. It could be that this initial idea will morph into a totally different proposal over the next steps.

3 | CLARIFYING QUESTIONS
Once the initial proposal has been laid out, other team members present can ask comprehension questions to ensure they've understood. The tension-holder isn't expected to have all the answers right away but does their best to elucidate where they can. This is important because a well-informed decision requires a thorough understanding of both the problem and the proposed solution. It's important to note that at this point opinions should not yet be expressed explicitly or implicitly. There will be space for that in the next step.

4 | REACTION ROUND
Taking turns, each team member (besides the tension-holder) shares their initial feedback on the proposal, from the perspective of their roles, including the regenerative ones. They can also put forth other proposals for how to solve the original tension.

Each role speaks for itself only, and no interruptions, discussion, or comments from others are allowed. At this point, the tension-holder jots down the points they find most valuable, but doesn't modify their proposal yet.

5 | AMENDING AND CLARIFYING THE PROPOSAL
After all team members have had the chance to share their reactions, the focus shifts back to the person who sensed the tension and made the original proposal. Thanks to the reaction round, they now have a wealth of new perspectives and feedback to consider, and if they wish, they can amend and clarify the proposal. If this is done, the new proposal is reviewed together once more.

6 | SAFETY ROUND
One by one, each team member says if they have safety concerns regarding the latest proposal. A safety concern means a concern that the proposal may cause ir-

reparable harm, which is why it constitutes a veto from the person. In rIDM, there are two different types of safety concerns:
- Reasons why the proposal might harm or set back the **team** or **organization**.
- Reasons why the proposal might cause harm to **the planet** or **future generations**.

As usual, the key question is whether the proposal is safe enough to try. By asking the whole team to consider the risks from their perspective, we create a comprehensive safety net to catch all important aspects of the proposal.

7 | INTEGRATION

As soon as a safety concern is voiced, it gets integrated into the proposal. This happens via a dialog between the tension-holder and the objector. Together, they try to modify the proposal to assuage the safety concern, while still resolving the original tension. Usually, the objector proposes an amendment directly.

Once they've integrated the safety concern, a new safety round is initiated. If no more safety concerns arise, the proposal is deemed safe enough to try and thereby accepted.

In practice, it may feel weird that there's no room for debate and discussion at this point. However, this structured and disciplined approach is exactly where the rIDM approach draws its power from: it ensures that every voice and perspective gets heard and a responsible decision is made without the team getting mired in endless discussions. This makes sense, because the decisions aren't set in stone anyway but can be revised and revisited as new tensions arise.

PREVENTING HARM TO THE PLANET AND FUTURE GENERATIONS

It's possible that, especially in the early phases of their transformation journey, the team might not be able to integrate all of the regenerative safety concerns that arise. However, they shouldn't let this slow them down. In fact, they've already taken an important step by bringing these goal conflicts into the light. To keep up momentum, we recommend that they make a decision that's safe enough to try for now, while recognizing that they can't yet solve all of the goal conflicts. Those that seem irresolvable are captured in the tension stash or Goal Conflict Navigator, to be worked on at a later point, possibly with other stakeholders. This ensures that these goal conflicts don't just get swept under the rug.

INVOLVING THE REGENERATIVE STANDARD ROLES

In order to give voices to the standard regenerative roles in the rIDM-process, the person in question needs to speak not only for themselves, but also for parts of

Module 2: Direction   207

the Earth, for future generations, and for those marginalized in the space the team operates in. In practice, this means that team members who hold one of these roles speak twice in each round: once from the perspective of the standard role and once from the perspective of their role as a team member. Differentiating these perspectives into two separate roles and speaking in turns helps ensure that each role gets the space and attention needed to arrive at a good decision.

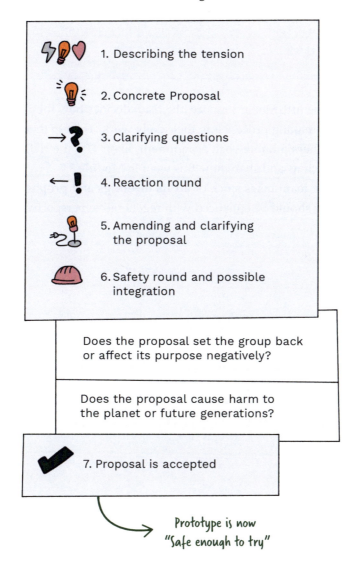

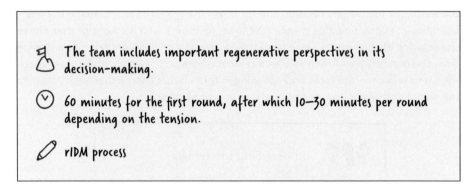

To wrap up the fifth Stellar Practice, the team decides how they'll anchor this new decision-making process into their daily work. To help them do this, we usually give them a **homework assignment**, like: "Use the rIDM to make at least two decisions and share how this went in Module 3."

Finally, the team takes stock of **all its meetings** and proposes where decision-making should be enhanced with regenerative perspectives and methods.

Good meetings are a prerequisite for regenerative decisions

What makes good meetings good is their structure. That's why, on the Stellar Journey, we help teams understand the significance of meetings and offer inspiration for how to design them. And meetings are important for a number of reasons:

- Meetings are where **team habits** are formed or reshaped. This is where team members get a shared, live experience of the way they work together. It's where they grow their knowledge base and develop a shared language. And of course, all of this also shapes the team's collaboration culture.
- Meetings are key for team **effectiveness**. Most people probably know how frustrating it is to spend way too much time in meetings where the goals, required participants, and agenda are all ambiguous. When these aspects are clearly defined, and the team finds a good meeting rhythm, the result is usually improved flow and efficacy.

Meetings form an important **bridge** between the team's first run-through of the Stellar Practices, when external facilitators typically guide them, and subsequent rounds, when the team continues its Stellar Journey independently. The goal is that they learn the skills to carry on by themselves – sensing and resolving tensions as they go. Of course, they can only do this if they have the tools to integrate tensions and adapt the main elements of the Stellar Approach to suit their ever-changing reality.

Inner Work in Module 2

The team has now completed all of the contents of Stellar Practices 4 and 5. As before, we conclude Module 2 with our inner work rituals:

- The **Virtue Coach**, now focusing on the second Stellar Virtue, "Creative Joy."
- The **Pause and Nurture Hope** ritual helps us discuss what makes us hopeful.

A Creative Joy work-out with the Virtue Coach

Creative Joy is a combination of optimism and creativity. You may remember this feeling from when you were a child – getting totally lost in the flow of discovering or creating something new. This boundless creative energy is something that a few lucky people can still access as adults, and it's what we try to tap into with this Virtue Coach exercise.

The steps in the exercise are exactly the same as in Module 1, except here we use the following guiding questions:

- On a scale of 1 to 10, how much joy do you currently get from developing and trying out new ideas?
- Think back to a moment in the past when you were brimming with drive and creativity. How would you describe the situation?
- What exactly was it that gave you this boundless energy? What was fun about what you were doing? What unleashes your creativity?
- What image, sound, or gesture do you currently associate with this creative joy?

Pause and Nurture Hope

Hope is the force that keeps us from succumbing to apathy. The more we learn about the polycrisis and our own role in it, the more important it becomes to give the team some initial experiences of their shared impact and efficacy. This gives them hope. More precisely, it gives them *Constructive Hope*, which is distinct from *False Hope*.

False Hope is the hope that someone or something, whether a technological breakthrough, Elon Musk, or even God, will step in and solve all our problems. What makes these scenarios particularly appealing is the implicit hope that maybe we can keep the party going and don't need to change our consumption habits after all. Unfortunately, this kind of hope is not helpful, because it relies on *someone else* doing something, leading us to avoid and distance ourselves from our problems instead of taking action.

Constructive Hope, on the other hand, is the hope that our individual and collective efforts can help us meet the challenges of the polycrisis. This hope depends on each of us understanding our own contribution and the next step that we can take toward a better future – no matter how small.

By taking matters into our own hands, we can act despite all the uncertainties, getting a first-hand experience of how change *is* possible. And if we as a team can create change, so can others too.[18]

We briefly mentioned the Pause and Nurture Hope ritual at the end of Module 1, but we actually employ it in each module, and we'll elaborate on the details now.

1 | PAUSING
The team takes a moment of silence, one to three minutes long, to reflect on this question: "How do I feel, looking back on this day?"

2 | SHARING HIGHLIGHTS
One by one, each team member briefly shares any feelings they currently sense. Others listen carefully, without judging or commenting, as all feelings are valid here. The team can also do a second round of sharing, if they feel they wish to say more after hearing their colleagues speak.

3 | ANSWERING THE GUIDING QUESTIONS
In this ritual, we connect reflecting on our feelings with how we can make an impact. That's why each team member now takes a few minutes to jot down their thoughts around the following two questions. The notes are meant only for themselves and don't need to be shared with anyone else.
- How am I in this moment? What feelings do I sense?
- This is the next step that enables me to make a difference and gives me hope ...

4 | DISCUSSING IN PAIRS
The team forms pairs to discuss their reflections confidentially.

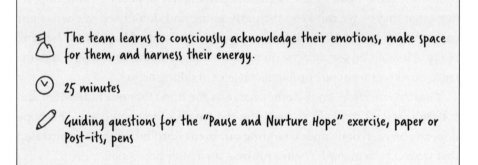

The team learns to consciously acknowledge their emotions, make space for them, and harness their energy.

25 minutes

Guiding questions for the "Pause and Nurture Hope" exercise, paper or Post-its, pens

Resilience in Module 2

In Module 2, team members learn about another framework to help them keep track of their energy budget – the Three Regulation Systems[19]:

- **The threat system** is rooted in our basic survival instinct, and it's constantly looking for anything out of the ordinary. If it detects something threatening, whether a wooly mammoth stampeding or a new message in our email inbox, the body automatically triggers a stress response, thereby narrowing our perception. This allows us to focus on this very important task of dealing with the threat to protect ourselves and our loved ones. This system is responsible for the primitive reactions of fight, flight, or freeze.

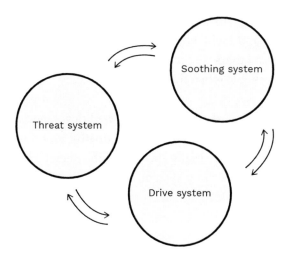

- **The drive system** is responsible for the fleeting but pleasant feelings that motivate us to do whatever we need to in order to survive and succeed. This can range from satisfying our basic needs to striving for larger achievements. When we get what we want, the system releases dopamine, which feels *really* good – for a moment.
Evolution has shaped our threat and drive systems to activate quickly and easily, which is why they can create a stress trap for modern humans. Those of us with potent threat and drive systems, but relatively undeveloped soothing systems, can fall into a stress spiral that usually ends in burnout.
The drive system is constantly looking for potential rewards. If it can't find any in our relatively safe environment today, it can trigger the threat system over something trivial just to get the short-lived pleasure of resolving the "threat." Those of us with strong threat and drive systems run the risk of falling into a stress spiral that usually ends in burnout. To balance things out, a potent soothing system is also needed.

- **The soothing system** is geared more toward long-term regulation than the other two. It releases oxytocin and has a balancing and restorative effect, evoking feelings of trust, connection, empathy, and security. Our perception is clear and lucid, enabling mindful social behavior and peaceful coexistence with others. Creativity, play, and exploration also tend to become more accessible when this system is engaged.

Ideally, all three systems should be equally well developed and active. If the threat or drive systems dominate, we lack empathy for others and lose sight of the long-term perspective in life and that of the planet. However: "Without a well-developed (…) soothing system, it's not possible to experience deep satisfaction in a state lacking threats or incentives. Instead, one feels emptiness and/or boredom."[20]

The three forces that can bring balance

To restore balance, it's helpful to reflect on a few questions: When and how often does each of these systems guide my actions? What makes it easier or more difficult for me to switch between these systems? The following exercise can help explore these questions further.

1 | INDIVIDUAL REFLECTION
Each team member makes a pie chart based on the question: "What proportion of time is each of these systems active in me?" This answer should be based mainly on the work context as currently experienced by the team members.

2 | PRESENTING THE RESULTS
Working either as a team or in small groups, the pie charts are briefly presented and the following questions pondered:
- What situations come to mind where I've switched from one system to another?
- What would I like to change about the split of my pie chart?

3 | LETTING PICTURES SPEAK FOR THEMSELVES
A set of visually inspiring cards is laid out in the room, or, in the case of a virtual workshop, shared digitally. Each team member briefly examines the cards and then spontaneously, intuitively, without overthinking it, picks one or more cards to rep-

resent the qualities of their soothing systems. Each then retreats to a quiet spot with their cards.

The facilitator reads out the following instructions to help team members to mentally connect with the pictures and their atmosphere:
- What feelings do these pictures evoke in you? What bodily sensations do you perceive?
- What would you need in order to strengthen these qualities in your life?
- To strengthen or expand anything in life, regular rituals can be useful. So what would be a good ritual to help you strengthen these qualities? It doesn't need to be elaborate or grandiose, but rather something small that's easy to put into practice. What ideas spring to mind?
- Look over the pictures once more and take five minutes to jot down what's important to you right now in terms of reinforcing these qualities in your life.

Any outcomes from the above are kept private. Finally, the team can, if they so wish, agree on a simple shared rule that will help them as a team to monitor their soothing systems going forward.

 Team members get to know the three regulatory systems and begin to understand which systems are most prominent for them.

 60 minutes

 Inspiration cards, paper or Post-its, pens

To wrap up the second module, we process the tension stash, review the Goal Conflict Navigator, and plan the next sprint, again meant to take place in the four to six weeks between Module 2 and Module 3.

Ideally, the goals that we set for ourselves in the beginning of the module can now be checked off:

- ☑ The team has a clear vision of how exactly they'll make their regenerative contribution over the next three to five years.
- ☑ Team members know how to use tensions to develop processes in an iterative way.
- ☑ The team has applied circular thinking to its own circle of influence and identified initial steps to close loops.
- ☑ The team has created roles necessary for its regenerative development journey.
- ☑ The team has learned to incorporate regenerative perspectives into its decision-making.
- ☑ The team knows how to use regenerative routines in its meetings and has revised its existing meetings accordingly.
- ☑ The team becomes even more confident in managing its internal resources.
- ☑ The team's sprint backlog has been updated, with clear to-dos defined for the next four to six weeks.

218   The Stellar Approach

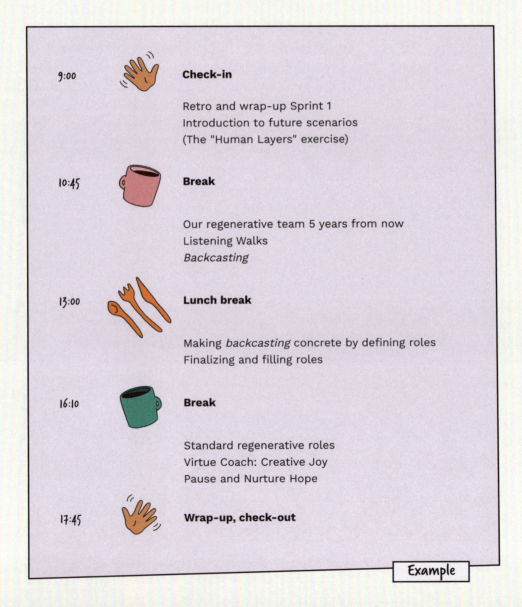

Module 2: Direction   219

Workshop Agenda Module 2
Day 2

9:00 — **Check-in**

Consent and integrating regenerative perspectives into decisions

10:30 — **Break**

Run-through rIDM
Closing loops

12:40 — **Lunch break**

Closing loops (continued)
Sprint planning and kick-off for Sprint 2

15:15 — **Break**

Resilience: the three regulation systems
Processing tensions

17:45 — **Wrap-up, check-out**

Example

Module 3: Impact

And so we arrive at the last module of the Stellar Approach. At this point, the team has been on the Stellar Journey for just over two months and has had two sprints to launch projects and build new habits. Now, it's time to ensure that the newly acquired competencies actually drive lasting impact.

It's important to note that, in the Stellar Approach, impact doesn't need to be immediate or linear. Sometimes, we underestimate the time it takes for our actions to yield benefits, but that doesn't change the fact that we're having an impact. It's not about the outcome this week or quarter but about the effect on future generations. And to gauge this impact, the team needs to define meaningful indicators.

Additionally, the team will also learn how it can *stay* effective. This is the core of the seventh Stellar Practice, and we've already touched upon it in some of the exercises at the end of the first two modules.

To get started, we'll kick off Module 3 with a retro, meaning a quick review of the outcomes of the second sprint.

We'll get to know the final Stellar Virtue, "Perseverance," while spending most of the workshop time on the topics of impact and self-efficacy – covered by Stellar Practices 6 and 7.

6. **Making Progress Visible:** How can we measure our own impact? How can we share and talk about our impact with other parts of the organization?
7. **Staying Effective:** How can we ensure that we stay effective and replenish our strength?

We consider Module 3 successfully completed if we've achieved these goals:

- [ ] The team has identified useful indicators for measuring its regenerative success.
- [ ] The team understands how to use storytelling and narratives to win over partners and supporters in the organization.
- [ ] The team has established habits and routines to foster its own resilience, thereby helping it stay on the regenerative path in the long run.
- [ ] The team is motivated for the journey ahead and knows how to navigate the uncertainties and dilemmas it will inevitably encounter.
- [ ] The team has established a sprint routine to support its regenerative contribution.
- [ ] Team members have the means to support each other as they continue to develop and grow.

Stellar Practice 6: Making Progress Visible

How can we measure our own impact? How can we share and talk about our impact with other parts of the organization?

Many conventional businesses use dashboards to gauge their progress in a desired direction, and in this respect, regenerative ones are no different. However, the scope of what's tracked is broader: regenerative success requires metrics beyond mere financials and economic KPIs.

With the sixth Stellar Practice, the team learns to define and update meaningful indicators for their progress on the regenerative path.

To start, we consider pre-existing metrics in the organization, such as those included in sustainability reporting. These can be useful already, but typically the team also needs to break them down into something more tailored to its own work. This helps the team to assess its own impact more directly and make its progress visible to the rest of the organization.

Besides measurement, the sixth Stellar practice also explores the importance of storytelling, because we humans tend to be moved more by stories than by facts or numbers. This is why the team also learns to frame its progress in narratives so as to communicate to and win support from other parts of the organization.

What is regenerative success, and how do we measure it?

In organizations with regenerative aspirations, success isn't just a matter of profitability. Financial success is only the goal in as much as it coincides with "relational success," meaning the fostering of healthy relationships with key stakeholders in surrounding systems (see page 67).

Module 3: Impact   223

To understand this effect on stakeholders more deeply, we can use the basic idea of the IOOI model (Input, Output, Outcome, Impact).[21] In the model, we describe the desired impact we want to have, determine the indicators for said impact, and define how we'll measure them. This approach lets us keep an eye on both our footprint *and* handprint (see box).

Footprint and handprint

The term **"ecological footprint"** usually refers to the emissions that our own activities cause either directly or indirectly. It's important we understand and reduce our footprint so we don't exceed the planetary boundaries. Here, organizations and companies play a key part, because not only do they account for the majority of emissions overall, but they can also shape the behavior of consumers through the products and services that they offer.

Meanwhile, our **handprint** captures the positive effects of our activities, be they ecological or social. Our handprint shows our commitment to changing societal conditions – including structures, rules, laws, and overall societal awareness of what needs to be done – to help more people make sustainable or regenerative decisions. This can mean things like forging partnerships or actively participating in legislative processes to help set standards across the entire industry. It could also mean simply bringing up the topic of sustainability when talking to other people. This can extend our impact far beyond what would be possible by merely reducing our footprint.

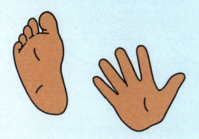

The Stellar Approach

Typically, the IOOI model is applied to individual projects, but in the Stellar Approach we use it to gauge the team's overall regenerative performance and impact.

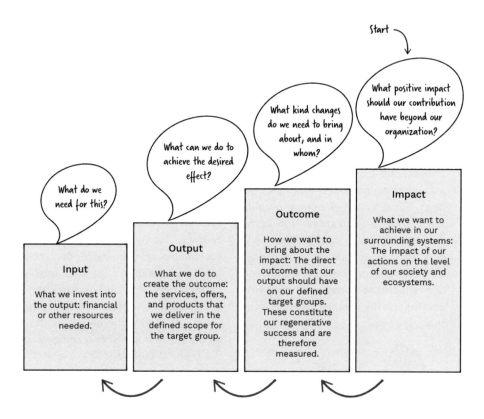

To understand the model better, let's consider as an example a team working in a logistics company, responsible for packing goods before shipment. We'll focus specifically on the aspect of circularity here.

- The team's desired **impact** is to make the greatest possible contribution to a global reduction of the plastic waste that ends up in oceans, landfills, and incinerators.

- The **outcome** they're aiming for is that their target group, comprising their major customers, permanently changes their mindset and behavior when it comes to the handling of shipped goods. Specifically, they should come to see packaging materials as something precious to be used frugally.
- The team's **output** consists of investing, together with one of their largest customers, in an innovation project to test circular packaging (footprint). Meanwhile, they're also launching an industry-wide network for reusable packaging (handprint).
- The required **input** includes the time and money needed for this work, as well as specialist knowledge and supporting partners

Measuring regenerative impact

We want to understand if our contribution is having the desired impact, and in doing so, nail down the right indicators for measuring regenerative success. To achieve this, we start with the desired impact and work our way backward to the inputs required.

PREPARATION
Between Modules 2 and 3, one or two team members are tasked with a little homework assignment: reviewing the organization's sustainability reports, if available. Often, this might already spur some ideas for indicators that the team can directly influence through its decisions. Depending on the scope and complexity of these indicators, it may even be worth having a quick pre-workshop discussion to understand them better with those in charge of sustainability topics in the organization. Then, at the beginning of the workshop, the relevant indicators can be briefly presented to the rest of the team and left somewhere visible for easy reference during the discussion.

The team begins its dive into the topic of measuring impact with a short discussion round, using a whiteboard or flipchart to capture their thoughts around the following questions:
- What does success mean in our organization today?
- How do we define success in our team?

- What are the quantitative, measurable indicators that reflect our success?
- Do we see a difference between impact and success? If so, how would we describe that difference?

To end on, we present the model to the team and begin working on its four phases.

1 | IMPACT: WHAT CONTRIBUTION DO WE WANT TO MAKE ON THE LEVEL OF OUR SOCIETY AND ECOSYSTEMS?

To formulate the team's desired impact, we use as a starting point the team's **regenerative contribution** from Module 1, which describes their intended part in making the organization more regenerative. When they crafted it, the team already considered their societal and ecological stakeholders, meaning that the desired impact on society and ecosystems is usually fairly clear already.

Building on this, the team can now formulate its desired impact on these two important surrounding systems that it's embedded in. Sometimes, some initial ideas for indicators may already crop up at this stage. Usually though, the desired impact is defined so broadly that truly meaningful and measurable indicators can only be defined in the next step.

2 | OUTPUT: IN ORDER TO HAVE THIS IMPACT, WHAT KIND OF CHANGES DO WE NEED TO BRING ABOUT, AND IN WHOM?

Here, we focus on the question of which **changes** we need to bring about in which **specific target groups** in order to further our desired impact. To understand this, the team chooses its most important target groups, possibly using the *Regenerative Business Canvas* to recall its relevant stakeholders throughout the value chain.

Next, the team breaks up into small groups, each picking one of the chosen target groups. For each target group, they define possible indicators and gauges to measure them with, as well as – if possible – specific goals for them. To help structure this process, we provide the team with pre-prepared worksheets.

Module 3: Impact   227

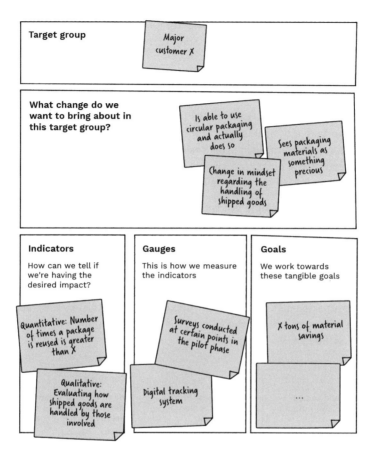

3 | BRINGING THE INDICATORS TOGETHER
The small groups present their results to each other and share feedback. Together, the team aligns on a **manageable set of indicators** deemed important for measuring its regenerative outcomes.

A good rule of thumb here is that less is more. It's much easier to embed a few easy-to-follow metrics into the team's daily work and develop them further than it is to try to implement too many indicators or ones that are too complicated. If it turns out later that something important is missing, it can always be added in.

The team agrees on who takes responsibility for gathering the necessary data as well as the point in time or cadence for sharing the status of the indicators, for example via a report or in a meeting.

At this point, it's time for a refreshing break.

4 | OUTPUT: DO OUR OUTPUTS CONTRIBUTE TO THE DESIRED OUTCOMES?

In this step, we take a critical look at the team's **outputs**, meaning the products or services the team delivers. Using the desired outcomes above as a guide, we can see to what extent the outputs contribute to these outcomes, as well as identify gaps and spot where changes may be needed.

To do this, we can use a simple start-stop-continue framework: Outputs that contribute to the desired outcomes and that the team already delivers – or that it has already made plans for in the previous modules – can be put in the Continue column. Ideas for additional outputs that would contribute to the desired outcomes can be placed in the Start column. Finally, outputs with dubious outcomes can be put in the Stop column. Depending on the team size, they do this either as a team or in small groups. It's just important to keep in mind that this exercise applies only to the outputs they create for the target group, not preparation for them, internal team tasks, or the like.

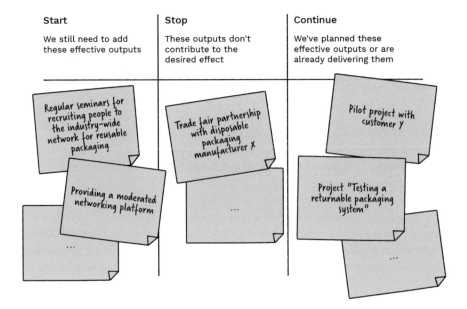

Module 3: Impact 229

5 | INPUTS: WHAT DO WE NEED FOR THIS?
To end the exercise, we discuss the **inputs** required. We work through the Start and Continue columns from the step above, considering as we do: What *additional* financial or other inputs does the team need to deliver these outputs? What skills? How much time do we as a team need to invest in these? All of this is captured on a whiteboard or flipchart.

We set a time limit for this discussion round and, as usual, capture any arising tensions in the tension stash.

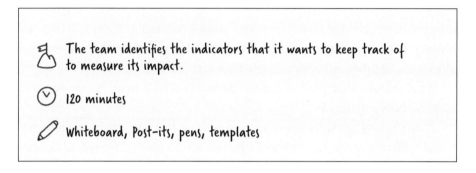

- The team identifies the indicators that it wants to keep track of to measure its impact.
- 120 minutes
- Whiteboard, Post-its, pens, templates

Storytelling: A good story will get you everywhere

The team now has a clearer understanding of how to define its desired regenerative impact and measure the outcomes. But to make this impact a reality, the team needs to win over relevant stakeholders who will support them. In our experience, external support is almost always needed, for example from allies and sponsors within the organization, but also from customers, suppliers, associations, and other players outside of the organization.

To win this support, the team needs *good stories*.

A good story resonates on a deep emotional level, creating meaning and building trust faster than any dossier of facts. Yet despite all these advantages, storytelling is surprisingly rare in the world of business today. Perhaps dull facts seem like a safer bet. But stories have always been the right medium when the goal has been to convey information memorably. And luckily, the skill of crafting good stories can be learned.

Whether we tell the story via slides, video, or even face-to-face without any visual aids is something we can decide later. The most important thing now is determining the *message* to convey.

An offer you can't refuse

Of course, targeting stakeholders with stories tailored to them is a trick we already know from the field of marketing, where studies have shown that stories are 22 times more memorable than mere facts.[22]

We also know that good stories sell products at least twice as effectively as facts. So how is it done?

To really work, a story needs to be simple, surprising, credible, and emotional.[23] What's more, stories should be tailored to reach different audiences. In the following exercise, we'll practice crafting a story for a specific stakeholder.

PREPARATION
The team picks out a tension that can't be resolved without winning someone over from outside the team. They can use the Goal Conflict Navigator or the Regenerative Business Canvas as inspiration for this.

1 | STAKEHOLDER MAP
The team places the tension in the middle of the stakeholder map. Silently, using Post-Its, they add in people – *not* roles or entities – who are needed to resolve the tension. This could mean someone who has to agree to a change before it can be made, someone who's blocking the way, or someone whose help is needed to deliver the output. They also note each person's current attitude toward the tension, using a scale of -- to ++ to describe how supportive they are likely to be in solving the tension.

Throughout this process, no discussion should take place. The team members simply read each other's Post-Its, using them as inspiration to think of yet more relevant stakeholders.

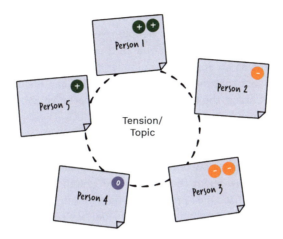

2 | FINDING THE RIGHT PERSON

Next, they draw a matrix on another whiteboard, with the Y-axis denoting the person's influence, and the X-axis the extent to which they are affected by the change.

Together, the team positions the most important stakeholders somewhere within the matrix. This exercise can highlight if there are any highly influential people who aren't really affected by the change. It's important that they be won over because they can be highly unpredictable forces otherwise.

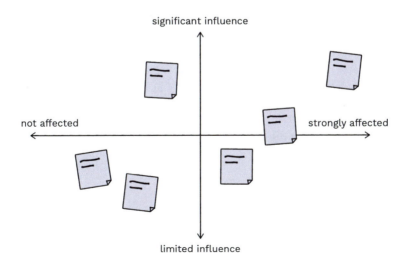

For the time being, we can ignore all the Post-Its in the bottom half of the matrix ("limited influence"). Of the influential people remaining, we choose a particularly relevant one for resolving the tension at hand. Their relevance could stem from, for example, their status as an important multiplier, them being strongly impacted by the change, or the fact that the team isn't sure if they can count on this person's support. In the next steps, the team gets to craft a narrative about its regenerative initiative, tailored specifically for this person.

3 | CREATING A PROFILE
Working together, the team now draws up a profile of the person in question. They put everything they know about them up on the whiteboard: What's their current role at the company? What's their professional background and career path? What do they have planned next? What kind of situations do they seem relaxed or tense in?

It's also alright to engage in a little benevolent speculation: What motivates the person, and what matters most to them? Most importantly: What aspects of our initiative might interest or benefit them? Where in our initiative is there added value for this person?

4 | PUTTING THE PUZZLE PIECES OF THE STORY TOGETHER
Building on the findings from the impact exercise, the team now begins to craft a story that will captivate the person in question. Helpful questions to ponder include: What impact are we aiming for that is relevant for this person? Which of the desired outcomes will interest this person the most? For which outputs do we need their support the most?

The team splits up into three small groups, each focusing on one of three parts that will be later put together like a jigsaw puzzle.[24]

- **Puzzle Piece 1: Setting the stage**
  Clarity and credibility: How do we see the situation today, and what are we planning?
- **Puzzle Piece 2: Eyes on the prize**
  Emotion and surprise: Why is our initiative so valuable, for this person too?
- **Puzzle Piece 3: Call to action**
  Tangibility: What support do we need?

The small groups have 30 minutes to craft sentences or snippets of sentences as guided by the questions in the next step. We don't recommend that they merely answer each question directly, because the real value comes from the process of working together as a group, building on the ideas of others.

If a piece doesn't fit with the specific context of this discussion, it can be adapted or discarded.

Hint: *It's a good idea to use a Post-It for every individual idea or sentence, as this makes it easier to rearrange and replace them later on.*

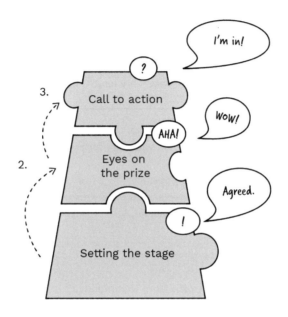

Puzzle Piece 1: "Agreed."

Setting the stage: How do we see the situation today and what are we planning?

1. Credibility: Our starting point

We connect with the other person and describe the current situation so that they can only say: "Agreed. That's exactly how it is."

Guiding questions:
- What specific challenge do we see in the organization on the path to regenerative sustainability?
- What motivates our team to embark on this new path?

2. Clarity: Our initiative
We describe our initiative as simply as possible, aiming to pique curiosity.

> Guiding questions:
> - How can we depict our initiative with a striking, memorable image?
> - What's our part in this initiative?
> - Can we quantify this in numbers?

Hint: *You can best grab the audience's attention by launching right into the exciting part of the story – how it all came to be can be filled in later. So be sure to put in the extra effort to make the opening scene very captivating.*

Puzzle Piece 2: "Wow!"
Eyes on the prize: Why is our initiative so valuable, for this person too?

1. Surprise: The outcome we're aiming for
We wow our audience with the potential outcome – or impact – of our plan, described as vividly and surprisingly as possible.

> Guiding questions:
> - What stakeholders will benefit and what will that look like from their perspective?
> - How will our organization profit from the initiative?
> - What will we be able to see in the company that wasn't there before?
> - Can we quantify this in numbers?

2. Emotion: Why this is important for you
Now, we focus on a concern or need of this person, which will be addressed by our initiative.

> Guiding questions:
> - What added value is there in the initiative for this person?
> - What does this added value look like in concrete – ideally visual – terms?
> - How is this person affected by it?

Hint: *Here, we can use the profile that was created in step 3. One option is to show a before-after comparison that makes it clear how the person's world will change when our initiative is implemented.*

Puzzle Piece 3: "I'm in!"
Call to action: What support do we need?

1. Credibility: What we as a team will accomplish
>We briefly summarize what our contribution is to the initiative.

Guiding questions:
- What have we already done to get this initiative moving?
- Where have we hit blockers?
- What goal conflicts do we face?

2. Tangibility: Why it all depends on you
The person learns why exactly we need their support.

Guiding questions:
- What exactly do we need, and what does this person's support look like (described in vivid detail)?
- What part will they play in our initiative?
- What image can we use to convey this?

Hint: *We feel a connection with others especially when we're scared together, laugh together, or oppose something together. Even small, simple stories can evoke emotions in the other person. Perhaps, for example, we can share some of the mistakes we've made and what we've learned from them. Or we can talk about conflicts we've settled or wins that we've celebrated.*

To make this more concrete, let's revisit the example of the logistics team from before, who now find themselves wanting to win over their company's CFO with their story. You can find a rough outline of it below.

EXAMPLE: PUZZLE PIECE 1
Whatever we do, we can only reach our Scope 3 sustainability goals by working together with our partners. The next thing we need is a proof of concept for viable circular packaging that we can share publicly. By doing so, we'll be pioneering something that may well transform our entire industry. **("Agreed.")** What's more, we have a concrete plan for how to make this into a success story.

EXAMPLE: PUZZLE PIECE 2
By championing circular packaging to our customers, we give them the opportunity to reduce their own footprint. This means we're effectively solving another problem for them, besides the transport and storage of packages, bringing us closer together as partners. And you'll have a truly visionary, high-profile project in your portfolio to meet the demands of the board to future-proof our business. **("Wow!")**

EXAMPLE: PUZZLE PIECE 3
Our team has planned out several steps already, but the first and most important one has already been taken: we managed to convince customer X and producer Y to partner with us in creating the prototype. Now, we need inputs A, B, and C in order to design and test the prototype. We'd like you to come on board as a sponsor and mentor because we value your commitment and dedication. **("I'm in!")** What next steps would you recommend that we take?

At the latest here, it's time to take a refreshing break.

5 | DISCUSSION AND INTEGRATION
The team comes together to present their puzzle pieces to each other and fit them together, removing overlaps and adjusting as needed. Their goal, as always, is to arrive at a narrative that's safe enough to try.

We recommend that the team makes the story undulate back and forth between what *is* and what *could be*. Here, it's helpful to draw the storyline as an actual line on a whiteboard. Ideally, it should resemble a rollercoaster ride, darting up and down for dramatic effect through the points gathered earlier, and finally seasoned with a pinch of humor.

Toward the end of the second puzzle piece, we should try to create an aha moment, where the person realizes that they want to be part of the success of this initiative. We don't spell this out explicitly, because just like a joke can only be funny if the person gets it themselves, so too the person needs to have this epiphany for themselves. There will be time to go into the details of what we expect from this person later, in Puzzle Piece 3.

It's worth noting that the starting point and request to the person should take up less than a quarter of the story as a whole. This is because people always remember best what they hear last, which makes the ending especially important to get right. That's why the discussion should never end with the request, but rather the person should be reminded of the value that's in it for them, as described in Puzzle Piece 2.

At the very end of the meeting, the team will deviate slightly from the conventional storytelling approach to ask the person directly how the story felt for them. By listening to their feedback, they can refine the story further for the next person.

6 | DRESS REHEARSAL AND CELEBRATION
The team finds someone in the organization who hasn't had anything to do with the process so far and asks them to take 15 minutes to listen to the story and share their feedback. To give some context to this "test subject", the team shares any necessary background information and explains whose perspective the person should try to adopt while listening. Here, props like accessories, clothes or even wigs can be useful for immersing into the test subject's role and for making the scenario more vivid.

The team then tells the story as if they were speaking to the person they aim to convince, and the test subject gives feedback as if they were that person: Was the story convincing? What stuck in their mind? What questions came up? The team takes notes of the answers and uses them to potentially adjust and finalize the story afterward.

Finally, it's time for the team to celebrate this newly minted story with a round of cheers and applause, before determining the next steps.

The team members get clear on which stakeholders from their surrounding systems they need to win over for their own transformation journey. They also develop a story to do so.

150 minutes

Storytelling cards, Whiteboard, Post-its, pens

Stellar Practice 7: Staying Effective

How can we ensure that we stay effective and replenish our strength?

All transformations require energy and fortitude, but it's particularly taxing to navigate the complexities and uncertainties of regenerative transformations. And just as natural systems need time to regenerate and have limits that can't be crossed, so too do people. Ultimately, to be able to take responsibility for the well-being of the planet in the long run, we need to also care for ourselves.

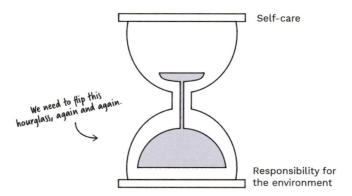

The seventh and final Stellar practice focuses on the inner equipment that team members need for their journey. Regenerative teams know to make time not just for doing, but also for *being*, meaning for reflecting on and working on their inner selves.

Since we do inner work in all the modules, you already know some of the elements of the seventh Stellar Practice:

- The **Pause and Nurture Hope** ritual deepens a person's connection to their own emotions and their fellow team members.
- The **Virtue Coach** ritual helps the team use its own resources and better understand the experiences of colleagues.

- The **boat analogy** is useful for building micro-habits that boost resilience.
- The **Three Regulatory Systems** remind the team to nurture its own soothing system, enabling it to restore calm in challenging times.

To complement these, in Module 3, we focus on three inner competencies that are key in the Stellar Approach:

- **Relationship capabilities:** To contribute meaningfully to life on this planet, we need to be capable of forming relationships. Here, we distinguish between our relationship with ourselves (self-contact), our relationship with others (empathy), and our relationship with the world (field competencies).[25]
- **Resilience and regenerative ability:** While the team will have some triumphs on the Stellar Journey, it's no walk in the park. They will likely encounter delays, inertia, and even dead ends that will force them to turn back. The key to overcoming all of these obstacles is *resilience*. We know from the domain of personal development that resilience doesn't just mean bouncing back after a crisis, but actually becoming stronger in the process. To foster this trait, we need to see ourselves as living systems that need time for rest and regeneration if they are to be productive in the long run. We also need to learn to actively practice self-care.
- **Tolerating ambiguity and mastering dilemmas:** This competency is closely tied to resilience. Periods of great transition are often marked by paradoxes and goal conflicts that may be hard to resolve. This is why it's so important to cultivate the ability to tolerate conflicting states or needs, without lunging for the easy either-or solutions. This way, development can proceed while the paradoxes are gradually worked out.

In the seventh Stellar practice, we introduce two methods for strengthening the team's interpersonal relationships and enhancing their competency in dealing with dilemmas. We then bring the guided Stellar Journey to an end with the rituals from the previous modules, as well as some individual reflection and peer counseling.

Dealing with dilemmas competently

A dilemma is a challenge that's inherently unsolvable: "Within this logic, there are no solutions to be found, or only unsatisfactory ones."[26] Very likely, most of the items we've saved in the Goal Conflict Navigator so far involve a dilemma of some kind.

On the path to regenerative economic activity, we're sure to run into plenty of ambiguities, dilemmas, and paradoxes, simply because we're changing the rules mid-game. We'll encounter tough questions like: Which of these goals is *most* important? What do we do about the other ones that are also kind of important? Whom are we prepared to disappoint?

As we move toward making regenerative decisions, it's useful to recognize dilemmas and deal with them in a deliberate, mindful way. Otherwise, we run the risk of getting stuck in a *dilemma cycle*.

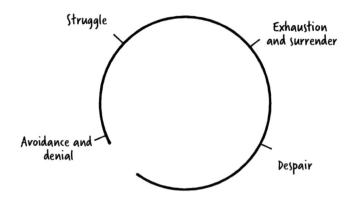

- **Avoidance and denial:** We avoid making a decision and focus on something else.
- **Struggle:** We realize that we need to confront the problem and struggle to find a solution that satisfies everyone, even if it comes at great personal sacrifice.

- **Exhaustion and surrender:** We couldn't solve the dilemma and give up the pointless struggle.
- **Despair:** We're unable to cope with the situation, and this weighs on us, though the severity of the burden depends on the individual.

From dilemmas to opportunities

A dilemma implies that there are only two potential choices ("di" meaning "two" in Greek). By reframing the situation as a "tetralemma" ("tetra" meaning "four"), we often discover that, actually, there are more options than first seemed.[27] We explore this idea further in the exercise below, which can help the team better understand its own reactions to dilemmas and to manage them consciously.

1 | REMEMBER
The team splits up into pairs. Each person brings to mind a situation where they had to make a choice, but there was no obviously correct one. They recall this situation as vividly as possible. To find inspiration, they can also review the Goal Conflict Navigator since it probably contains some dilemmas at this point. This phase should take no more than three minutes in total.

Next, everyone spends a few minutes taking notes and asking themselves which of the four reactions in the dilemma circle they had at the time and how did these reactions manifest.

Then each person shares with the other person what they remember about their thoughts and feelings at the time.

2 | RESEARCH
Next, the pair applies the tetralemma model to each of their situations, which means examining four perspectives, plus an additional one.
- The one: A possible solution
- The other: The opposite solution

The Stellar Approach

- Both: A solution that encompasses both of the above
- Neither: An altogether different solution
- Something else entirely: A completely new viewpoint and approach to the situation

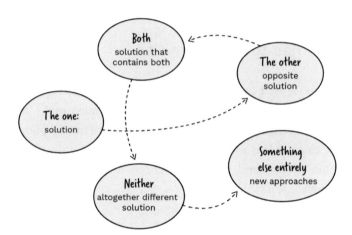

Each pair then writes the names of the perspectives on blank cards and lays them on the floor. Person A walks, at their own pace, from one marker to the next, pausing at each one to consciously sense their physical and mental reactions, sharing them as they go: What possibilities come to my mind here? What thoughts emerge? How does standing here feel?

Meanwhile, Person B writes down what A says, keeping the entire process calm and serene. This is to ensure that Person A can envision new possibilities and formulate their thoughts and feelings clearly. Once Person A is done with all five perspectives, the two switch roles.

3 | DEBRIEFING
Both team members take some time to debrief, asking:
- How was this process for us?
- What did we learn?
- What learnings will we apply going forward?

Finally, the team comes together to share their highlights and to capture ideas for how the entire team can benefit from the learnings.

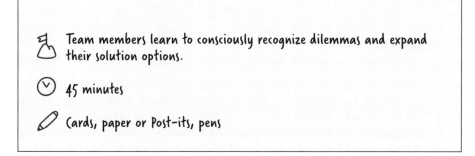

Strengthening relationships in the team

To conclude the seventh Stellar Practice of "Staying Effective," team members reflect once more on how they can support each other in monitoring their own energy balance. To help them do this, we use the *Circle Way*[28] exercise, which fosters stronger connections in the team.

The Circle Way is rooted in the fact that in nearly every culture around the world, people have traditionally gathered in circles to discuss important matters, for example around a fire. This is because a circle offers a simple but structured way of assembling people together. Often, these meetings also had rules to ensure that people spoke to each other respectfully. We use this time-honored way of coming together because it enables a different discussion culture, defined by openness, mindful expression, and focused listening.

Coming together with the Circle Way

The Circle Way is a way of bringing this traditional form of human discourse into the present day. Before starting, the team needs to agree to a few key principles:

- The circle is a confidential space; what's discussed there stays in the room.
- We ask for what we need and offer what we have.

- We listen attentively, with compassion and curiosity.
- We use the breaks for introspection and realignment and then come together again.

1 | PREPARATION

In the Circle Way, a team member first introduces a topic that's relevant to the team. This person also assumes the role of the host of the meeting. To prepare, they pick a suitable location – somewhere quiet, private, and ideally outdoors. Once there, the team forms a standing circle, and the host places an object in the middle to symbolize the theme. This sets the focus for the meeting. They also place another object in the center to act as a kind of "talking stick," which signifies that the person holding it now has the floor. This "talking object" is a simple way to structure and order the speaking turns.

For the first Circle Way meeting in Module 3, we usually propose the same topic: *"How can we as a team ensure that we stay effective and remember to care for our soothing systems?"*

We also ask if anyone in the team would like to be the host for this topic, or, alternatively, if anyone would like to propose their own topic around the theme of resilience.

2 | OPENING THE FLOOR

- The team chooses a *guardian* role, which we'll describe in just a moment. The team also decides which standard regenerative role is most relevant to the topic at hand. The holder of this role will have a part to play later on.
- If this is the first Circle Way meeting for anyone in the group, the team reiterates and reaffirms the principles listed earlier.
- The team does a quick check-in round, answering the following questions: Why have I accepted this invitation? What do I bring with me? How do I feel here in the circle right now?
- The host sets the circle's intention and explains what the object in the center means: "The reason we're here is …"

3 | DISCUSSION

After the host's introduction, participants can begin sharing their thoughts on the topic. One person takes the talking object from the center, which indicates that only they are allowed to speak, and they're not to be interrupted *under any circumstances*. They're afforded the undivided attention of the circle until they've fully finished expressing their thoughts. They then pass the talking object to the person

Host
Introduces a topic relevant to the team, for example a difficult decision stemming from the team's regenerative tensions. They invite the other members to exchange ideas.

Guardian
Safeguards the needs, time, and energy of the group. Signals the team to take a brief moment of silence, if perceives a need for one or is asked to do so.

Standard Regenerative Roles
Speaks from the perspective of the Earth, future generations, or marginalized groups: How do I perceive what's been said? What does it mean for me? Would I like to add something?

---

next to them, who speaks and passes it on again. In this way, everyone can be sure that their turn to speak will come.

Everyone takes turns sharing what's inside them, speaking from their own personal perspective, and drawing inspiration from what they've heard from others. However, they never comment on or judge what has been said before. If someone doesn't want to speak, they can simply pass the talking object forward.

Should the guardian role get the feeling that the group needs time to process what's been said, they can signal a moment of silence after a speaking turn, for example by ringing a bell. This moment can last for a minute, or even longer, as determined by the guardian. During this time, the team remains standing in the circle, using the time to contemplate what's been said. Other team members can also ask the guardian role to signal one of these breaks.

After each one of these moments, the person holding the standard regenerative role that was chosen for this meeting gets the talking object. They reflect on what they've heard so far:
- As a representative of the Earth's systems/future generations/marginalized groups, how do I perceive what's been said?
- What does it mean for me, in my day-to-day life?
- Is there something I want to add from my perspective?

Once this role is done speaking, the talking object is then passed further along the circle.

The discussion doesn't end until there's no one left who still wants to contribute, which makes the duration of the circle hard to predict. The 60 minutes mentioned below are only a guideline.

4 | CLOSING

Once the discussion is over, the team has a final feedback round, reflecting on the question: "What have I learned and what will I take home with me?"

The host then proposes possible next steps, closes the circle, and bids the participants farewell.

 The team knows how to prepare for tough decisions or topics by engaging in a profound and sincere discussion with each other.

 60 minutes

 An object to symbolize the topic, a talking object, role cards for the host, role cards for the guardian and standard regenerative roles

Inner Work in Module 3

All of the exercises in the seventh Stellar Practice relate to the inner workings of change processes. In addition to the Tetralemma and Circle Way exercises, Module 3 also includes the **Virtue Coach** and **Pause and Nurture Hope** rituals, this time focusing on the third Stellar Virtue, "Perseverance."

A Perseverance workout with the Virtue Coach

Perseverance is paramount in any transformation. Changes typically take longer than we predict, there's often organizational inertia to overcome, or it can take several tries before the right approach is found.

To persevere through it all, we need to manage our energy reserves prudently right from the start and also allow ourselves time to regenerate after big pushes. After all, we're engaged in an "infinite game"[29] of sorts – one that never ends. This means that success depends on our ability to stay effective.

We'll follow the same steps as in Modules 1 and 2, but the guiding questions are different:

- At the moment, how easy is it for you to pursue your plans in life persistently (on a scale from 1 to 10)?
- Think back to a time when you continued to pursue an endeavor despite many obstacles and setbacks. Describe that scenario vividly – what was it like?
- What allowed you to persevere? What pushed you to keep going?
- What image, sound, or gesture do you associate with your perseverance?

Completing the module and the Stellar Journey

As always at the end of a Module, we process the tension stash, review the Goal Conflict Navigator, and plan out the next sprint. Since Module 3 marks the end of the facilitated Stellar Journey for the team, we take a bit of extra time here to ensure that the team has what they need to continue their regenerative journey on their own. We also review all the work packages together with the team and ensure that everyone is clear on the next steps.

To end on, we take some time for individual reflection via journaling and for a peer consultation exercise. These are meant to ensure that the team can continue their journey with the greatest possible inner clarity.

In journaling, your thoughts count

In this exercise, each team member gets to explore their own thoughts in writing:

First, everyone finds themselves a quiet, comfortable spot, where they feel at ease writing. The moderator then reads out a list of questions, one at a time.

Team members take roughly two minutes per question to jot down their thoughts, with some flexibility depending on the question. The questions will be shared later, so they don't need to waste time writing those down. Here are the questions:
1. What are your biggest wishes and hopes for the journey that lies ahead?
2. How far off do these hopes seem? Do they beckon somewhere in the distant future, or are they already within reach?
3. Do you sense any fears or anxieties? If so, what are they?
4. What's holding you back, personally? (This could include, for example, certain behavioral habits or thought patterns.)
5. What would you need to let go of to make your hopes a reality?
6. What are the 3–4 most important tasks or challenges that you foresee for your team on the Stellar Journey?
7. Do you foresee any hazards that could stop you in your tracks?
8. As a regenerative team, what do you need to implement your ideas in this organization?
9. What do you personally need from the team in order to stay balanced even during difficult times?

> Team members find out what they need to successfully complete the last Stellar module and move forward with the next steps.
>
> 15 minutes
>
> Paper or Post-Its, pens

Case-based peer consultation

After the journaling exercise, team members get the chance to discuss their personal concerns and thoughts more deeply via a peer consultation exercise. To get started, they split up into small groups of four to five people.

At the end of the module, we guide the team through the case-based consultation format below. But we also encourage the team to continue to use formats like this regularly to support each other's development. This could mean having fixed peer-group meetings or ad hoc sessions with changing participants. The idea is that every consultation focuses on a specific concern, following a structured approach, with everyone taking turns to moderate.

1 | PREPARATION
Each small group determines whose issue will be tackled in the session, and this person acts as the presenter of the case. In addition, a timekeeper role is assigned – their job is to ensure that the group follows the process and doesn't exceed the time limits, while also participating as a reflection partner like the others.

2 | PRESENTING THE ISSUE
The presenter of the case describes the issue that they uncovered in the journaling exercise. This could be a specific concern or a question that they want the team to address. Whatever the issue, they describe it in detail, explaining whom it affects, what their own role in it is, what attempt they've made to solve it, and so on. Finally, they define the "consulting assignment" for the team.

3 | CLIENT INTERVIEW
The consultants take a few minutes to ask clarifying questions so as to better understand the issue. Here, it's important that everyone speaks in turn. No actual advice should be given yet.

4 | FORMING HYPOTHESES
The presenter of the case now turns away from the consultants so as not to see or distract them, but the presenter should still be able to hear the discussion and take notes. The consultants formulate hypotheses, speculating based on what they heard. They can make conjectures and possibly voice some initial ideas for solutions. Still, no recommendations or advice should be given yet.

5 | QUICK RESONANCE CHECK WITH THE CASE PRESENTER
The case presenter now shares some feedback based on what they heard:
- Which hypotheses resonated with me the most?
- What really made me stop and think?
- Which idea do I want to explore further?

Please note: This is *not* about confirming or correcting the hypotheses made, but indicating which ones resonated the most.

6 | DEEP DIVE
The consultants go deeper into the points that resonated most, developing and discussing ideas and proposals for how to solve the original issue.

7 | REVIEW
Finally, the group reviews how the consultation went and shares feedback around the following questions:
- What can we learn from this?
- How do we feel now? To what extent does the presenter of the case feel supported?
- How well did this peer consultation format work?

Module 3: Impact 251

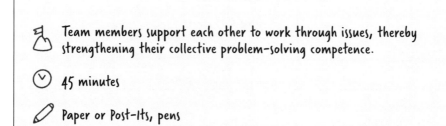

> 🧪 Team members support each other to work through issues, thereby strengthening their collective problem-solving competence.
>
> ⏲ 45 minutes
>
> ✏ Paper or Post-Its, pens

As we reach the end of Module 3, we take a moment to reflect on where the team started the Stellar Journey and where it stands now – a retro meeting of sorts. We also ensure that they've anchored into their daily work some core concepts like working with tensions, sprints, and the Goal Conflict Navigator. This enables them to seamlessly and confidently continue their journey from here on out, still going one step at a time. Ideally, at this point, the team has achieved the following goals.

- ☑ The team has identified useful indicators for measuring its regenerative success.
- ☑ The team understands how to use storytelling and narratives to win over partners and supporters in the organization.
- ☑ The team has established habits and routines to foster its own resilience, thereby helping it stay on the regenerative path in the long run.
- ☑ The team is motivated for the journey ahead and knows how to navigate the uncertainties and dilemmas it will inevitably encounter.
- ☑ The team has established a sprint routine to support its regenerative contribution.
- ☑ Team members have the means to support each other as they continue to develop and grow.

Workshop Agenda Module 3
Day 1

9:00	👋	**Check-in**
		Retro and wrap-up Sprint 2 Introduction to the topic of impact
10:30	☕	**Break**
		Measuring the impact of the team's contribution
12:45	🍴	**Lunch break**
		Storytelling Puzzle
16:00	☕	**Break**
		Pause and Nurture Hope Virtue Coach: Perseverance
17:45	👋	**Wrap-up, check-out**

Example

Module 3: Impact   253

Workshop Agenda Module 3
Day 2

9:00		**Check-in**
		Sprint planning and kick-off for Sprint 3
10:30		**Break**
		From dilemmas to opportunities
		Journaling
		Peer consulting for issues arising from journaling
12:45		**Lunch break**
		Presenting the *Circle Way*
		Circle Way team session on resilience
15:30		**Break**
		Processing tensions
		Retro on the Stellar Journey
17:00		**Deep Check-out, celebrating accomplishments**

Example

The key takeaways from this chapter

The team's Stellar Journey has taken them through all three workshop Modules: Context, Direction, and Impact. Each module has focused on certain Stellar Practices and Virtues.

Throughout the journey, the team grows its regenerative competence, develops new habits, and works on its own mindset. It learns how to incrementally contribute to bringing economic activity into balance with the vital ecosystems around us. What's more, team members gain the tools to continuously strengthen their relational skills, resilience, and ability to handle dilemmas.

During the sprints between modules, the team implements some first projects to make its regenerative contribution a reality. Throughout the Stellar Journey, it also learns how to independently use tensions, sprints, and the Goal Conflict Navigator to make incremental progress.

As they reach the end of the Stellar Journey, the team has everything it needs to continue on its own. It understands all the core components of regenerative economic activity and knows how to adapt when new information comes to light along the way.

The Big Picture: The Stellar Approach as a Part of the Regenerative Transformation

Even though we've completed the last module, the Stellar Journey is never really over.

Once teams have been through all three modules, they have the tools to make their own actions incrementally more regenerative and to bring other stakeholders along for the ride. But this is far from the end. Rather, the transformation is just beginning.

Especially in larger organizations, a broad transformation needs more than just teams making their Stellar Journeys. It's still true that organizations, at their core, consist of the countless daily decisions made by teams. However full-scale transformation projects are so complex that they demand some minimum level of architectural planning and oversight to support the teams.

Just as before, there are no proven, ready-to-use instructions to follow here. But there are some work packages that we consider essential, which is why we'll briefly introduce them in this chapter. They fall into two main categories:

- The conditions and success factors required for successful transformation processes.
- The building blocks of an overarching regenerative transformation process.

Conditions and Success Factors

Change processes are, by their very nature, unpredictable and complex. To at least increase our likelihood of success, we need to ensure that the conditions are as favorable as possible. Happily, through our own work with clients, we've identified eleven important conditions and success factors for the Stellar Approach[1] …

The organization's resolve must be clear

A regenerative transformation is not a walk in the park. Strongly held beliefs will be constantly questioned and business models will get revised or even completely revamped. Enduring all of this turbulence requires a deep conviction that this journey is necessary for the future viability of both the organization and our society as a whole. In other words, the organization needs to have a strong *resolve* to embark on this path.

The organization's leadership plays a key part here. Unless the leaders are on board with a transformation, its chances of success dwindle. And this holds especially true in regenerative transformations, which always involve stepping into uncharted territory. Such profound transformations can only succeed if the company leadership …

- … understands the need for transformation.
- … is eager to pioneer and help shape the rules of a regenerative economy.
- … communicates the need for and their commitment to change clearly and unequivocally.
- … takes time to understand what's going to be done
- … sets a good example.
- … keeps the organization's owners in the loop and involves them in the journey.

Bring all leaders along for the journey

When we talk about the importance of leadership, we don't just mean the top management that has the power to start – or stop – the regenerative transformation. We also mean the subsequent leadership levels, which are just as important in anchoring and advancing the transformation throughout the organization.

To get all management levels involved, we recommend using different formats to co-develop the overarching narrative of the transformation, including its ambition level. (See the "Strategic Alignment" workstream below.) Here, it's important to listen not only to supporters but also the skeptics, who often point out some unspoken objections or overlooked obstacles that will otherwise come as surprises later.

Creating islands of success within the organization

We know that a regenerative transformation can't succeed if the leadership isn't on board. But where the rubber really hits the road is in the operational teams of an organization. This is where the vast majority of micro decisions are made day in and day out, and they are what can move the organization toward more or less regenerative action.

Moreover, these teams can act as torch-bearers for the wider organization. In general, regenerative change is fuelled by success stories, as they show others what's possible and inspire them to start their own journey. These success stories don't need to involve the whole organization but can just demonstrate solid impact in a limited circle of influence.

This is why the Stellar Approach is so focused on teams: They provide a small arena, where decisions can be gradually shifted in a more regenerative direction. What's more, they can create concrete, small-scale solutions that inspire other teams to follow suit, thereby enhancing the regenerative innovation potential of the entire organization.

No team is like another

We define a team as a group of people who work on something together out of their own accord. This could be a functional, cross-functional, or leadership team. We've designed the Stellar Approach specifically for these kinds of teams, which is why it may not work for groups outside of this definition, for example, if they only work together rarely or don't actually pursue shared goals. Nor is the Stellar Approach intended to fix problematic teams that are, say, in the throes of conflict, about to disband, or that have grown so large and bloated that members barely know each other. These teams are also important and can be helped, but it's not what we specifically created the Stellar Approach for.

Find and support strong internal change agents

In any transformation, external facilitators can only provide impulses for action, but the actual transformation has to occur from within the organization. And this requires strong internal change agents who take responsibility for driving the desired change. In the Stellar Approach, these are often people who already have some experience with the topics we deal with, such as sustainability.

It's also important that some of these change agents hold leadership positions, because they can then use their organizational power to make the transformation smoother. In order to convince leaders to take on this role, it can be helpful to explain that sustainable and regenerative organizational development will be a key aspect of leadership in the future.

Focus on pioneers

Pioneers are needed at the beginning of every transformation. These are the people and teams who are willing to throw themselves into the transformation head first, even when a lot of it is still unclear. This is why pioneers should always be volunteers who take pride in forging a path for others.

At the outset, the Stellar Approach is just a prototype – it has to be gradually adapted to the needs of the organization. This means that the module workshops will inevitably be a bit rocky for the first pioneering teams, but this will smooth the way for those that follow. This is why it's worth picking the first teams carefully to ensure they have an early-adopter mindset suited for pioneering work.

Communicate continuously

Communication constitutes the basic building block of organizations, and especially in change situations, continuous communication is vital, because employees will expect a lot of transparency. Basic questions like "What's the reason for this journey?", "What's the rough destination?", and "How can I contribute?" will need to be answered and revisited again and again. This is the only way to ensure that the entire organization has clarity on the desired direction.

What's more, there should also be room for the organization to share successes and failures and to talk about their progress and solutions, so that everyone can learn from each other's experiences. This means establishing the right spaces and formats for this, both within organizational units like departments, but also across the organization as a whole.

Don't expect miracles

Change takes time. And while it's true that we as humanity don't have an abundance of time to transition into a regenerative economy, there's not much we can do about it. After all, even a blade of grass won't grow faster by pulling on it. This is why it's important to have realistic expectations for the organization's regenerative development, appreciating that many small steps and decisions will be needed along the way.

Unrealistic expectations only result in seeming failures that can make the whole transformation project look bad. To avoid this dynamic, it's worth communicating clearly from the start that a regenerative transformation is more a marathon than a sprint. It'll take a long time and will never be truly over. It can lead to some activities being phased out, business models being iterated on, or even the creation of new ecosystems with entirely new market rationales. And even though we've designed the Stellar Approach to make the transformation so gradual that the overall performance of the organization shouldn't be disrupted along the way, there might still be bumps in the road.

The bottom line: expecting or promising miracles is a surefire way to be disappointed.

Be part of the solution (and have fun while you're at it)

The looming threat of the climate catastrophe and other societal crises forms a pretty bleak backdrop for any sustainable or regenerative transformation. But even though the topic is a serious one, we should try not to fall into "crisis depression," which can sap our motivation and lead to a downward spiral.

Neurological research tells us that anxiety and worry hamper our ability to think in a creative, solution-oriented way. So while it's important to acknowledge feelings like regret and grief, it's also vital to see the regenerative transformation as an interesting, or even fun design task. The prize: healthy people living on a healthy planet.

Overcome path dependencies

Though we may imagine that we're free to do whatever we choose, we're actually constrained by innumerable path dependencies – political, economic, and organizational. These drastically reduce the number of possible options available. Often, major societal shifts actually stem from the realization of how extremely restrictive these path dependencies are and how they effectively create a lock-in effect that leaves very few options on the table. This is often when new paradigms and patterns are introduced that radically change the playing field, opening up more possibilities again.

To succeed, the regenerative transformation needs individuals and groups in organizations who can recognize path dependencies and have the courage to break free from them. These are the people who understand that change won't happen overnight but who will nevertheless push steadfastly toward something new. In our experience, the organizations that cultivate this mindset across all decision-making levels are the ones that also evidence the greatest innovation potential in the regenerative transformation.

Expect surprises along the way

Does any larger endeavor ever really go to plan? No matter how good our planning is, there will always be unforeseen challenges along the way.

Of course, an organization should have *some idea* of what it wants to achieve in the next 10, 20, or 30 years. But at the same time, it's good to recognize that things will probably turn out very differently.

Moreover, it's important to keep an eye on how things change out in the world and to react appropriately. New requirements will crop up, and the organization needs to figure out what a mature response is.

Unfortunately, many of the trends we see are exacerbating the already dire state of the world. This is why it's especially important to embrace any positive trends that could help the regenerative transformation effort.

The Building Blocks of a Broader Regenerative Transformation Architecture

Shaping a successful regenerative transformation demands some foundational know-how of transformations and workstreams that are specific to the goal of sustainability or regenerativity. The precise transformation architecture is always a case-by-case question, but we've found some key elements to be essential across the board.

Scouting and preparation

Major transformations aren't measured in weeks but in months or even years. This means they require a plan that provides some initial direction but can also be adapted later on.

The first question that often comes up in a regenerative transformation is who has authorized it. Often, the mandate comes from top management, but sometimes also from sustainability officers or dedicated transformation teams. Whoever it is, we need to clarify the assignment with them before we get started:

- Why does the organization want to make this journey? Does it already have a vision or strategic ambition to strive for?
- Is the leadership of the organization on board? What private agendas or interests should we be aware of?
- What about the owners, what's their part in this process?
- Are the employees on board? Are they ready to make this change?
- Do we have some data on the status quo, like say a materiality analysis, baseline measurements, or something else?
- What does the current context look like: What workstreams and building blocks are already in place? How can they be incorporated into the transformation architecture?
- What workstreams or building blocks are still missing?

The Stellar Approach

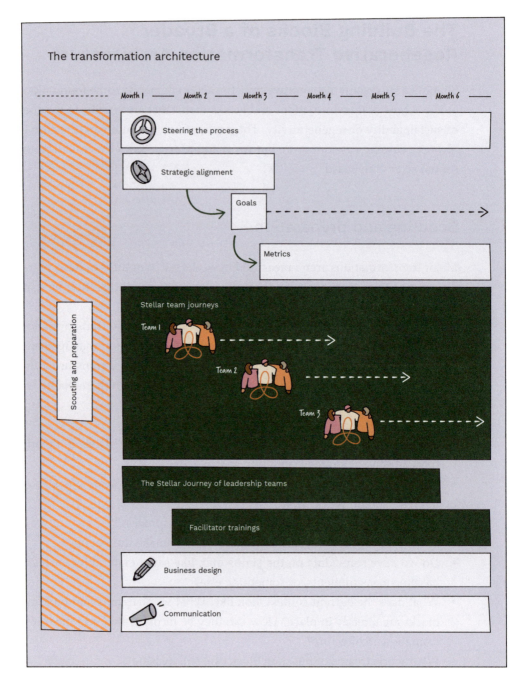

- How have the responsibilities and roles for the individual work packages been distributed? What does the overall project design look like?

Once we've clarified these questions, we can map out the concrete transformation architecture, in which the Stellar team journeys are but one of many elements. A steering team is usually tasked with coordinating the various workstreams.

Usually, the first teams to embark on the Stellar Journey are "pilot teams," who have volunteered for the task. Their experiences help us to learn quickly and adapt the methodology to suit the organization. For example, the pilot team's journey might show us that the organization already has an advanced understanding of sustainability and regenerativity, which would allow us to skim through the first module and spend more time on the others.

To help us pick these pilot teams, we use the following guiding principles:

- **Volunteers only:** The teams should want to embark on this journey of their own accord, not because someone else told them to.
- **Apply within:** It often makes sense to have teams apply for the spots in the process, because this gives the most motivated teams a better chance.
- **Pioneers and early adopters wanted:** Regenerative economic activity is still largely uncharted territory, which is why the first teams embarking on the Stellar Journey should be open-minded and eager to try something new.
- **Have a taste of your own medicine:** Another important consideration is that leadership or steering teams in an organization should also experience the Stellar Journey themselves as early as possible in the transformation. This gives them credibility, as they'll actually know what they're talking about.

Another major component in this scouting and preparation phase is analyzing the impact of organizational activities, commonly referred to as "materiality." A materiality analysis and any necessary baseline measurements are especially important here. Key questions include:

- How do our various business activities affect the environment, the climate, or the well-being of our employees?
- How do our emissions fall into the different scopes?
- Where does the organization currently stand, based on what indicators?

Organizations subject to the Corporate Sustainability Reporting Directive (CSRD) have to deal with these questions regularly anyway, but it's also important for smaller companies to use them to determine their starting point for sustainable or regenerative transformation.

The outcomes of the materiality analysis form the foundation for other work packages, like, say, formulating the ambition for the transformation, defining goals for it, or developing business models further.

Steering the process and managing stakeholders

In a broader transformation architecture encompassing multiple workstreams, we typically work with central steering teams. Depending on the organization and the scope of the project, these teams can have varying accountabilities, but usually at least the following:

- Monitor the architecture and coordinate the workstreams.
- Take responsibility for adjusting and iterating on the architecture along the journey.
- Bring in additional expertise where needed.
- Ensure periodic checkpoints or retrospectives to digest learnings about the process.
- Keep track of the diverse stakeholders in the process and orchestrate interventions as needed.

It's important that certain key perspectives be represented in the steering team, such as the perspective of the leadership, the business, sustainability, communication, and so forth. But in addition to these, it's important to include the standard regenerative roles too, so that the Earth, future generations, and marginalized groups also have a seat at the table. That said, in order to work effectively, the steering team should only comprise roughly 6–8 people, and to fully focus on the transformation, they should free up a substantial chunk of their time.

Another crucial workstream in any successful transformation is stakeholder management, because there are always people who can accelerate or hinder the change process. Both the supporters and the skeptics can provide valuable insights for the transformation, as long as they're integrated into the process in the right way.

To summarize the relevant stakeholders, we can use the simple stakeholder mapping exercise as in the storytelling exercise on page 231. This can help us understand each stakeholder's proximity to the process and their likely attitude toward the transformation. It can also be a helpful tool for categorizing stakeholders based on their decision-making power and the extent to which they'll be impacted by the transformation.

Strategic alignment

The strategic alignment workstream comprises four key elements for creating high-level alignment and coherence: ambition, purpose, narrative, and governance.

Ambition

A regenerative transformation cannot succeed without steadfast organizational resolve. Along the journey, *business-as-usual* patterns will likely be challenged, which is why it's critical that the organization's intention and strategic ambition are clearly defined and expressed.

In most organizations, this intention originates at the leadership level. That's why it makes sense to clarify questions around strategic alignment early on with top management and, if applicable, also with the owners, meaning investors, shareholders, and so on.

270   The Stellar Approach

To determine the level of the organization's ambition, we use a spectrum spanning the space between a degenerative and regenerative economy:

- On the lowest level, only the minimum legal standards are met.
- On the second level, these requirements are slightly surpassed.
- The third level targets a best-in-class position in the industry.
- The fourth level meets requirements as outlined by scientific research.

To make these four levels more concrete, we define the ambition across three dimensions[2]:

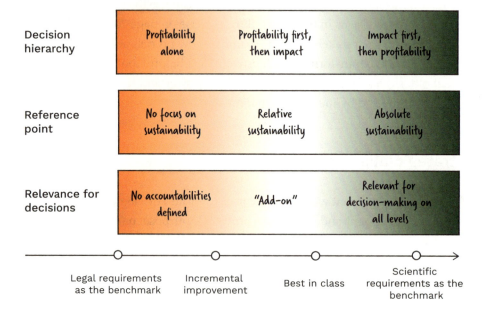

- **Decision hierarchy:** On the path of regenerative transformation, most organizations will face short-term conflicts between profit and impact. Therefore it's important to develop a shared view of where the organization wants to position itself on this dimension. In other words, when the inevitable goal conflicts come up, what's more important to us: profit or impact?[3] What decision-making heuristics can guide us in these moments?

- **Reference point:** The reference point determines what kind of sustainability the organization's ambition relates to. The lowest level implies that sustainability plays no part in the organization's activities. The medium tier means setting relative sustainability targets, like: "Reduce CO_2 emissions by X percent compared to the year Y." The highest level means defining the sustainability ambition in absolute terms, in line with the scientific understanding of planetary boundaries (see page 60).
- **Relevance for decisions:** This final dimension clarifies how the strategic ambition is integrated into the organization's accountabilities. On the lowest rung, there are no clearly defined accountabilities to support the ambition at all. On the intermediate level, the ambition is mostly just an add-on to the core business of the organization. And on the highest level, the ambition is relevant for and embedded into decision-making across the organization.

Purpose

Depending on the formulation of the strategic ambition, the organization's purpose might also need to change. Some organizations already have a purpose statement, while others opt for strategic elements like a vision or mission. But in our experience, purpose is a concept that's well-suited to a regenerative world, because it provides clear direction and fosters coherent decisions that contribute to a larger goal.

Purpose is the answer to the question of why the organization exists – its raison d'être. In the world of *business-as-usual*, the answer would typically revolve around making money and ensuring that the organization survives. But as we move closer to *business-as-the-world-needs*, where organizations don't just avoid harm but strive for positive ecological and/or social impact, the more the purpose will grow to encompass this contribution.[4]

To help craft a compelling organizational purpose, we use tools like Simon Sinek's *Golden Circle* (complemented with an element of "Who?") and the *Integration Playoffs* described on page 165. The purpose statement should serve as a regenerative compass for the entire organization, allowing individual teams to align their regenerative contributions based on it.

Narrative

Another crucial strategic element is the narrative around the regenerative transformation. As discussed earlier in regard to storytelling, stories connect with people in a unique way (see page 229). Stories help us construct meaning, make our ideas understandable, and draw people into our journey.

This is why it makes sense to invest time and effort into the story that's told about the regenerative transformation. The strategic ambition and purpose should serve as a basis, and the methodology presented in the sixth Stellar Practice can help. Questions that the narrative should answer include:

- Why are we embarking on this journey?
- Why now, of all times?
- What do we want to change by making this journey? What do we want to keep as is?
- What milestones or goals have we set for ourselves?
- How will we navigate on this journey? How will we deal with the obstacles we'll encounter and the developments we can't foresee?
- How will we stay in contact and communicate on this journey?

Governance

A final element of strategic alignment is how the regenerative ambition will be embedded into the organization's governance. To ensure a consistent and coherent approach, some key governance elements need to be aligned on:

- How will the regenerative transformation be embedded into existing strategy elements, like the vision, mission, and goals? Do they need to be developed or refined further to fit the regenerative transformation?
- How do we incentivize performance in the organization? Do we need to change something there?
- What criteria guide decisions in the organization and what key decision-making heuristics are used? Do we need to change something there?
- How do we measure success in the organization, and how should this be evolved?

Answering these questions and enacting possible changes will take time. Happily, there's no need to do everything at once, but rather the issues can be tackled in individual projects. It's just important to not forget this area. Otherwise, discrepancies can arise that create ambiguity and confusion if left unresolved for too long.

What's more, in practice it's inevitable that some tensions around the governance can't be foreseen and will only emerge along the way. That's why knowing how to work with tensions is also valuable for dealing with these issues (see page 133).

Goals

The strategic ambition and materiality analysis form the foundation for setting goals. Based on these two elements, it's possible to identify the most relevant social and ecological focus areas to work on.

These areas can also align with Stellar Principles or other regenerative frameworks, like the Doughnut Model, but they're always highly context-dependent. One organization focuses on freshwater consumption and healthcare, while another company with a different business model concentrates on climate change and education, for example.

Specific goals with **clearly defined timeframes** can then be set within these focus areas. To do so, a few general principles come in handy:

- *Ecological goals:* Wherever possible, these should be defined in absolute terms. This is because, at the end of the day, the Planetary Boundaries constitute clear, absolute limits for the impact of humanity. Hence, individual organizations would also conform to these "budgets." Tools like *Science-Based Targets (for Nature)*[5] can help define these absolute goals.
- *Social goals:* These can be defined as relative goals, but they always need to be context-sensitive, meaning that they're benchmarked against the minimum standards of each local environment. For example, the wage level should also always be benchmarked against the local minimum

living wage. Moreover, these goals also need a clearly defined timeframe.
- *Economic plausibility:* As we've already mentioned before, there are costs associated with transitioning to a regenerative business focused on its holistic impact. In the medium term, these costs can be seen as an investment into new business models and greater organizational resilience, but in the short term, these benefits will not yet be apparent. Therefore, when defining the above goals, it's important to also make hypotheses as to their likely effect on costs and revenues, both immediately and over time.
- *Footprint and handprint:* Alongside footprint goals aimed at reducing the organization's harmful impact, it's important to also set handprint goals. As a reminder, these denote the positive impact that sustainable or regenerative actions have on others, both directly, but also indirectly by inspiring them to follow suit. Growing the organization's handprint can in fact be very profitable, since there are significant business opportunities in creating new products and services to address global challenges. Many companies have already begun to include their corporate handprint in their sustainability reporting, alongside their footprint.

Metrics

Goals are only useful in steering our actions if they're measured. Hence, it's vital to establish meaningful indicators for these goals. There may already be well-established standards for some areas, such as the different scopes of CO_2 emissions, but in others, measurement is still challenging. This is changing through recent advances in research though. For example, it's now possible to reliably depict the impact of individual organizations on biodiversity.

If no baseline measurement was made in the scouting phase, one should be planned into the overall architecture to enable better quantification of the journey ahead. Sometimes the baseline can also help fine-tune the timeframe for and other specifics of the contributions to the goals.

Since the Stellar Approach focuses on teams, it often makes sense to set up dashboards to bring together the contributions of individual teams on the outcome level and link them to the overarching organizational goals.

Stellar team journeys

The Stellar team journeys constitute the heart of the Stellar Approach, but there's no one right time to start them up with the pilot teams. In some transformations, it may make sense to first work on the strategic ambition, overarching goals, and metrics, so that the teams have a sense of direction on their journey. But often, it's best that the pilot teams start their journey right away so they can quickly get useful results and generate learnings that help shape the overall transformation.

Whatever the right approach, the regenerative transformation will in any case require that regenerative knowledge and habits be spread throughout the organization. This means that, sooner or later, there will come a time for each and every team to define its own contribution to the overall regenerative journey and begin making its work incrementally more sustainable and regenerative.

A Stellar Journey spans roughly three months, and depending on the size of the organization, teams typically start their journeys at slightly staggered times. This way, the experiences of Team 1 will help adjust some parameters by the time Team 2 gets underway.

Prior to Module 1, each team has a two-hour kickoff meeting where it …

- … is told what to expect in the process going forward.
- … takes stock of the seven practices as they currently stand and sets development goals for its journey through the Stellar modules.
- … gets the preparatory homework for Module 1.

This kick-off is also where we make sure that the team is truly ready to start the Stellar Approach. In other words:

- Does everyone know what to expect, and are they ready for this shared journey?
- Is this really a team, meaning a group of four to twelve people who spend most of their working hours pursuing a common goal together? Or is it more a discussion forum or a group that happens to share an interest?

When we accompany a transformation project, we typically advise and support the first three to eight teams in their journeys. In parallel, we train internal Stellar facilitators who can assist us as co-moderators. This all happens in coordination with the steering team or sustainability officers, of course. Once these internal facilitators feel up to the task, they can completely take over and replace us in this workstream.

The Stellar Journey of leadership teams

As stated before, a sweeping regenerative transformation can only succeed if the leadership is fully committed to it. Therefore, in addition to the tools for finding strategic alignment that we've already covered, we highly recommend that the leadership tier of the company also start their own Stellar Journeys. This way, they will actually know what they're talking about with regard to the transformation, can steer the overall process in an informed way, and give their input to shaping the Stellar content early on.

The Stellar Journey of leadership teams comprises the same basic building blocks as everyone else's: the four Stellar Principles, the seven Stellar Practices, and the three Stellar Virtues. But there is a twist: leadership teams will also spend time preparing for their roles in the Stellar process. This is so that they can help, for example, deal with goal conflicts that other teams will inevitably encounter but which they can't resolve on their own. Here, the leadership team can help process these conflicts for example by leading, coaching, or making tough decisions.

Facilitator trainings

To help the Stellar routines gain a lasting foothold in day-to-day work, every team needs skilled facilitators. They ensure that things like routines around meetings and discussions are adhered to and that the sprint backlog is processed smoothly. This is why we supplement the Stellar team journeys with in-depth facilitator training. To minimize the training workload, we typically group people from several teams together into cohorts.

The training sessions focus on improving the participants' facilitation skills, getting them to feel more comfortable with the Stellar process, and teaching them how to master even difficult situations. In addition to this process-related emphasis, we may also do deep dives into regenerative topics as needed.

Business design

Another common element in regenerative transformations is that existing business models are refined or completely revamped. Sometimes, this can happen in the course of the Stellar team journeys, for example in a sprint project. But often, it's worth thinking of this topic as a distinct innovation project that should take place within the transformation architecture.

The first step in this workstream is segmenting the portfolio of existing business models based on the actions that each model needs so it supports the overarching goals. Again, the outcomes of the scouting and preparation phase are useful here.

Whether refining existing business models or creating entirely new ones, the best approach is an iterative one. In practice, this means several rounds of prototyping, learning, and improving along the way from the initial idea to the "finished" business model. Agile methods like design thinking and scrum are often useful tools here, as long as they're supplemented with a "life-centric" or "planet-centric" perspective (see page 82).

Another proven method for developing new regenerative business models is harnessing the collective intelligence of the organization. For example, curated and managed intrapreneurship programs can combine entrepreneurial drive with regenerative perspectives, resulting in innovative new approaches and generating learnings for the whole organization.

Communication

The importance of communication cannot be overstated. All change processes live and die by communication.

In-house, the focus should be on conveying the narrative and the "why" of the transformation, as well as on supporting communication between different teams and workstreams. This is why – as mentioned before – the communication perspective should ideally be represented in the steering team.

Communication toward the outside world should focus on sharing the regenerative transformation journey with external stakeholders. Transparency, honesty, and integrity are of the utmost importance here. It's completely fine to not have all the answers to all the questions at the outset – after all, this is largely uncharted territory we're venturing into. But it's important to not overpromise, because external stakeholders seldom forgive apparent greenwashing, *especially* if the company in question is claiming it wants to become regenerative.

The key takeaways from this chapter

Larger transformation processes are always complex and follow unpredictable paths. That's why there are no proven, ready-to-use instructions for a regenerative transformation. What we do have, however, are building blocks that help craft the broader transformation architecture.

Stellar team journeys are an effective and decentralized way to share regenerative knowledge and habits throughout the organization, thereby incrementally enhancing its regenerative maturity.

If necessary, the Stellar Journeys can be supplemented with additional elements around organizational ambition (leadership and strategic alignment), operationalization (goals and metrics), innovation projects (business design), and communication (narratives, storytelling, external communication).

Leadership plays a vital part in the regenerative transformation, because developments on the team level can affect the fundamental business logic of the organization, necessitating decisions or authorizations at higher levels.

The architecture is overseen by a steering team comprising key perspectives on the transformation, including regenerative ones.

Part 3

Food for Thought and the Way Forward

We're at the end of the book, so now at the latest it's time to get a little personal [cue Barry White]:

- How old are you right now?
- How many years do you think you have left?
- How's the world going to change in those years?
- What would the world be like if organizations and businesses actually made life better instead of eroding its foundations?
- What could your personal contribution – big or small – be to creating such a world?

In complex environments, we have to accept that we can't know exactly what kind of solutions we'll discover in the future. So our challenge today is less about understanding everything, but rather about taking action and working to make things a little bit better, day by day.

As we said in the introduction to this book, we can't hope to resolve all the paradoxes and systemic entanglements of the polycrisis today. But we did promise that we'd encourage you to take the first steps and just get going.

In transformations big or small, the Stellar Approach offers a decentralized way to start taking those first steps.

Humanity faces a monumental challenge, which is why many of us grapple with feelings of powerlessness and directionlessness. Ideally, the Stellar Approach should replace those feelings with a sense of "I know what to do, and I'm ready to get started."

Just remember: it's not a panacea or silver bullet, but rather a work in progress that will continue to evolve over the coming years.

We believe that for a company to become truly regenerative, some organizational development must also happen. This is because a true regenerative transformation will necessarily affect all three sides of the organization:

- The "display" side: what we communicate to the outside world, how we present ourselves, what we offer.
- The formal side: goals, structures, roles, processes, and so forth.
- The informal side: the organizational culture and informal structure of the company.

What's more, the transformation will also require many different functions and experts to collaborate and various workstreams to be synchronized.

There's one question that we often encounter in organizations: "If we apply the core principles of the Stellar Approach, does that mean the entire organization will automatically become regenerative and we can all just high-five?"

The answer: not necessarily.

The Stellar Approach focuses mainly on the organization's service provision and its relationship with its environments because these are key areas for taking regenerative action. That said, for an organization to be fully regenerative, it needs to take into account some other dimensions too.

That's why we want to end this book by presenting an organizational model that goes beyond the Stellar Approach and zooms out to the bigger picture. For all the pioneers, thought leaders, and change-makers out there, here is the *"Life-Centric Organization."*

(In general, we tend to use the terms "regenerative," "life-serving," and "life-centric" pretty interchangeably, because they all share the view that life itself should be the focus of economic and organizational activity.)

The 5+1 Model: The Life-Centric Organization

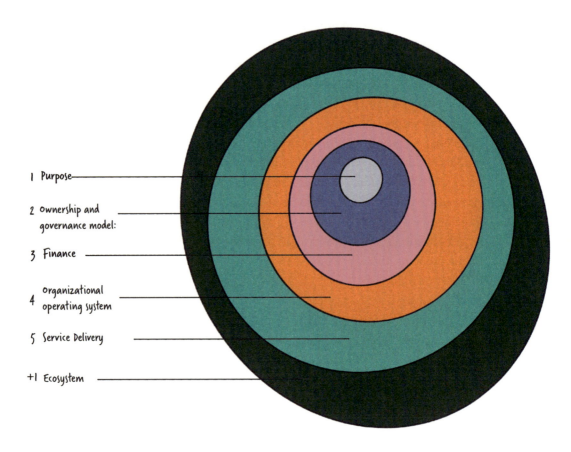

1 Purpose
2 Ownership and governance model:
3 Finance
4 Organizational operating system
5 Service Delivery
+1 Ecosystem

If the thought of immersing yourself into *yet another* model fills you with trepidation, don't worry. We know that, by now, you've already waded through a veritable sea of approaches, models, and tools.

That's why this last part of the book is meant to be *light* reading – something you'd peruse in a hammock by the beach or right before bedtime. Some of the elements we describe will already be familiar from the first two parts of the book, but you'll also find some fresh new ideas peppered throughout.

The entire field of regenerative organizations is still in its infancy, so you can think of this model as our contribution to the ongoing discussion around its development. Our hope is that it will inspire some readers to join us on our journey.

The Life-Centric Organization model is based on six levels that we consider essential for an organization aiming to become comprehensively regenerative. We frame this as "5+1," because five of these levels are internal to the organization, whereas the sixth transcends the limits of the organization as a system:

1. Purpose:	From "Profit over impact" to "Impact over profit"
2. Ownership and governance model:	From short-term value creation to long-term responsibility
3. Finance:	From profit focus to financial resilience
4. Organizational operating system:	From hierarchical structures to a living organism
5. Service Delivery:	From linear exploitation to reciprocal value creation
+1 Ecosystem:	From fighting over scarce resources to co-evolution

In a moment, we'll take a closer look at these six dimensions, but before that, we want to walk you through the four important principles that underlie a life-serving organization. They shine through all six dimensions and help bind the organization together. They're intertwined and act as balancing forces to each other, as you'll soon see.

To explain them, we'll need to dive into some systems theory, but in the spirit of keeping this light reading, we'll endeavor to keep these parts short. Especially if you're not familiar with systems theory, don't worry too much about understanding every word or concept in detail.

Think of this as food for thought, and you're free to just nibble where you like.[1]

The organizational principles of a life-centric organization

Principle of Meaning

"Without meaning, society and every social system would simply cease to exist."[2]

Meaning can be defined as the gap between what is and what's possible, and the social system's entire raison d'être is to close this gap. This is why there's an assumption in systems theory that if meaning in a system were ever lost, it would be immediately recreated in order to sustain the system.

Meaning also serves a fundamental and indispensable function in organizations, because it reduces complexity. Meaning – often formalized as the organization's purpose – limits the available options to those that serve the purpose, thereby providing direction for all communications and decisions. One way to think about it is that when things get complex, meaning provides a shining beacon to focus on.

What's more, meaning also serves an important function in linking people (or "psychic systems," as they'd be called in systems theory) to each other and to organizations. If someone doesn't find meaning in their contribution to the organization or understand the meaning of the organization as a whole, their bond with the organization – and other people in it – weakens.

The principle of meaning works from the inside out: it originates within the organization and extends outward toward the external environment, being continually updated at the edges as the organization makes sense of new information.

Principle of Value Creation

The value creation principle acts as a counterbalance to the principle of meaning, working from the outside in. No matter how strong the sense of meaning of an organization, it also needs to create value for its environments or it has very little reason to exist. This is particularly evident in the private sector: if customers stop buying or paying for an organization's services, the organization's economic long-term survival becomes impossible.

But the value creation principle also affects non-economic sectors, although sometimes its impact is only evident in the long term. There too, if an organization doesn't generate value for its environment, it's basically just keeping itself busy. This can lead to the environment eventually questioning why the organization even exists, as can happen for instance when taxpayers challenge the necessity for a public institution.

What's more, if no value is created for the environment, the organization can also lose its meaning, resulting in its disintegration from within.

Principle of Self-Determination

Organizations are social systems and as such strive to sustain and reproduce themselves. This is a basic law of systems that we already mentioned in Part 1 when discussing the economic system (see page 76).

Similar to the principle of meaning, the principle of self-determination also works from the inside out: What happens in a system is determined by its structure, so in this case, the inner structure of the organization. Any external influences are processed according to the system's unique structures.[3]

As a closed system, the organization generally determines for itself what decisions it makes, how it uses its communication channels, and in what way it guides its own development.

Principle of Interdependence

As we saw in the first part of the book, a system's development is constrained by the boundaries that its environments set, which is why co-evolution with those environments is so crucial. Hence, the principle of interdependence acts as a counterbalance to the principle of self-determination – though in principle an organization acts autonomously, it's also interdependent with its environments.

In the context of regenerative organizations, this is perhaps the principle that needs focus most urgently, as it goes beyond mere economic interdependence between customers and supplies, extending to competitors, ecosystems, and the biosphere as a whole. The bottom line is that an organization can only thrive in the long run if its various environments thrive too.

With these fundamental organizational principles in mind, we can now turn to the 5+1 levels of a life-serving organization.

Purpose: From "Profit over impact" to "Impact over profit"

Purpose is the heart and soul of any regenerative or life-centric organization and the formal definition of the organization's meaning. It's a concept we've already touched upon many times in the book, but to recap, it encapsulates the reason for the organization's existence: Why do we exist? Why does the world need us? How should we evolve if we realize the world no longer needs us in this way?

This level is the wellspring of the Principle of Meaning. Events within and outside of the organization shape the sensemaking process, influencing what is seen as meaningful, what's possible, and how meaning is further developed.

As mentioned before, the principle of meaning is counterbalanced by the principle of value creation. Unless an organization provides its environments with valuable services, its survival – and the purpose it pursues – will be in jeopardy in the long term.

In the transition to regenerative economic activity, purpose plays a pivotal part. In conventional economic activity, it's easy to define an organization's purpose: it exists to generate profit so that it can survive ("Profit over impact"). But when we add non-economic environments to the equation and start basing the organization's business model on contributing to planetary and societal health, the purpose expands. Accordingly, the purpose of regenerative organizations centers on achieving the desired impact and consciously navigating potential conflicts between impact and profit ("Impact over profit").

Ownership and Governance Model: From short-term value creation to long-term responsibility

The ownership of property is a core construct in our economic system. It's what enables all of the actions and operations that are economic in nature. The added value of owning property stems from the fact that it can be freely sold, used as a store of value or as collateral. All of these are facilitated and protected by legal systems and institutions. What's more, it's only through ownership that creditor-debtor relationships can arise, and consequently, money itself.[4]

Many of the major challenges that the economic system currently faces can be traced back to ownership and its knock-on effects. In particular, the rise of financialization, meaning the growing importance of credit and capital markets, wouldn't be possible without property. Managing property responsibly is key to developing a regenerative economy, and in fact, it's something that many nation states' constitutions demand.

Regenerative organizations need to find ownership and governance models that bring short-term and long-term interests into a viable and future-proof coexistence. As is often the case, this is a "both/and" issue: Short-term ownership interests may well be justifiable sometimes, but, from a regenerative perspective, they always need to be balanced with a long-term outlook that prioritizes future generations and the well-being of our planet. Concepts like *responsible ownership* and *steward ownership* are promising approaches for this that highlight how responsibility is an integral part of ownership.[5]

Finance: From profit focus to financial resilience

Following our reflections on the level of ownership, it's logical to wonder how economic processes in regenerative organizations can be designed, and what a life-serving approach to capital and money could look like.

Just as was the case on the ownership level, this too goes into the *deep design* of an organization.[6] After all, economic processes very much structure and define the system, especially in the case of organizations in the private sector.

Key questions to answer on this level include:

- How can we include non-economic forms of capital, like natural and social capital, in our measurement of success?
- How much money do we as an organization need? How should we use any potential surplus?
- What types of capital do we invest in? How can we systematically support the regenerative transformation through our investments?
- How can we create internal accounting practices that make regenerative considerations an integral part of our decision-making processes?
- How can we ensure that our economic operations are dynamic and agile enough to keep up with the complexity of real life?

The last question especially tends to resonate with finance professionals. The business world has been discussing agility and iterative approaches for years, spurred on by the growing complexity of the world. Yet, in the field of finance, many still cling to their annual budgeting routines and traditional linear controlling tools. (This despite commendable pioneering efforts such as the *Beyond Budgeting* movement.)

This is why, in our own organization, we've developed an approach to finance that allows for decentralized, purpose-driven economic management. We call this *"New Finance,"* and it's divided into seven main methods. Together, they gradually shift economic planning and management into a more agile direction, while also enabling open discussion about potential conflicts between purpose and profit. You can read all the details in the book *New Finance*.[7]

Organizational Operating System: From hierarchical structures to a living organism

On this fourth level, we examine how an organization works together and what processes, structures, and cultures define it. Key questions include:

- How is leadership organized?
- How is responsibility allocated?
- How are decisions made?
- How does communication flow in the organization?
- How does the organization handle conflicts?
- How does it learn and evolve?

The organizational operating system connects the internal levels of a regenerative organization – purpose, ownership, and finance – with the external service delivery toward customers and other stakeholders.

Until recently, most organizations operated in relatively stable environments. Of course, it's not that changes didn't happen 50, 100, or 200 years ago, but the pace of change was slower back then. These days, organizations operate in highly volatile environments: Conditions are in constant flux, and each week brings new challenges to deal with. The only survivors in these complex environments are those that adapt constantly.

Regenerative organizations have an edge here because they see themselves as living organisms. Hence, they have an organizational operating system that enables a great deal of responsiveness in their processes, structures, and culture. This could perhaps be termed the "complexity competence" of the regenerative organization, which is almost as unwieldy a term as the "interdependence competence" from Part 1 (see page 77). The bottom line is that, instead of a *"Command and Control"* approach, these organizations opt for the more organic and agile *"Sense and Respond."*

To shape transformation processes on the level of the organizational operating system, we've developed a framework called "The Loop Approach." It's a sister curriculum to the Stellar Approach, focused on helping organizations evolve from hierarchies of people into something more akin to a living organism. Many of the basic ideas of the Loop Approach – for example, iterative and tension-based work, a strong emphasis on development, and the focus on teams – are also mirrored in the Stellar Approach. If you'd like to learn more about the Loop Approach methods, we recommend checking out the eponymous book.[8]

Service Delivery: From linear exploitation to reciprocal value creation

All of the levels we've examined so far relate to the inner workings of an organization. But at the service delivery level, the organization comes into contact with its external environments: customers, suppliers, the public, competitors, and both human and non-human stakeholders. We'll take a closer look at this broader ecosystem soon, but for now, we'll focus on the service delivery level that acts as a bridge between the organization's inner workings and the surrounding ecosystem.

This means that the concept of service delivery here must touch on both sides, starting with the internal:

- How do we deliver services within the organization?
- How do we manage our own resources?

What about externally:

- How do we deliver our services?
- How do we engage with our human and non-human stakeholders?
- How do we ensure that our relationships with these stakeholders are healthy?

This is where the principle of self-determination within the organization meets the principle of interdependence, relating to the environments around it.

In the 5+1 model, the Stellar Approach fits into this level and the subsequent ecosystem level. It helps shape transformation processes with a focus on service delivery and also answers the question of how organizations can gradually transition from degenerative service delivery (linear exploitation) to a regenerative approach (reciprocal value creation).

"+1" Ecosystem: From fighting over scarce resources to co-evolution

This level transcends the boundaries of the organization, bringing us fully into the realm of customers, partners, and other relevant stakeholders. As mentioned before, these include both human stakeholders and non-human entities like bees that pollinate plants and forests that sequester CO_2. These can be considered the "natural partners" of an organization.

This level is where the principle of interdependence stems from: our own survival is contingent on curbing our developmental drive where it harms the systems we depend on. In the first part of the book, we termed the goal "co-evolution" (see page 76).

The more we begin to think of our ecosystems in this way, the more our view of our shared coexistence with them also changes.

We start to understand that as a part of several systems, we're always partners with the environments that make our existence possible – economically, socially, and existentially. This is perhaps most relatably and practically expressed in the phrase: "I am because you are."

It's impossible for any individual organization to create meaningful regenerative results in isolation. That's because regenerativity is a trait of the entire system that can only take hold if cooperative and *reciprocal* relationships are built throughout that system.

Here, reciprocity simply means the willingness to give something to get something, be it in supply chains, sourcing operations, customer relations, local communities, or with natural partners.

Regenerative organizations need to understand their own needs and boundaries while remaining porous enough to form partnerships and respond to the needs of their ecosystem partners.

This is why it's so critical for regenerative organizations to build up their co-creative capabilities, be intentional about their decision-making, and establish a governance system that clearly defines who, including ecosystem partners, should have a say in decisions.

There you have it: the Life-Centric Organization model. It comprises 5+1 levels and offers a blueprint for a comprehensive regenerative transformation, spanning from the core of why the organization exists to its outermost dependencies.

For most organizations, it would be overwhelming to try to tackle all of the levels simultaneously. But at the same time, it's important to note that the levels are interconnected and need to be considered somewhat collectively. As an example, the Stellar Approach can lead to changes in the organization's purpose, economic processes, and collaboration modes.

Interdependencies are something we simply need to learn to live with.

Some Encouragement for Your Regenerative Development Journey

We're slowly reaching the end of our journey through the wilderness of regenerative organizations.

But before we wrap things up with a final check-out, we'd like to offer you some inspiring affirmations. After finishing the book, you can keep coming back to these whenever you find yourself in need of encouragement.

Every job is a sustainability job. Given the societal challenges we face today, there's not a job or role in the world that should ignore sustainability questions. If we want the sustainable and regenerative transformation to succeed, we need everyone to contribute, no matter what their line of work.

Don't underestimate your own circle of influence. Whether you're an executive, manager, or employee, you can make a difference. You won't be able to single-handedly save the world, but you can still contribute and make a real impact. And it may well turn out to be a greater one than you know: in complex environments, no one can predict what contribution will lead to what change.

Acknowledge the contradictions. The transition from conventional to regenerative economic activity will inevitably result in contradictions and goal conflicts between what the organization does and what the world needs. So consider yourself and your colleagues "sensors" that can help bring these contradictions and conflicts to light. After all, this is the first step toward solving them.

Harness the power of small steps. If there's no clear solution to a problem yet, the only thing we can do is set a rough direction and start making our way, one step at a time. Global transformations don't usually happen in a single giant leap, but rather through many small steps taken all across the world. So if taking one little step seems pointless or insignificant, just remember that many great changes have sprung from such modest beginnings.

Focus on the footprint and the handprint. The regenerative transformation isn't just about measuring, reporting, and reducing the footprint. Perhaps even more important is the work of designing, developing, and innovating in order to grow the handprint. Alongside reducing emissions, all organizations are called upon to create regenerative innovations, like new processes, materials, technologies, and business models. And this is only possible if many people in various roles use the creative leeway they have to foster innovations and inspire others.

Find some supporters. At the outset of the regenerative transformation, you might sometimes feel like a troublemaker: raising uncomfortable questions, challenging the way things are done, and forcing the organization to examine its impact. But the more you wave your flag and voice your concerns openly, the quicker you'll realize that you're not the only one in the organization who feels this way. You can count on the fact that, in every organization, there will be potential allies who share your views. To find them and encourage them to rally around you, all you need to do is start talking about the regenerative transformation. It'll probably resonate more often than you'd guess.

It's OK to still want to make money, but please take a more long-term view than today! The relative market stability of the *business-as-usual* era is now coming to an end. The future of business will revolve much more around contributing to the creation and restoration of resilient societies and infrastructures. We'll see much more focus on renewable, regenerative, and circular processes and technologies, as well as on relocalization, rewilding, equality, and social cohesion. While there'll still be money to be made, it will mainly come from supporting planetary and social metabolic processes. It's high time to reorient our business models in this direction, lest they become obsolete.

Dare to rewrite the story. Look at the world around you. Simply put, you could say that it's composed of three elements: First, living processes – flora and fauna, the giant metabolic process of biology. Second, there's everything that our human civilization makes: buildings, products, technologies, and so forth. And finally, there are stories. Capitalism, the economy, money – at the end of the day, these are all stories. And they're powerful ones, there's no doubt about that, but they're only stories nonetheless – social constructs that are by no means immutable. And right now, it looks like humanity is writing a new chapter in the story of the economy. So if ever there was the perfect time to ask questions and to pick up a pen to help author this story, it's now.

The key takeaways from this chapter

A comprehensive regenerative transformation of an organization requires change on many levels.

The Life-Centric Organization model depicts these as 5 (+1) levels:
- Purpose
- Ownership and governance model
- Finance
- Organizational operating system
- Service delivery
- +1 Ecosystem

Not every level needs to be worked on at once, but it's good to keep in mind that there are dependencies between them.

If the task at hand seems overwhelming, just remember that you can't know everything at the outset, and pathways and solutions will emerge as you go. The regenerative transformation needs everyone to contribute in their own circle of influence. So make your way step by step, connect with like-minded people, foster a culture of voicing contradictions openly, take honest stock of where you stand, and find your spark for creating something new. Bon voyage.

Check-out

We started this book with a check-in, and now we'll end it with a *check-out*. This is a chance to slow down and reflect, to just be present with your thoughts for a moment.

Remember how, in the first chapter, we asked you what you'd need to get out of this book to consider your decision to read it a resounding success? Well, whatever it was, we hope that it has lived up to as many of your expectations as possible. We also hope it has encouraged you to take action in your circle of influence. Because at the end of the day, it's only together that we can make a difference.

And the good news is that change is already afoot. It's not a linear process, and it's often slower than we'd like, but it is happening. And as the challenges we face steepen, so too do our efforts to innovate: As we speak, companies and start-ups are springing up that increasingly prioritize regenerativity over pure profit. Established companies too are beginning to question if, after all, they have a raison d'être beyond short-term profits. People across all kinds of organizations are recognizing and facing up to their responsibilities. Networks are forming to foster vocal and widespread discussion around the very themes of this book. And like-minded individuals are coming together to fight for a more life-serving economy.

Just remember: while it's important that we take our responsibility seriously, we shouldn't take it *too* seriously. Try to have some fun along the way. And bring others with you. If you're not sure what the first steps could be for you to start making a difference, just drop us a line at stellar@thedive.com. We'd love to hear from you!

In the last pages of the book, you'll find some further reading suggestions, as well as some additional tools and a glossary of regenerative concepts. To go even deeper, feel free to visit our website. There you'll find printable DIY tools and interactive training sessions to help turn your learnings into action. We'd also be thrilled to get to know you in person in one of our workshops. You can find all the details at https://www.stellar-approach.com/en.

If you found this book useful, please feel free to pass it on; perhaps someone else would benefit from reading it too.

Now that we have finished all the writing, editing, correcting, deleting, deep-diving, and reviewing, we're checking out. We do so with the feeling that, at least for now, everything has been said. We explained how we see the world and its potential for change, at this moment. And we look forward to possibly seeing things a bit differently tomorrow or the day after – hopefully with a greater and deeper understanding. Last but not least, we're excited to see that, all around us, more and more people and organizations are lacing up their shoes and taking the first steps on their own journeys.

After all, we are the generation that holds the future in our hands. Good luck, everyone!

Appendix

Checklist for Workshops

Stellar workshops can take place in person or virtually, though some of the techniques tend to work better when participants are physically together in one room. In the best case, they can even venture out into nature for a bit. However, if an in-person workshop isn't possible, the techniques can be adapted for a digital setting, albeit with a few constraints.

Whatever the medium, the following conditions need to be met:

- ☑ All team members are present and have cleared their schedules for the workshop. If they need to make important phone calls, this can be accommodated with scheduled breaks.
- ☑ Before starting the series of workshops, team members have gotten sufficient briefing on the purpose of the sessions and the goal of the Stellar Journey.
- ☑ It's clear who the moderator is and who's responsible for the structure of the session. Ideally, there should be two trainers present, at least one of whom has experience as a Stellar trainer.
- ☑ There's an agenda that participants can clearly see and use to orient themselves during the session.

For in-person workshops, the following additional criteria should be taken into account:

- ☑ The workshop is held away from the team's usual workplace, ensuring that team members can focus on the content without being distracted by their regular work.
- ☑ The space should be quiet and private enough that the team members don't need to worry about anyone eavesdropping on what they say.
- ☑ The space should allow the team to sit in a circle of chairs and be large enough for movement and interactive work. Rooms with big conference tables don't work.
- ☑ If feasible, the workspace should offer easy access to nature, as some Stellar methods work best outdoors.
- ☑ The space should have plenty of writable walls, whiteboards, or flipcharts.
- ☑ Additional materials to include: at least one timer, Post-its in various sizes and colors, enough pens, sticky dots, scissors, and tape.
- ☑ During breaks, there should be ample amounts of sugar-free drinks and snacks that don't cause one's insulin levels to spike, such as fruits or nuts.
- ☑ Lunch should be quick and light enough for participants to be productive in the afternoon.

For virtual workshops, we recommend ensuring the following:

- ☑ The entire workshop and the methods to be covered should all be prepared in a digital working environment so that all participants can collaborate. Possible tools for this include Miro or Mural.
- ☑ The moderators ensure that all participants are comfortable navigating the digital workspace and that any technical issues are addressed.
- ☑ The participants have ensured that they won't be disturbed during the workshop.
- ☑ Participants are "seated" in a virtual circle. All participants' names are visible, making it easier to follow a speaking order in certain formats, such as check-ins or check-outs.

☑ Participants have stocked up on plenty of snacks and drinks. They also have a timer, such as the stopwatch on their phone, as well as a pen and paper ready for taking notes.
☑ The agenda should allow for enough breaks. Participants should have the chance to engage in physical activity during these breaks or even in the workshop sessions themselves.

Basic Concepts in Sustainability and Regenerative Economic Activity

The United Nations Sustainable Development Goals (SDG)

What it is
- The 17 Sustainable Development Goals (SDGs) are political objectives set by the United Nations to ensure global sustainable development on economic, social, and environmental levels.
- Adopted in 2015, these goals have an initial time frame of 15 years, ending in 2030.
- There are 17 main goals from the three areas – *biosphere, society, and economy* – replete with 169 sub-goals or objectives.

What it can be used for
The goals can help structure sustainability discussions. As the UN sees it, these are the critical elements needed to preserve our habitat. Many companies use the goals as a basis for their sustainability agendas. The problem is that often individual topics are tackled in isolation, which obscures the systemic connections between the various issues. The SDGs also largely leave open what contribution is "enough" for each issue.

How it can be helpful on the way to a regenerative economy
The SDGs can be understood as an initial, human-centric approach to several dimensions of sustainability. The sub-goals describe many critically needed global changes. However, they're not wholly regenerative goals, as they only partially take into account the complex interconnections between different subsystems on our planet

Basic Concepts in Sustainability and Regenerative Economic Activity

Guiding questions
- What SDGs does our organization directly and indirectly impact with its activities?
- What concrete effects do we as a team have in these areas?
- Where should we become (even more) active?

More information
thedive.link/en/UNSDGs

Scope 1–3

What it is
- The scope concept, established by the *Greenhouse Gas Protocol*, differentiates between various categories of emissions in the calculation of corporate greenhouse gas emissions.
- Scope 1 includes direct emissions from sources owned or controlled by the company, for example from natural gas, refrigeration, or the company's fleet of vehicles.
- Scope 2 covers indirect emissions caused by the process of generating energy that the company purchases.
- Scope 3 encompasses all other indirect emissions that occur in the company's value chain. This includes upstream emissions (from goods and services bought) as well as downstream emissions (from goods and services sold). Therefore, the company can't control these emissions directly, but they are directly influenced by the company's value chain.
- Scope 3 emissions usually constitute the largest share of a company's emissions, but they're rarely mentioned in balance sheets or corporate goal statements.

What it can be used for
The scope concept helps to differentiate the various circles of influence of a company. It facilitates standardized and comparable reporting and helps set objectives and define strategies to reduce the footprint.

How it can be helpful on the way to a regenerative economy
Scopes provide a starting point for evaluating the effects of a company's business models. They can prompt deeper reflection on our own responsibility toward the living environmental systems around us. However, it's worth noting that they are very much focused on the footprint, accounting only for CO2 emissions and equivalents. In other words, it only addresses one of the nine planetary boundaries.

Guiding questions
- What strategies for reducing our footprint exist within our organization, and how far along are we in implementing them?
- What ideas emerge if we radically rethink our business model with the goal of reducing our Scope 3 emissions to zero?
- How can these ideas help us balance our relationships with our stakeholders, both human and non-human?

More information
thedive.link/en/Scopes

Science Based Targets for Nature (SBTfN)

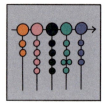

What it is
- The Science Based Targets for Nature (SBTfN) are developed by the "Science Based Targets Network."
- They guide organizations in setting targets aimed at the conservation and restoration of biodiversity and ecosystems, an approach known as "Nature Positive."
- In addition to climate-impacting emissions, the SBTfN also cover the following earth systems: biodiversity, land use, oceans, and freshwater. The targets

- are continually refined by the Science Based Targets Network based on new scientific findings and data.
- The SBTfN make far more tangible how CO_2 emissions and decarbonization are connected to other ecosystems. This makes plain the importance of actually preventing or remediating damage locally, instead of compensating for it elsewhere.
- In 2023, a pilot phase for quantifying targets began. In it, 17 partner companies focus on the areas of freshwater and land use, with others to be addressed in subsequent years.

What it can be used for
With the Science Based Targets for Nature (SBTfN), organizations can describe and quantify their impact on ecosystems. Businesses can use the SBTfN to set firm and absolute goals in line with the planetary boundaries.

How it can be helpful on the way to a regenerative economy
The SBTfN serve as a foundation for establishing company targets that are consistent with scientific insights. By pursuing these goals, businesses help to preserve and strengthen biodiversity and ecosystems. Furthermore, the SBTfN can also be used as a basis to develop political actions and regulatory strategies.

Guiding questions
- Which SBTfN areas are relevant to our organization?
- Local focus: Where in the world do we impact these areas? What exactly is our impact?
- How can we create local conditions that enable regenerative cycles?

More information
thedive.link/en/SBTfN

Ecosystem Services

What it is
- Ecosystem services were developed in 2001 as part of the "Millennium Ecosystem Assessment" on behalf of the United Nations.
- They catalog the regenerative services provided by Earth's ecosystems, including the provision of food and raw materials and the regulation of the weather to avoid extreme events. They aim to make the value of nature's services to humans more tangible through a quasi-economic lens.
- In 2011, the value of all ecosystem services was estimated at $125 trillion annually.[1]
- Already in 2017, over 15 000 scientists warned that most ecosystems are seriously endangered and that the chances of preserving them are poor.[2]

What it can be used for
This model can help businesses better understand externalities. Usually, the services provided by ecosystems are considered free, so damaging them through our economic decisions is tolerated. To begin reducing these externalities, it's vital to understand the importance of these services and the fragile equilibrium of the ecosystems that provide them.

How it can be helpful on the way to a regenerative economy
The absence of ecosystem services as a factor in price setting represents a significant flaw in the current economic system. Having an overview of these crucial functions can lead to more focus on preservation, for example if the services are integrated into pricing mechanisms. These services are recognized in "Science Based Targets for Nature" (see page 308) and will also be part of the European Sustainability Reporting Standards (ESRS E2-4) from 2024 onward.

Basic Concepts in Sustainability and Regenerative Economic Activity

Guiding questions
- Which ecosystem services do our business models depend on?
- How would our business models change if we were to pay a fair amount for these services?
- How can we take the value of these services into account when we design our processes and business models?

More information:
thedive.link/en/EcosystemServices

The *Safe and Just Space* in Doughnut Economics

What it is
- Introduced by economist Kate Raworth in 2012, the Doughnut Economics model outlines the safe and just space of a viable, future-proof economy.
- The model's outer limits are defined by planetary boundaries. To conserve the resources that the survival of humanity depends on, our economy needs to operate within these scientifically established, absolute thresholds.
- Meanwhile, the doughnut's inner edges describe factors related to societal stability, mirroring the social goals of the UN's SDGs. This social foundation indicates the minimum levels of these factors needed to enable a viable, future-proof coexistence for all humanity.
- Whereas we shouldn't exceed the planetary boundaries, we also can't undercut the social dimensions.
- In between the two limits is the playing field where we can act in an ecologically safe and socially fair way.

What it can be used for
This model can help businesses recognize their overall responsibility – both human and economic – toward the world. The exercise on page 149 can provide a tangible experience of the safe and just space. Additionally, the Doughnut Economics Action Lab (DEAL) offers a variety of tools that can help apply the model in business.

How it can be helpful on the way to a regenerative economy
A key component in changing business practices is that individuals understand the responsibility they have to operate in the safe and just space. Unlike models that focus solely on measurement and footprint reduction, Doughnut Economics also paints a positive vision of what there is to gain.

Guiding questions:
- Which planetary boundaries are relevant to our business model? How can we ensure that we operate within these limits?
- How does our organization benefit from the social foundation? What are we doing to strengthen it and establish fair minimum conditions?
- How can our economic activities contribute to humanity moving into the safe and just space of the doughnut?

More information:
thedive.link/en/Doughnut

Infinite Games

What it is
- The concept of finite and infinite games was introduced by James P. Carse in 1986.[3]
- The goal in finite games is to win, whereas the goal in infinite games is to keep playing.
- Finite games are played according to set rules, ending with clear winners and losers.
- In infinite games, the rules, boundaries, and participants can change over time so that the game can keep going.
- Simon Sinek has extended this idea to the world of business[4]: Organizations usually pursue specific annual objectives, aiming for success in a limited time window. But this approach overlooks the long-term nature of our economic system and the planet as a whole. Our environment is playing an infinite game.

What it can be used for
By embracing the infinite game, organizations can set themselves up for long-term success. This requires them to be agile and responsive to ever-changing conditions. A long-term vision beyond merely pursuing profit is key to achieving stability and bolsters both the resilience and innovative potential of the organization.

How it can be helpful on the way to a regenerative economy
Organizations that see themselves as playing an infinite game collaborate with other organizations to achieve shared objectives and adjust the rules as needed. Understanding that competition is only a temporary aspect of the game can pave the way for radical new regenerative business models.

Guiding questions
- Where in our organization do we see some finite game rules?
- If we embraced an infinite game mindset, what strategies would be useful for us?
- What rules of ours would we like to change, and how would this alter our perception of the situation?

More information
thedive.link/en/InfiniteGames

Biomimicry

What it is
- Biomimicry, also known as bionics, applies learnings from nature to design healthier and more sustainable technologies for humans.
- By studying strategies that living beings use to satisfy their needs efficiently, we can find solutions that are in harmony with the principles of life, thus safeguarding the foundation for life on Earth.
- One example is "fog harvesting," where nets are used to capture moisture from the air. This approach was inspired by the desert beetle, a hardy insect that survives thanks to its unique shell, where many small bumps collect condensation from the morning mist and channel it into the beetle's mouth. This method has proved to be a cost-effective, environmentally friendly, and practical way to obtain drinking water in poor and remote areas.

What it can be used for
Companies can use biomimicry as inspiration when developing new products, materials, or processes.

How it can be helpful on the way to a regenerative economy
Through biomimicry, we can explore a solution space that is regenerative by design thanks to being inspired by how life on Earth survives and thrives. All life grapples with the same challenges as us, whether in keeping warm, filtering water, generating energy, or something else. Other creatures can show us how to conserve valuable resources and behave in ways that don't cause harm to ourselves or others.

Guiding questions
- In what areas of our economic activities do we knowingly cause damage to environmental systems but currently see no alternatives?
- What problems are these current activities intended to solve?
- Which creatures in nature face similar challenges? What strategies of theirs could inspire us?

More information
thedive.link/en/Biomimicry

Permaculture Principles for Organizations

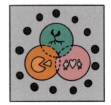

What it is
- The approach of permaculture stems from agriculture, combining the terms "permanent" and "culture." The approach offers long-term oriented practices focused on the harmonious interplay between natural dynamics.
- The twelve principles of permaculture describe the basic features of regenerative agricultural systems and lifestyles. Their aim is to fulfill ecological goals, conserve natural resources, protect biodiversity, and bolster communities.
- Organizations can adopt these principles by integrating natural operating principles into their business practices and consciously considering the social effects they have on their employees and local communities.

Basic Concepts in Sustainability and Regenerative Economic Activity

What it can be used for
The permaculture principles can help organizations (or individual departments within them) to make their decisions regenerative. By applying these principles, it's possible to find solutions that don't just focus on individual parts but take a holistic view of the whole system. The principles are most potently experienced in a natural setting, like a permaculture garden, as this provides a strong basis for translating them into practical actions.

How it can be helpful on the way to a regenerative economy
The permaculture principles open up fresh perspectives on organizations as living systems. This includes designing self-regulating system dynamics; the efficient use and conservation of resources; closing loops; cultivating vibrant relationships; developing decentralized solutions; promoting diversity; valuing change; and using interfaces with other systems to find creative solutions.

Guiding questions
- What do we see when we assess our organization's economic actions through the lens of permaculture principles?
- How can we develop our activities further so as to apply and adhere to as many of these principles as possible?
- What impact would this have on our processes or business models?

More information
thedive.link/en/Permaculture

Inner Development Goals (IDG)

What it is
- The "Inner Development Goals" (IDG) are a framework aimed at promoting individual and collective development on an inner level. The goals set within this framework emphasize the inner dimension of change, focusing on personal maturity, and awareness. The IDGs cover areas like emotional intelligence, self-reflection, mindfulness, empathy, and ethical conduct.
- This framework was developed by a non-profit initiative consisting of the 29k Foundation, Ekskäret Foundation, and The New Division. It was first introduced in 2020 as a complement to the Sustainable Development Goals.

- It distinguishes between five dimensions of inner development: *Being, Thinking, Relating, Collaborating, and Acting*, further broken down into 23 skills and qualities across the categories.

What it can be used for
The IDG can be seen as a roadmap for personal development, focusing on inner growth in particular. They help promote inner development processes in individuals and teams. They offer a concrete, ever-evolving toolbox of methods to deepen our understanding of ourselves and our relationship with the world.

How it can be helpful on the way to a regenerative economy
The IDGs aim to cultivate qualities essential for sustainable and regenerative business practices. By promoting empathy, cooperative behavior, and ethical awareness, they contribute to a corporate culture where interdependencies with social and ecological systems are seen as a natural prerequisite for the organization's own existence.

Guiding questions
- How do each of us gauge our individual abilities across the different IDG dimensions?
- How about as a team, where do we stand in relation to them? In which of the five dimensions do we see a need for what kind of further development?
- How could the IDGs support our inner development, both as individuals and as a team?

More information
thedive.link/en/IDGs

References and Further Reading

Here we list the sources that we've referred to in the text, as well as some reading recommendations that we consider to be particularly valuable in the field of regenerative economic activity. [Brackets indicate our own translations of German sources.]

References

Ahmed, N. M. (2023). The Planetary Emergency is a Crisis of Spirituality. https://ageoftransformation.org/the-planetary-emergency-is-a-crisis-of-spirituality/

Achterberg, E., Hinfelaar, J. & Bocken, N. (2016). Master Circular Business With The Value Hill. https://assets.website-files.com/5d26d80e8836af2d12ed1269/5dea74fe88e8a5c63e2c7121_finance-white-paper-20160923.pdf

Baldwin, C. (1998). Calling the Circle. The First and Future Culture. New York: Random House.

Bateson, G. (1972). Steps to an Ecology of Mind. San Francisco: Chandler Publishing Company.

Bauhardt, C. (2015). Feministische Kapitalismuskritik und postkapitalistische Alternativen. [Feminist critique of capitalism and post-capitalist alternatives]. Aus Politik und Zeitgeschichte (p. 32–39). https://www.bpb.de/shop/zeitschriften/apuz/211047/feministische-kapitalismuskritik-und-postkapitalistische-alternativen/

Beck, K. & Buddemeier, P. (2022). Green Ferry. Das Ticket ins konsequent nachhaltige Wirtschaften. [Green Ferry. The ticket to consistently sustainable economic activity]. Hamburg: Murmann.

Breidenbach, J. & Rollow, B. (2019). New Work needs Inner Work: A handbook for companies on the way to self-organisation. 2nd edition. Munich: Vahlen.

Carse, J. (1986). Finite and Infinite Games, New York: Free Press.

Chenoweth, E. & Stephan, M. J. (2011). Why Civil Resistance Works: The Strategic Logic of Nonviolent Conflict. New York: Columbia University Press.

Costanza, R., de Groot, R., Sutton, P., van der Ploeg, S., Anderson, S. J., Kubiszewski, I., Farber, S., Turner, R. K. (2014). Changes in the global value of ecosystem services, Global Environmental Change, 26 (p. 152–158). https://doi.org/10.1016/j.gloenvcha.2014.04.002

Coulon, E. (2023). Regenerative Thinking Starts With Breaking Down Social Constructs. https://gdruk.com/inspire/regenerative-thinking-starts-with-breaking-down-social-constructs

de Yonge, J. (2022). The CEO Imperative: How can you put regeneration at the heart of creating value? https://www.ey.com/en_ro/sustainability/the-ceo-imperative-how-can-you-put-regeneration-at-the-heart-of-creating-value

Dixson-Declève, S., Gaffney, O, Ghosh, J., Randers, J., Rockström, J. & Stoknes, P. E. (2022). Earth for All. A Survival Guide for Humanity. New Society Publishers.

Dyllik, T. & Muff, K. (2015). Clarifying the Meaning of Sustainable Business: Introducing a Typology From Business-as-Usual to True Business Sustainability. Organization & Environment. https://doi.org/10.1177/1086026615575176

Fraser, N. (2012). Feminism, Capitalism, and the Cunning of History: An Introduction. FMSH-WP-2012-17. https://shs.hal.science/halshs-00725055/document

Fraser, N. (2022). Cannibal Capitalism: How our System is Devouring Democracy, Care, and the Planet – and What We Can Do About It. London/New York: Verso Books.

Fullerton, J. (2015). Regenerative Capitalism: How Universal Principles And Patterns Will Shape Our New Economy. Capital Institute.

Greenwood, T. (2023). Is spirituality the missing pillar of sustainability? https://tomgreenwood.substack.com/p/is-spirituality-the-missing-pillar

Growth that Matters, AB (2021). Inner Development Goals: Background, method and the IDG framework. https://static1.squarespace.com/static/600d80b3387b98582a60354a/t/640605519559993bd30bc15f/1678116201110/IDG_Report_Full.pdf

Hayashi, A. (2021). Social Presencing Theater: The Art of Making a True Move. Cambridge, Mass.: PI Press.

Heath, C. & Heath, D. (2010). Made to Stick: Why Some Ideas Survive and Others Die. New York: Random House.

Heinberg, R. & Miller, A. (2023). Welcome to the Great Unravelling: Navigating the Polycrisis of Environmental and Social Breakdown. Corvallis: Post Carbon Institute.

Hickel, J., Dorninger, C., Wieland, H. & Suwandi, I. (2022). Imperialist appropriation in the world economy: Drain from the global South through unequal exchange, 1990–2015, Global Environmental Change, Volume 73. https://doi.org/10.1016/j.gloenvcha.2022.102467

Jaspers, L., Ryland, N. & Horch, S. (Eds.). (2022). Unlearn Patriarchy. Berlin: Ullstein.

Klein, S. & Hughes, B. (2019). The Loop Approach. How to Transform Your Organization from the Inside Out. Frankfurt/New York: Campus.

Konietzko, J., Das, A. & Bocken, N. (2023). Towards regenerative business models: A necessary shift? Sustainable Production and Consumption, 38, . 372–388.

Kortendiek, B., Riegraf, B. & Sabisch, K. (2019). Handbuch Interdisziplinäre Geschlechterforschung [Handbook of Interdisciplinary Gender Studies]. Heidelberg: Springer.

Kumar, S. (2017). Soil, Soul, Society: A New Trinity for Our Time. Brighton: Leaping Hare Press.

Lerche, A. (2023). New Finance. Gestaltung zeitgemäßer Finanzprozesse in Purpose Driven Organizations [New Finance. Designing Modern Financial Processes in Purpose-Driven Organizations]. Stuttgart: Schäffer-Poeschel.

Levermann, A. (2023). Die Faltung der Welt. Wie die Wissenschaft helfen kann, dem Wachstumsdilemma und der Klimakrise zu entkommen [The Folding of the World. How Science Can Help Us Escape the Growth Dilemma and the Climate Crisis]. Berlin: Ullstein.

Liu, P. R. & Raftery, A. E. (2021). Country-based rate of emissions reductions should increase by 80% beyond nationally determined contributions to meet the 2 °C target. Communications Earth & Environment 2, 29. https://doi.org/10.1038/s43247-021-00097-8

Luhmann, N. (1995). Social Systems. Stanford University Press.

Luhmann, N. (1988). Die Wirtschaft der Gesellschaft [The Economy of Society]. Frankfurt: Suhrkamp.
Luhmann, N. (2018). Organization and Decision. Cambridge University Press.
Maté, G. & Maté, D (2022). The Myth of Normal: Trauma, Illness, and Healing in a Toxic Culture. New York: Avery.
Maturana, H. R., & Varela, F. J. (1987). The Tree of Knowledge: The Biological Roots of Human Understanding. Boulder: New Science Library/Shambhala Publications.
Olk, C., Schneider, C. & Hickel, J. (2023). How to pay for saving the world: Modern Monetary Theory for a degrowth transition. Ecological Economics, Volume 214, 107968. https://doi.org/10.1016/j.ecolecon.2023.107968
Oxfam (2023). Climate Equality: A Planet for the 99%. https://oxfamilibrary.openrepository.com/bitstream/10546/621551/2/cr-climate-equality-201123-en.pdf
Parrique T., Barth J., Briens F., Kerschner, C., Kraus-Polk A., Kuokkanen A., Spangenberg J. H. (2019). Decoupling Debunked. Evidence and arguments against green growth as a sole strategy for sustainability. https://eeb.org/wp-content/uploads/2019/07/Decoupling-Debunked.pdf
Pfeifer, S. (2019). Stressregulation durch das Zuneigungs- und Fürsorgesystem. Wie wir unsere biologische Ausstattung zu etwas mehr Glück und Zufriedenheit nutzen können. [Stress regulation through the care and soothing system. How we can use our biology to be a little bit happier and content] IBP Institut Magazin 7, 2019. https://www.ibp-institut.ch/files/client_data/Dokumente/IBP/Publikationen%20Shop%20Downloads/IBP%20Artikel/Artikel_Wie%20wir%20unsere%20biologische%20Ausstattung%20zu%20etwas%20mehr%20Gl%C3%BCck%20und%20Zufriedenheit%20nutzen%20k%C3%B6nnen_Magazin%207_SP_191002.pdf
Potting, J., Hekkert, M., Worrell, E. & Hanemaaijer, A. (2017). Circular Economy: Measuring Innovation In The Product Chain. https://www.pbl.nl/sites/default/files/downloads/pbl-2016-circular-economy-measuring-innovation-in-product-chains-2544.pdf
Raworth, K. (2017). Doughnut Economics: Seven Ways to Think Like a 21st-Century Economist. White River Junction: Chelsea Green Pub.
Richardson, K., Steffen, W., Lucht, W., Bendtsen, J., Cornell, S. E., Donges, J. F., Drüke, M., Fetzer, I., Govindasamy, B., von Bloh, W., Feulner, G., Fiedler, S., Gerten, D., Gleeson, T., Hofmann, M., Huiskamp, W., Kummu, M., Mohan, C., Nogués-Bravo, D. (. . .) & Rockström. J. (2023). Earth beyond six of nine planetary boundaries. Science Advances, Volume 9, Issue 37. https://www.science.org/doi/10.1126/sciadv.adh2458
Rieß, B. (2010) (Hrsg.). Corporate Citizenship planen und messen mit der iooi-Methode. Ein Leitfaden für das gesellschaftliche Engagement von Unternehmen. [Planning and measuring corporate citizenship with the IOOI method. A societal engagement guide for companies]. Bertelsmann Stiftung.
Ripple, W. J., Wolf, C., Newsome, T. M., Galetti, M., Alamgir, M., Crist, E., Mahmoud, M. I., Laurance, W. F., 15 364 scientist signatories from 184 countries (2017). World Scientists' Warning to Humanity: A Second Notice, BioScience, 67 (12, 1026–1028). https://doi.org/10.1093/biosci/bix125
Robertson, B. (2015). Holacracy. The New Management System for a Rapidly Changing World. New York: Henry Holt & Company.

Rosling, H., Rosling Rönnlund, A. & Rosling, O. (2018). Factfulness: Ten Reasons We're Wrong About The World – And Why Things Are Better Than You Think. New York: Flatiron Books.

Scharmer, C. O. (2016). The Theory U. Leading from the Future as it Emerges. Oakland: Berrett-Koehler Publishers.

Schmid, B. & Hipp, J. (1998). Macht und Ohnmacht in Dilemmasituationen. [Power and powerlessness in dilemma situations]. ISB Wiesloch. https://www.isb-w.eu/campus/medien/schriften/1998SI0024D_024-MachtUndOhnmachtInDilemmasituationen-Schmid-Hipp_1998.pdf

Sharpe, B. (2013). Three Horizons: The Patterning of Hope. Bridport: Triarchy Press.

Simon, F. B. (2009). Einführung in die systemische Wirtschaftstheorie. [Introduction to systemic economic theory]. Heidelberg: Carl Auer.

Sinek, S. (2019). The Infinite Game. New York: Portfolio.

Varga von Kibéd, M. & Sparrer, I. (2000). Ganz im Gegenteil. Tetralemmaarbeit und andere Grundformen systemischer Strukturaufstellungen. [Quite the contrary. Tetralemma work and other basic forms of systemic structural constellations]. Heidelberg: Carl-Auer.

Vogel, J. & Hickel, J. (2023). Is green growth happening? An empirical analysis of achieved versus Paris-compliant CO_2–GDP decoupling in high-income countries. Lancet Planet Health (7) 2023; e759–769. https://www.thelancet.com/action/showPdf?pii=S2542-5196%2823%2900174-2

Weick, K. E. (1995). Der Prozess des Organisierens. [The process of organizing]. Frankfurt: Suhrkamp.

Zautra, A. J., Hall, J. S. & Murray, K. E. (2010). Resilience: A new definition of health for people and communities. In: J. W. Reich, A. J. Zautra & J. S. Hall (Eds.), Handbook of adult resilience, S. 3–34. Guilford, New York: Guilford.

Further reading

A sustainable and regenerative economy

B Corp Climate Collective (2021). The Climate Justice Playbook for Business. How to centre climate action in Climate Justice? https://www.bcorpclimatecollective.org/climate-justice-playbook

De Fraguier, N. & Vasconcellos, S. (2023). The Regenerative Enterprise: Leading change at a time of planetary crisis. Self-published.

Jackson, T. (2021). Post Growth: Life After Capitalism. Cambridge: Polity Press.

Mackey, J. & Sisodia, R. (2013). Conscious Capitalism: Liberating the heroic spirit of business. Boston: Harvard Business Press.

Polman, P. & Winston, A. (2021). Net Positive: How Courageous Companies Thrive by Giving More Than They Take. Boston: Harvard Business Press.

Reed, B. (2007). Shifting from 'sustainability' to regeneration. Building Research & Information, 35 (6), 674–690. https://doi.org/10.1080/09613210701475753.
Schumacher, E. F. (2010). Small is Beautiful. Economics as If People Mattered. New York: Harper Perennial.
Stahlhofer, N., Schmidkonz, C. & Kraft, P. (2018). Conscious Business in Germany: Assessing the Current Situation and Creating an Outlook for a New Paradigm. Cham: Springer.
Tàbara, J. D. (2023). Regenerative sustainability: A relational model of possibilities for the emergence of positive tipping points. Environmental Sociology, 9 (4). https://doi.org/10.1080/23251042.2023.2239538
Vasconcellos, S. & De Fraguier, N. (2021). The Positive Handbook for Regenerative Business: A practical guide with a compass to empower changemaker companies to unleash positive impact. The Positive Movement.
Wahl, D. C. (2016). Designing Regenerative Cultures. Bridport: Triarchy Press.
Wunderman Thompson Intelligence (2023). Regeneration Rising: Sustainability Futures.

Systems theory

Meadows, D. H. (2008). Thinking in Systems: A Primer. White River Junction, Vermont: Chelsea Green Publishing.
Polanyi, K. (1944). The Great Transformation. The Political and Economic Origins of Our Time. New York: Farrar & Rinehart.

Understanding nature

Jordan, M. & Hinds, J. (2016). Ecotherapy: Theory, Research and Practice. Basingstoke: Palgrave Macmillan.
Luisi, P. L. & Capra, F. (2014). The Systems View of Life. A Unifying Vision. Cambridge: Cambridge University Press.
Mancuso, S. (2021). The Nation of Plants. New York: Other Press.

Transformation

Bendell, J. (2023). Breaking Together: A freedom-loving response to collapse. Bristol: Good Works.
Göpel, M. (2023). Rethinking Our World: an invitation to rescue our future. Melbourne: Scribe Publications.
Scharmer, C. O. & Kaufer, K. (2013). Leading from an Emerging Future. From Ego-System to Eco-System Economies. San Francisco: Berrett-Koehler Publishers.

Circular design

Benyus, J. M. (2009). Biomimicry: Innovation Inspired by Nature. Boston: Mariner Books.
Ellen MacArthur Foundation (Hrsg). (2014). A New Dynamic – Effective Business in a Circular Economy. Ellen MacArthur Foundation Publishing.

Webster, K. (2017). The Circular Economy: A Wealth of Flows. 2nd edition. Milton Keynes: Lightning Source Inc.

Permaculture

Morrow, R. (2022). Earth Restorer's Guide to Permaculture: The revised and updated third edition of the author's Earth User's Guide to Permaculture. Victoria: Melliodora Publishing.

Growth, Green Growth, Degrowth

Hickel, J. (2019). Is it possible to achieve a good life for all within planetary boundaries? Third World Quarterly, Vol. 40. https://doi.org/10.1080/01436597.2018.1535895

Millward-Hopkins, J., Steinberger, J. K., Rao, N. D., Oswald, Y. (2020). Providing decent living with minimum energy: A global scenario. Global Environmental Change, Vol. 65. https://doi.org/10.1016/j.gloenvcha.2020.102168

O'Neill, D. W., Fanning, A. L., Lamb, W. F. et al. A good life for all within planetary boundaries. Nature Sustainability (1) 2018, S. 88–95. https://doi.org/10.1038/s41893-018-0021-4

Colonialism

Faloyin, D. (2022). Africa Is Not A Country: Breaking Stereotypes of Modern Africa. London: Harvill Secker.

Goodchild, M. (2021). Relational Systems Thinking: That's How Change Is Going to Come, from Our Earth Mother. Journal of Awareness Based System Change, 1(1), S. 75–103. https://doi.org/10.47061/jabsc.v1i1.577

Feminism and the patriarchy

Endler, R. (2021). Das Patriarchat der Dinge: Warum die Welt Frauen nicht passt. Cologne: DuMont.

Fraser, N. (2019). Feminism for the 99%: A Manifesto. New York: Verso.

Hooks, B. (2000). Feminism is for everybody. London: Pluto Press.

Complexity

Dörner, D. (1997). The Logic Of Failure: Recognizing And Avoiding Error In Complex Situations. Revised edition. New York: Basic Books.

Taleb, N. N. (2012). Antifragile. Things That Gain from Disorder. New York: Random House.

Leadership

Hutchins, G. (2022). Leading by Nature: The Process of Becoming A Regenerative Leader. Wordzworth Publishing.

Hutchins, G. & Storm, L. (2019). Regenerative Leadership: The DNA of life-affirming 21st century organizations. Wordzworth Publishing.

Sandford, Carol (2017). The Regenerative Business: Redesign Work, Cultivate Human Potential, Achieve Extraordinary Outcomes. London: Nicholas Brealey Publishing.

Resilience

Denyer, D. (2017). Organizational Resilience: A summary of academic evidence, business insights and new thinking. BSI and Cranfield School of Management.

Inner Processes

Macy, J. & Brown, M. Y. (2014). Coming Back to Life: The Updated Guide to the Work That Reconnects. Gabriola Island, B. C.: New Society Publishers.

Macy, J. & Johnstone, C. (2022). Active Hope. How to Face the Mess We're in with Unexpected Resilience and Creative Power. First revised edition. Novato, CA: New World Library.

Solnit, R. (2019). Hope in the Dark: Untold Histories, Wild Possibilities. Chicago: Haymarket Books.

Storytelling

Hopkins, R. (2020). *From What Is to What If.* White River Junction, Vermont: Chelsea Green Publishing.

Business design and innovation

Graeber, D. (2019). Bullshit Jobs. The Rise of Pointless Work, and What We Can Do About It. A Theory. London: Penguin Books.

van der Pijl, P., Lokitz, J., Wijnen, R., van Lieshout, M. (2020). Business Model Shifts. Six Ways to Create New Value For Customers. Hoboken: Wiley.

van der Pijl, P., Lokitz, J., Solomon, L. K. (2016). Design a Better Business. New Tools, Skills, and Mindset for Strategy and Innovation. Hoboken: Wiley.

Sinek, S. (2009). Start with Why. How Great Leaders Inspire Everyone to Take Action. New York: Penguin Publishing.

Ownership

Heinsohn, G. & Steiger, O. (2012). Ownership Economics: On the Foundations of Interest, Money, Markets, Business Cycles and Economic Development. London: Routledge.

Regenerative Glossary

Acceleration The use of fossil fuels on a massive scale has accelerated almost every aspect of human activity. This acceleration can be seen in, for example, economic → growth, population growth, as well as in rising → inequality and environmental challenges. In mathematical terms, this acceleration would be described as exponential, while in physical terms, it can best be termed as a self-amplifying effect. Unfortunately, it serves to exacerbate → systemic crises / the polycrisis.

Ambiguity Ambiguity means having multiple meanings or interpretations. Today's world is characterized by a high degree of ambiguity, → paradoxes, and related → dilemmas stemming from digitalization, globalization, and the → polycrisis. People who have high ambiguity tolerance can perceive and tolerate uncertainties, ambiguities, and contradictions well.

Backcasting Backcasting is a strategy exercise for plotting future pathways. It begins with a vision or a desired future scenario and works backward to determine the steps required to reach it. It results in concrete action plans outlining the path to the future.

Backlog In agile project management, a backlog refers to a collection of open tasks and items that need to be processed. You can think of it roughly as a "working memory" where things can be put aside for now. In the context of the Stellar Approach, the backlog is part of the → sprints. To-dos, work packages, and accountabilities that arise from the processing of → tensions are stored and made visible in the backlog, providing the → team with high transparency regarding any outstanding tasks.

Biodiversity Biodiversity refers to the variety of life on our planet. It is an essential part of → nature. It can be divided into three distinct organizational levels: species diversity (including animals, plants, fungi, and bacteria), genetic variability within these species (such as different apple varieties), and ecosystem diversity, meaning diversity in the kinds of ecosystems where these species coexist and interact (for example marshes, deserts, and rainforests). Biodiversity is crucial for overcoming → systemic crises and fostering sustainable societies. Unfortunately, the environmental damage caused by humans has caused biodiversity to decline for decades already and continues to gravely threaten it. We have already surpassed the → planetary boundaries for both species diversity and genetic variability.

Business Design Business Design can be used in innovation work to develop or refine business models. Typical features are the use of interdisciplinary → teams and an → iterative approach. An idea is prototyped and refined through several iterations before it becomes a ready business model. Traditional business design is heavily user-centric. As we see it, this user-centric perspective should be complemented with a life-centric or planet-centric view to design business models compatible with a → life-serving economy.

Circle of Influence The Circle of Influence is a concept designed to help individuals identify and understand opportunities to shape circumstances and outcomes. It also illustrates the systemic interdependencies in which we operate. Described first by Stephen Covey, this framework distinguishes between the Circle of Control (aspects we can directly control), the Circle of Influence (aspects we can influence but not control), and the Circle of Concern (aspects that affect us but are beyond our influence).

Circular Design Circular Design means designing products, services, and processes in such a way that the underlying resources can be kept in circulation for as long as possible. This requires circular thinking, which entails looking for ways to close loops while keeping an eye on all interdependencies. Based on the waste hierarchy, we can differentiate between ten different levers of circularity: Refuse, Rethink, and Reduce relate to usage and foregoing usage entirely, as well as to manufacturing processes. Reuse, Repair, Refurbish, Remanufacture, and Repurpose have to do with extending service lives. Recycle and Recover are about reprocessing materials in a sensible way.

Climate change Climate change can refer to both the warming and cooling of the climate, which is why it should not be confused with → global warming. As a component of the broader → polycrisis, climate change means global warming driven by the increased emissions of → greenhouse gasses (GHGs) from human activities, intensifying the natural greenhouse effect and leading to further warming. The phenomenon is commonly referred to as human-made climate change. Its impacts are wide-ranging, from higher temperatures to more frequent extreme weather events. It's also driving increased rates of species extinction, thereby contributing to the decline in → biodiversity.

Co-Evolution Co-evolution refers to a system's ability to develop its vital environments alongside itself in order to ensure its own survival. In → systems theory, a distinction is made between systems and their environments. All types of living systems have the drive to maintain and sustain themselves. However, they often need their environments as partners in this endeavor. As an example, consider how we humans need the oxygen and water that's provided by our environment, the biosphere. This means it's sensible for us to act in a co-evolutionary way towards the planet.

Colonialism Modern colonialism, an aspect of imperialism, reared its head at the end of the 15th century. It involved European powers seizing foreign territories by subjugating local populations and exploiting them economically. This practice involved severe oppression, violence, slavery, discrimination, and genocide. The era of colonialism mostly ended after World War II, yet its legacy still shapes the structure of the → economy today. Thus, in the sustainability transformation toward a → life-serving economy, it's vital to include post-colonial perspectives to better address and dissolve colonial structures.

Complexity Complexity describes the diversity and interconnectivity within a system or process. A complex system comprises many interconnected elements that are often unpredictable and challenging to grasp. Living systems exhibit a high degree of complexity. Managing complexity requires understanding interactions and uncertainty, as well as recognizing emergent properties that can arise within complex systems (→ Systems Thinking).

Contribution In the Stellar Approach, the term "contribution" refers to the regenerative contribution of a → team to the entire → organization. The team articulates this regenerative contribution as an intention for how to utilize its area of responsibility and circle of influence to further the regenerative transformation. This provides clarity and a shared direction. The regenerative contribution is addressed in the third → Stellar Practice.

Cradle-to-Cradle Cradle-to-Cradle is an approach to sustainable production that aims for a closed material cycle, eliminating waste entirely. It contrasts with linear production

(Cradle-to-Grave), where a product ultimately ends up as waste. The concept was developed by Michael Braungart and William McDonough, who distinguish between two cycles: a biological cycle for consumable goods and a technical cycle for durable goods. The goal is for resources and materials to go around the cycle, again and again. The Cradle-to-Cradle principle is a rigorous application of → Circular Design.

CSRD and ESRS The CSRD (Corporate Sustainability Reporting Directive) is the EU directive governing non-financial reporting regarding → ESG aspects in the sustainability reporting of companies. Its predecessor was the Non-Financial Reporting Directive. The major updates in the CSRD include broader and more uniform reporting requirements, which were developed through the ESRS (European Sustainability Reporting Standards). Additionally, → materiality assessments now need to adhere to the principle of double materiality, giving a new and broader interpretation of what is considered material. What's more, reports now need to be audited externally and be included in the company's management reports. The CSRD also expands the reporting requirements to nearly 50 000 companies EU-wide.

Culture In the work context, culture usually refers to the shared values, norms, and beliefs that prevail in a company and affect collective behavior. The significance of corporate culture is perhaps best summarized by Peter Drucker's quote, "Culture eats strategy for breakfast," implying that a strong culture can influence success far more than any strategy. What's often overlooked, however, is that changing culture is very challenging. The obvious approach is to just write down all the desired values and beliefs and distribute them as a manifesto to employees. However, this usually yields minimal results. In → systems theory, culture is also described as the "undecidable decision premise."

Decisions Making a decision involves choosing the best option from two or more potential alternatives, taking into consideration any overarching → goals. Decisions create both intended and unintended consequences, which is why they always come with risks. Decisions play an important part in organizations because they drive activities, structures, and responsibilities, which also makes them a potential starting point for change.

Degrowth In contrast to → green growth, degrowth advocates emphasize an alternative type of qualitative → growth. The concept focuses on the well-being of people and nature, on time abundance, and on ensuring a good life for all. From the perspective of the degrowth movement, humanity is an integral part of the planetary ecosystem and should act accordingly, ensuring that → planetary boundaries are not exceeded. Furthermore, the movement strives for a just societal foundation to create a good life for everyone, similar to the principles of → Doughnut Economics.

Dilemma When you have to make a → decision between multiple options but none of them leads to the desired result, that's called a dilemma. Dilemmas often manifest in → goal conflicts which often arise in the process of a → sustainability transformation. Colloquially, this situation is known as being "caught between a rock and a hard place," and it can feel like an uncomfortable → paradox to face.

Diversity Diversity means variety, diversity, and heterogeneity. It involves not just acknowledging the different characteristics of individuals and groups but explicitly valuing and welcoming them. Diversity can be expressed via various dimensions, such as age, gender, and social background. An intersectional understanding of diversity recognizes that different dimensions of diversity interact, potentially leading to multiple layers of discrimination, for example due to both skin color and sexual orientation. Diversity strengthens → resilience because it allows us to draw on a broader base of knowledge, making us less vulnerable to crises.

Doughnut Economics Doughnut Economics is a model developed by British economist Kate Raworth. It's based on the nine → planetary boundaries, supplemented with the concept of a social foundation, comprising things like adequate access to education and housing. While the planetary boundaries mustn't be exceeded to ensure our sustained coexistence, the social foundation can't be undercut. The resulting space, known as the doughnut, is thus referred to as a → safe and just space for humanity.

Economy The term "economy" encompasses the public sector and businesses, institutions, private households, and individuals that participate in the market, create supply and demand, produce and consume, and sell and buy. In the economy, money serves as the medium of communication. The economic system is distinct from its social environments (such as the political system, healthcare system, or education system), its organic environments (for example the natural entities it interacts with, such as water cycles, soil systems, flora, and fauna, and people as organic systems), and from its psychic environments (people as psychological systems).

Ecosystem services Ecosystem services encompass the range of benefits that humans receive from the environment. They fall into four categories: provisioning services (such as the plants that we use for food or wood for building materials), regulating services (like water cycle management or natural air purification), cultural services (such as enabling tourism), and supporting services that allow the other ecosystem services to work (such as nutrient cycles and soil formation). Healthy ecosystems are essential for human survival, making it imperative to protect these ecosystems and their variety to preserve → biodiversity.

Energy Energy is central to our lives: we need it for warmth, light, mobility, and to power the infrastructure and machines of the → economy. It's a key driver of all our material → prosperity. At the same time, the unchecked extraction of fossil fuels has created massive problems that we've yet to resolve. Fossil fuels are part of the carbon cycle and the main source of anthropogenic greenhouse gas emissions (→ GHG), and by extension, global warming. To date, it has not been possible to decouple economic growth from energy use, which is why → climate change is continually being exacerbated.

ESG ESG stands for Environmental, Social, and Governance, covering the three fundamental pillars of sustainability. On the one hand, ESG refers to a set of criteria and conditions for how organizations should take → sustainability into consideration. On the other hand, it also provides a framework for non-financial reporting by companies and a set of criteria for assessing their sustainability. Especially in the financial market, ESG has become an important consideration in identifying long-term sustainable investments.

Externalities Externalities, also known as external effects, arise from the production and consumption of goods and services and affect → stakeholders who are not directly involved. They can be either positive or negative. Those impacted aren't compensated or charged because no relationship is created by pricing or market mechanisms. Negative external effects have significant and far-reaching consequences on the planetary ecosystem. Environmental pollution and greenhouse gas emissions (→ GHGs) have devastating effects on → biodiversity and → climate change, ultimately impacting our ability to stay within → planetary boundaries. The costs of this are rarely borne by those who cause them but are rather distributed across society.

Facilitator An important role that can help make meetings more effective. Their job is to direct the focus of the participants to whatever best serves the purpose of the meeting. In well-defined meeting formats, the role of the facilitator is to ensure the shared goals of the meeting are met and to follow the defined structure. The facilitator asks questions, grants speaking turns to participants, and generally directs the meeting to the desired outcome by using body language and verbal communication.

Financialization The term "financialization" describes a shift in the → economy and financial system, where the financial sector and markets are becoming increasingly prominent and intertwined with nearly all economic activities. This has led to increased speculation, the expansion of financial products and services, and an increase in short-term financial transactions. The consequences of financialization are multifaceted, affecting economic stability, income inequality, social structures, and environmental health.

Footprint (see also Handprint) The term "footprint" refers to the indirect and direct negative effects of our activities. Typically used in an ecological context, it represents the emissions we cause. This ecological footprint of both individuals and → organizations can be measured, and the aim is to reduce it by minimizing negative impacts. Businesses and organizations bear a great deal of responsibility here, as they contribute massively to negative emissions and also shape the choices available for individual consumers. Conversely, the → handprint highlights the positive effects of our actions.

GHG (Greenhouse Gasses) Greenhouse gasses are trace gasses that contribute to the greenhouse effect, thus increasing the surface temperature of a planet, such as Earth. Without this natural effect, the average surface temperature on Earth would be a frosty -18°C. However, the rise in greenhouse gas emissions caused by human activities is amplifying this natural phenomenon, resulting in → climate change, in this case, → global warming. This has led to international treaties like the Kyoto Protocol in 1997 and the → Paris Climate Agreement in 2015, which aim to regulate and reduce emissions of the eight most important direct greenhouse gasses, including carbon dioxide, methane, and nitrous oxide, with carbon dioxide serving as the reference value for others.

Global warming The term "global warming" should not be confused with → "climate change." Whereas the latter can refer to both the cooling and warming of the climate, global warming, or anthropogenic climate change, refers to the increase in average temperatures in the Earth's oceans and near-surface air. This is mainly due to the increasing emissions of greenhouse gasses (→GHG) from human activities, notably from using fossil fuels as an → energy source as well as from agriculture and forestry practices. This increase in emissions amplifies the natural greenhouse effect, resulting in rising temperatures. The effects of global warming include more frequent extreme weather events and rising sea levels.

Goal Generally speaking, goals state what's intended to be accomplished in the future and help direct behavior toward this desired outcome. Particularly in bigger → organizations, goals are essential for minimizing friction losses, meaning inefficiencies stemming from misalignment. Likewise, the goals of different organizational units need to be synchronized to avoid → goal conflicts. This requires a clear overall direction for the entire organization. The clearer the goal, the easier it is to work towards it. Especially in agile organizations that operate in complex environments, goals need to be continually adjusted.

Goal Conflict Navigator In the Stellar Approach, we use this tool for → goal conflicts that can't be immediately resolved. The Goal Conflict Navigator creates transparency around such conflicts and supports the team in taking action within their → circle of influence. The tool distinguishes between goal conflicts within the team, within the organization (including conflicts with other organizational units, leadership, and the owners), outside of the organization, and at the systemic level of the economic system.

Goal conflicts → Goals can either be in harmony with each other (goal harmony) or in competition with each other (goal competition). If goals are completely incompatible and contradictory, or cannot be achieved simultaneously, this constitutes a goal conflict. Goal conflicts often arise in the → transformation of organizations toward greater → sustainability or → regenerativity. This is because old patterns of economic activity get necessarily stretched and new ones are established. Making such goal conflicts transparent is a critical success factor in the regenerative transformation because it enables the associated → dilemmas and → paradoxes to be dealt with.

Governance Governance represents the "'G'" in → ESG, referring to the management, leadership, or organizational framework of an → organization. It manifests in the structures, rules, processes, → strategies, and → cultures of organizations. Governance should take into account external influences, such as legislation, and the needs of → stakeholders. Broadly, governance describes how organizations are led and managed. Key traits of good governance include transparency and integrity.

Green Growth The theory of Green Growth maintains a commitment to the quantitative growth of the → economy and the pursuit of → prosperity. It proposes that economic activity can be decoupled from its environmental impacts, typically seen as happening through innovative technologies. This then allows for growth, prosperity, and environmental protection to be reconciled. However, this approach faces a challenge from *rebound effects*, where increased efficiency is offset by increased consumption. What's more, research indicates that the necessary decoupling won't be fast or effective enough to keep pace with → climate change. This approach is contrasted with → Degrowth, which rejects the notion of quantitative economic growth.

Growth In today's economic system, the overarching goal of economic activity is growth. It's quantified by the Gross Domestic Product (GDP), which measures the total value of domestically produced goods and services. Over the last few decades, it's become increasingly clear that unlimited and indiscriminate economic growth is at odds with the ecological and physical limits of our planet. Moreover, evidence shows that even though growth has positive social effects, such as better healthcare, access to education, and increased life expectancy, it also exacerbates social inequalities. We currently find ourselves facing a → dilemma: In order to maintain social stability, we can't just bring economic growth to a halt without some kind of alternative. Meanwhile, we also need to manage growth more actively, to prevent the impending collapse of our ecosystems.

Handprint (see also Footprint) In contrast to the → footprint, the handprint focuses on the positive effects of our activities, be they environmental, social, or economic. The handprint represents our active contribution to shaping sustainable development. This can mean, for example, our efforts to modify societal conditions, such as the structures, rules, laws, and overall awareness of what needs to be done. This is done to encourage and enable sustainable decisions for more people. It could also mean advocating for legislation that sets standards for more sustainable behavior across an entire industry, rather than focusing solely on one's own → organization. Or it could entail bringing up the topic of → sustainability with → stakeholders whom the topic has never been broached with. This can potentially have a greater impact than merely reducing one's own footprint.

IDG The Inner Development Goals (IDG) are a set of skills designed to help us live meaningfully and sustainably while navigating the complex environments and challenges of today (→ polycrisis). The IDG framework outlines 23 key skills distributed across five categories: Being, Thinking, Relating, Collaborating, and Acting. They constitute the crucial skill set we need to be able to fulfill the Sustainable Development Goals (SDGs) and master the transformation to sustainable development.

Impact "Impact" describes changes due to activities, meaning changes that would not have taken place without said activities. An impact can be negative or positive, and it can arise from both action and inaction. Impact is a key component of the Stellar Approach: we use the → Regenerative Business Model Canvas to analyze the negative and positive impact of a team on its → stakeholders, and we apply the input-output-outcome-impact framework to define indicators for regenerative → success.

Inequality Equality and its opposite, inequality, are central themes in the history of society. Inequality describes a state of affairs where some people have more access to resources or enjoy better living conditions than others. This can manifest in access to education and sanitation, as well as in income and housing conditions. The UN's → Sustainable Development Goals aim to reduce such inequalities, and the → Doughnut Economics concept addresses inequalities with its social foundation. Many aspects of the → polycrisis threaten to exacerbate these inequalities, for example when it comes to income or the effects of → climate change.

Integrative election process The integrative election process is a structured approach for filling roles: (1) The role is presented. (2) Everyone can nominate candidates to the moderator. This should be done anonymously to avoid groupthink. (3) Once all nominations have been collected, team members explain why they nominated someone, focusing only on the positive attributes that qualify the nominee for the role. (4) After everyone has explained their reasoning, they can adjust their nominations if they wish. (5) The candidate who has gotten the most nominations is proposed to fulfill the role. (6) As with other proposals, safety concerns are asked for and, if necessary, addressed. This includes the proposed role holder. Once there are no more concerns, the role selection is considered → safe enough to try.

Interdependence Interdependence means mutual dependency. From a regenerative perspective, the planet and all its living beings constitute a vast metabolic system, where all parts are mutually interdependent. Likewise, → organizations don't operate in isolation but interact with various → stakeholders and systems.

IPCC The IPCC is the Intergovernmental Panel on Climate Change. This UN agency, commonly known as the World Climate Council, summarizes for political decision-makers the current state of → climate change research and its associated risks, along with strategies for mitigation and adaptation. Their goal is to establish a basis for informed, science-based global policy decisions. IPCC reports are recognized in the scientific community as credible and well-justified representations of the current state of climate change research.

Iterative An iterative process is one consisting of various phases that are repeated multiple times. Each repetition of an action or process creates interim results, which are then improved on further in the next iteration based on the feedback generated. In this way, working iteratively gradually approaches the desired goal. Iterative approaches involve testing, learning, and continuous improvement. They also make it easier to handle unpredictability, as ambiguities are reduced with every iteration.

Leadership Leadership refers to all activities designed to provide direction and reduce → complexity within an → organization. Leadership can be organized in different ways within a social group. While hierarchy remains the most common leadership structure in organizations, newer models focusing on situational or role-based leadership are increasingly prominent.

Life At the heart of the concept of regenerativity is the idea that the planet, including all human and non-human beings, constitutes a living system. All biological processes on Earth can be viewed as a vast, self-regulating metabolic process, where individual parts are constantly interacting in countless ways. It's these mutual relationships that define life. In the Stellar Approach, the → Stellar Principles are derived from the fundamental principles of life.

Life-serving economy A life-serving economy is centered around → life. It sees itself as being an embedded part of life and → nature. It strikes a healthy, long-term balance with its surrounding systems and makes a net positive contribution to life. In contrast to today's → economy, progress in a regenerative economy isn't assessed just through quantitative metrics but also through qualitative improvements and the level of well-being. We use the terms "life-serving economy," "regenerative economy," and "life-centric economy" synonymously.

Life-serving organizations Just as a life-serving economy is centered on life, so too are regenerative organizations. The goal of a life-serving organization is to contribute positively to life on this planet through its economic activities. The "5+1 Model" defines six main levels to consider when designing life-serving organizations: Purpose, Ownership and governance model, Finance, Organizational operating system, Service delivery, and Ecosystem.

Living systems design Living systems design goes beyond just serving human users, focusing on the whole of → life on this planet. It could, therefore, also be called regenerative design, life-centered design, or planet-centered design. This approach recognizes → complexity and requires → systems thinking.

Materiality analysis A materiality analysis is a tool for identifying key action areas in sustainability. The analysis is conducted with involvement from the organization's → stakeholders, enabling a holistic overview of the relevant → ESG criteria. The result is a so-called materiality matrix. A materiality analysis is mandatory for companies under the → CSRD. They need to adhere to the principle of double materiality, which deems a sustainability matter relevant if the company's activities have an impact on it (inside-out perspective) or if it results in risks or opportunities for the company (outside-in perspective).

Meeting At its core, a meeting is any gathering of two or more people in the context of work. This includes all scheduled regular meetings among teams or other groups, as well as any ad-hoc meetings with two or more participants. Meetings serve as a forum to exchange information, make decisions, and develop ideas and concepts. Often no tangible work results are created, which is why it can appear that no "real" work is being done there. In many → organizations, most people spend the majority of their time in meetings. This can lead to → tensions: "We spend so much time in meetings that we can't get enough work done." But it also creates an opportunity, whereby small improvements in meetings, for example introducing a → facilitator role, can boost productivity and motivation significantly.

Money Money is a universal measure and communication medium within the economy that's used to value goods and services and make exchanges easier. The transformative power of money can be risky in regenerative terms, as it's often used to enact changes and create new possibilities without considering their effects on environmental systems (→ externalities).

Multi-Capital Accounting Multi-Capital Accounting refers to various methods for a holistic measurement of success or the valuation of capital. It's based on the idea that an organization's performance depends on many forms of capital. Besides financial capital, it includes, for example, natural capital, meaning → nature and its → ecosystem services. The goal of Multi-Capital Accounting is to include externalities in accounting and decision-making. However, the term "capital" is used somewhat vaguely in many approaches to Multi-Capital Accounting.

Narrative Unlike everyday → storytelling, narratives are large, well-established stories that create meaning or convey values. And these aren't just any old tales but are often considered interpretations of the world that can steer entire societies. One example from today is the prosperity narrative, which is used to legitimize the doctrine of economic growth. Typically, narratives tend to be long-lasting and limited to specific cultures. New narratives often emerge during crises, as can be seen in the context of the necessary → sustainability transformation, where new potential narratives – such as "time affluence" or "the good life" – are challenging the growth narrative.

Nature Our perception of nature is inherently shaped by social, political, and economic relationships. In the regenerative paradigm, the separation between humans and nature dissolves. Humans are seen as a part of nature, continuously shaping their interactions with living non-human natural processes like ecosystems, animals, and plants. Unlike the infinite → growth that today's economy strives for, natural growth occurs in cycles of growth and decay.

Net Positive The term "Net Positive" refers to a mode of economic activity where an organization gives more to its environment than it takes. Thus, the benefits of an organization operating on a Net Positive basis extend well beyond traditional organizational boundaries. In a fully life-serving economy, which views the economy, society, and planet as interconnected living systems, all economic activities are Net Positive, because they focus on life on this planet, making a Net Positive contribution to it.

Net zero Net zero means a balance between carbon dioxide emissions and their removal from the atmosphere. As part of the battle against → climate change, various countries and organizations have adopted science-based net zero goals in line with the 1.5-degree target from the → Paris Climate Agreement. In contrast to climate neutrality, net zero includes all three → scopes in calculating the carbon footprint. What's more, it involves not just compensating for emissions but achieving a net zero state through carbon absorption by natural sinks, necessitating major investments into forests and bogs, for example.

Organization From a systems theory perspective, an organization is a social system composed of various elements, relationships, and processes that interact to pursue common → goals or purposes. An organization has distinct boundaries that separate it from its environment, and it functions as an independent entity that can respond to environmental changes. Organizations implement various strategies to manage → complexity, including → leadership, rules, and decision-making processes. Organizations can be subdivided into smaller units like → teams.

Paradox A paradox can be defined as a logically self-contradictory statement. In the → sustainability transformation, situations can occur that seem paradoxical because new patterns arise that contradict existing knowledge. For example, moving from a conventional understanding of the → economy to a grasp of the → life-serving economy can create paradoxes. To deal with paradoxes, it's worth recognizing that paradoxes are merely snapshots in time and solutions will emerge along the way, even if they're not yet visible.

Paris Climate Agreement At the 21st UN Climate Change Conference in Paris in 2015, 195 countries committed to limiting → global warming. The goal is to cap warming at 1.5 °C compared to the pre-industrial age, and if that's not possible, to at least stay well below 2 °C. This goal can only be reached through the consistent decarbonization of the → economy. Further goals of the Paris Agreement include reducing greenhouse gas emissions, adapting to → climate change, and redirecting investment flows into sustainable investments.

Patriarchy The word "patriarchy" originally meant the "rule of fathers." In modern usage, it denotes male dominance in almost all areas of life, including structural discrimination and disadvantages faced by other genders, as well as the associated violence and → inequality. The roots of patriarchy can be traced back to when humans adopted a sedentary lifestyle. Before this, gender equality was actually key to the survival of human communities: shared responsibilities in, for example, food provision, led to greater resilience and innovation. Over thousands of years, patriarchy has persisted through → narratives of men's divine or biological superiority, becoming a structural phenomenon where power and privileges are predominantly held by (white) men. Making the effects of patriarchal structures, behaviors, and thought patterns visible is the only way to attain gender equality.

Permaculture Permaculture is based on the cycles and ecosystems of → nature. The term was coined by Australians Bill Mollison and David Holmgren in the 1970s. It began as a method for sustainable agriculture and gardening but has grown into a global movement and a philosophy for sustainable living. Permaculture is founded on three ethical principles: Earth Care (mindful treatment of the Earth), People Care (mindful treatment of all people), and Fair Share (sharing and self-limitation). Moreover, permaculture includes twelve design principles, such as appreciating and leveraging diversity, taking small steps, and cooperating instead of competing. These design principles extend beyond land use and can be applied to other areas of life as well as to organizations.

Planetary boundaries Planetary boundaries refer to the Earth's ecological upper limits. They delineate the safe operating space for humanity. Exceeding these boundaries increases the risk of destabilizing Earth's ecosystems and endangering human life. The boundaries are defined based on current knowledge, with a built-in safety margin from potential → tipping points in subsystems. The concept of planetary boundaries was first published in 2009 by a research team led by Swedish scientist Johan Rockström, with updates in 2015 and 2023. Nine planetary boundaries have been defined: → climate change, biosphere integrity, freshwater use, land use, biogeochemical flows, novel entities, air pollution, ocean acidification, and ozone depletion. In 2023, the work of quantifying all of them was completed, and it was found that we've exceeded six of the nine boundaries.

Polycrisis The term "polycrisis" refers to a complex and interconnected crisis that affects various areas of society. A polycrisis occurs when multiple concurrent crises or challenges arise that amplify each other, threatening political, social, and economic stability. These crises can take various forms, such as political conflicts, economic problems, social unrest, environmental impacts, and public health emergencies. Addressing a polycrisis requires an interdisciplinary approach and collaboration between various stakeholders to develop holistic solutions and enhance societal resilience.

Practices A practice is a way of guiding actions so they become habitual through repetition. A practice includes skills and knowledge (skillset), the tools and resources (toolset), and ways of thinking and attitudes (mindset) that all make establishing and maintaining the practice more likely. In the Stellar Approach, we cultivate seven practices that support teams on their regenerative development journey.

Principles In this context, principles are something that helps to establish a common direction and to develop coherent solutions that support moving in this direction. In the Stellar Approach, we work with four principles that help us create a regenerative orientation: embedded, diverse, circular, and long-term.

Prosperity Prosperity, progress, and development are often used to legitimize the need for economic (→ economy) → growth. The → success of the economy is measured with the Gross Domestic Product (GDP), which mainly reflects material wealth. Critics argue that our current understanding of prosperity overemphasizes quantitative aspects, while more intangible factors like personal happiness or social inclusion are overlooked.

What's more, today's materialistic definition of prosperity comes with many negative → externalities that threaten long-term prosperity and societal stability.

Purpose Purpose helps → organizations reflect on why they exist in the world. It's the overarching common denominator and driving force of the organization: "Why does this organization exist? What difference do we want to make?" → Teams also can develop a shared purpose: "What's our team's → contribution? What's our mission?" And in fact, it's something that everyone can ask themselves about: "Why am I here? What do I want to contribute?"

Regenerative Business Canvas The Regenerative Business Canvas (RBC) is a tool for diagnosing and further developing business models (→ Business Design). The RBC outlines four phases in a linear value chain (Resource inputs, Production/Preparation, Usage, Residual waste/Incineration). The value creation process of a → team or → organization can be mapped onto these stages. The RBC also offers four approaches for closing loops: recycling, reprocessing, reusing, and extending the lifespan. In the Stellar Approach, we employ the RBC as part of the second → Stellar Practice.

Regenerativity Regenerativity represents an advanced stage of → sustainability. While the classic understanding of sustainability focuses on mitigating or avoiding harm ("do no harm," → Triple Bottom Line), regenerative approaches incorporate systemic perspectives, viewing life on this planet as a large system comprising various interconnected subsystems and aiming to contribute positively to the entire system (→ Net Positive).

Resilience Resilience is a term rooted in psychology. It means the ability to adapt and withstand changes or → crises without suffering lasting damage. The opposite of resilience is vulnerability. Resilience is relevant to individuals, societies, and → organizations. People and societies need to build up their resilience to cope with the impacts of multiple → systemic crises. Organizations, on the other hand, need resilience to thrive in our complex, dynamic, ever-changing world.

Roles In many organizational models, roles are used to divide responsibilities into clearly defined areas and then assign them to people. In Holacracy, for example, roles are meaningful clusters of accountabilities that are constantly being changed and expanded. In its simplest form, a role consists of a name, a purpose, and at least one accountability, meaning a recurring action associated with this role, for example, "Ensures a clear agenda is set for the meeting," or "Checks the content of reports for consistency."

Safe and just space The phrase "safe and just space" comes from Kate Raworth's discussion paper, "A Safe and Just Space for Humanity." It's closely tied to the concepts of → Doughnut Economics and → planetary boundaries, which delineate a safe operational area for humanity. The Doughnut Economics model supplements this with a social foundation that shouldn't be undercut. The combination of the two creates an ecologically safe and socially just space for humanity.

Safe enough to try In complex (→ complexity) environments, progress can only be made one step at a time, and → decisions must almost always be made under uncertainty. To help teams make choices under these conditions, we encourage adopting a "safe enough to try" mindset. The key question in it is: is the next proposed step safe enough to try, or are there significant safety concerns (for example because it could cause harm to the organization)? If there are no concerns, the next step can be taken. And if new → tensions arise along the way, they're addressed in the next step. The "safe enough to try" approach ensures that decision-making processes don't stall and teams can keep moving.

Science Based Targets (SBT) Science-Based Targets (SBTs) are goals set based on the most current scientific insights. The Science Based Target Initiative – made up of the Carbon Disclosure Project, the UN Global Compact, the World Resources Institute, and the World Wide Fund for Nature – develops methods for defining climate SBTs for companies. The Science Based Target Network expands on this work with SBTs for Nature. These provide a comprehensive methodology for defining similar science-based targets for environmental areas like freshwater, oceans, biodiversity, and land use, applicable to corporations and cities as well. SBT offers → organizations not only clear objectives but also a well-defined roadmap for tackling challenges like → climate change and the biodiversity crisis in their own operating area.

Scopes Scopes relate to the calculation of greenhouse gas emissions (→ GHG) by → organizations. An organization can emit greenhouse gasses either directly or indirectly. Direct emissions occur within the organization's control (Scope 1), while indirect emissions happen outside of its direct control (Scope 2 and 3). The distinctions between the three scopes are defined in the Greenhouse Gas Protocol, which is the internationally recognized standard for calculating greenhouse gas emissions. Scope 1 covers emissions from an organization's buildings and vehicles. Scope 2 captures emissions from the energy it buys, whether in the form of heat, electricity, steam, cooling or something else. Scope 3, typically the largest contributor, includes emissions from all activities upstream or downstream in the value chain, including from sourcing goods or from business travel.

SDG SDG stands for Sustainable Development Goals, a set of 17 global objectives established by the UN in 2016 with the goal of ensuring sustainable development on social, economic, and ecological levels until 2030. They are meant to guide politics, → the economy, civil society and science. The 17 goals are No poverty; Zero hunger; Good health and well-being; Quality education; Gender equality; Clean water and sanitation; Affordable and clean energy; Decent work and economic growth; Industry, innovation and infrastructure; Reduced inequalities; Sustainable cities and communities; Responsible consumption and production; Climate action; Life below water; Life on land; Peace, justice and strong institutions; and Partnerships for the goals.

Sprint Sprints are an agile project management method, where a predefined, short timeframe is dedicated to completing prioritized to-dos, enabling → teams to work highly efficiently during this time. We conduct sprints in the roughly four to six-week intervals between Stellar modules. This enables the teams to execute their first projects already during the Stellar Journey.

Stakeholder Stakeholders are individuals, groups, or entities that an → organization has a relationship with or whose interests are impacted by the organization's service provision. In the Stellar Approach, a stakeholder need not necessarily be human but can be any living system the organization interacts with, such as the local water system. In → systems theory, these would be called the organization's environments.

Stellar Practices See → Practices

Stellar Principles See → Principles

Stellar Virtues See → Virtues

Steward ownership Ownership is a key element of our economic system. In order to move toward a more → life-serving economy, we need a more responsible approach to the ownership of companies. Steward ownership focuses on the company's → purpose. Instead of distributing profits to owners, such companies prefer to reinvest profits into better pursuing their purpose. What's more, these companies are structured so that they can't be sold and are therefore isolated from speculation by market forces. This fosters independence, longevity, and → sustainability. There are various models for more responsible ownership, often implemented via foundations, and in the US, for example, a Perpetual Purpose Trust is a commonly-used model for steward ownership.

Storytelling In essence, storytelling is the purposeful use of stories to convince or excite an audience. It is often said that its effectiveness as a communication tool is due to the fact that passing down knowledge through stories has played an important part in human evolution. Meanwhile, critics warn that storytelling can be used to manipulate audiences since convincing stories are likely to be believed whether they're true or not.

Strategy Simply put, a strategy is a plan designed to achieve set goals. In an economic context, a strategy refers to how an → organization behaves in relation to its environment to meet its long-term → goals. There can be overarching strategies, like a corporate strategy, and narrower sub-strategies, such as a procurement strategy. Typically, strategy development is preceded by an analysis phase that informs the work. For sustainability-related strategies, for example, a → materiality analysis is conducted first. In complex environments, an → iterative approach to strategy tends to work better than a linear one.

Success In our society, success tends to be associated with (material) → prosperity resulting from economic → growth. Despite the prevalence of this → narrative, it's become increasingly clear in recent years that this definition of success comes with a swath of problems. For example, not everyone benefits equally from economic growth, and what's more, this type of success often creates negative social and ecological effects (→ externalities). In a → life-serving economy, the understanding of success is broader: success means economic viability but also having a positive → impact on relationships with surrounding (human and non-human) → stakeholders.

Sustainability These days, the term "sustainability" can have many meanings. One particularly influential definition comes from the Brundtland Commission, which said that sustainable development is "development that meets the needs of the present without compromising the ability of future generations to meet their own needs." Currently, the most widespread understanding of sustainability in the → economy is the three-dimensional → ESG model or the → Triple Bottom Line. Regenerative sustainability extends beyond this framework by emphasizing the importance of relationships in living systems.

Sustainability transformation "Sustainability transformation" describes the process of moving towards greater → sustainability and → regenerativity. In light of the current → polycrisis, sustainability transformation is a high priority for both companies and policymakers. The Stellar Approach is a framework designed to facilitate this transformation in the direction of a more regenerative organization, and by extension, toward a more → life-serving economy.

System crises See → Polycrisis

Systems theory When we speak of systems theory, we refer to the version developed by the German sociologist Niklas Luhmann. Systems theory differentiates between organic systems (like the bodies of living beings), psychological systems (like human consciousness), and social systems (like economic systems). The Stellar Approach is based on key insights from systems theory, such as the distinction between a system and its environment and the necessity of → co-evolution.

Systems thinking Systems thinking has no universally accepted definition, but it might be best described as a competency or way of thinking. Based on the ideas of → systems theory, systems thinking is the ability to better understand and design complex and dynamic systems. It represents a holistic approach intended to understand the consequences of our actions and make better decisions in guiding a system. Systems thinking is an important ability in the → sustainability transformation and in designing a → life-serving economy.

(EU) Taxonomy A key element for achieving the objectives of the European Green Deal, the EU Taxonomy is basically a classification system. It comprises criteria for determining whether companies' economic activities are environmentally sustainable. As per → CSRD, companies have to disclose in their sustainability reporting what parts of their economic activities are considered environmentally sustainable according to the EU Taxonomy. Similarly, financial market participants are required to report on the sustainability of the investments in their portfolios.

Team A team is a group of individuals who work collaboratively toward a common → goal. They deliver a service together and genuinely want to collaborate to do so. From an organizational perspective, a team is composed of roles that represent the various responsibilities that the team has. At the same time, a team also comprises individuals who, being psychological systems, have complex relationships with each other.

Team development Team development is a dynamic, long-term process. The → goal is to effect changes or improvements in the processes and structures of the → team. Team development processes can occur organically or be actively managed. In the context of the Stellar Approach, the goal of team development is to enable teams and their individual members to drive the regenerative development of an → organization.

Tension In the Stellar framework, the word "tension" doesn't have a negative connotation, but rather means a kind of unreleased energy potential that can serve as a starting point for change. People always carry various tensions in them – ideas, questions, emotions – which come to light as they work together towards a → goal. These tensions indicate a difference between what is and what could be. The tensions can be processed into actions that lead to small changes in the desired direction. That's why tensions of any kind should be seen as something positive: fuel for meaningful change.

Tipping point Tipping points are often discussed in relation to → planetary boundaries. A tipping point refers to a minor change that actually triggers a sudden and often irreversible change. Accelerating → global warming is a driver and likely result of tipping points being exceeded. In contrast, social tipping points can be seen as something positive, where small changes by individuals bring about significant changes in the behavior of the masses, for example in consumption patterns.

Transformation These days, the term "transformation" can mean any number of different things. In the Stellar Approach, it refers to a goal-oriented, fundamental change in a system. This kind of profound change is sometimes called a "second-order change". It's a long-term process, complex and unpredictable, and thus fraught with uncertainties. Along the way, → paradoxes and → dilemmas often crop up. A transformation comes to a (temporary) end when new structures have been established in the system. But eventually, they will be challenged too.

Transformation architecture A → transformation is a complex process that, in → organizations, requires a minimum level of planning and management to avoid everything descending into chaos. This is where transformation architecture comes into play: it's used to plan the various components needed for the transformation. In the Stellar Approach, we often work with a steering team tasked with coordinating the various workstreams that comprise the architecture. The transformation architecture should be designed to integrate new information along the way in an → iterative manner.

Triple Bottom Line The Triple Bottom Line represents the three pillars of → sustainability, focusing on attaining a lasting equilibrium between economic, environmental, and social performance. The term was coined by the British consultant John Elkington in the 1990s. By expanding the purely economic bottom line to include environmental and social aspects, the Triple Bottom Line aims to highlight the value and necessity of sustainability for the long-term survival of businesses. Critics argue that the Triple Bottom Line is often used as a mere veneer of sustainability. Consequently, Elkington himself has recently cautioned against using the Triple Bottom Line without properly understanding the complex interrelationships between the three pillars.

Virtues Virtues are qualities that guide a person's behavior and actions, helping them to develop in a desirable direction. In the Stellar Approach, we use the term "virtues" to denote the inner "equipment" that's useful for transitioning to regenerative economic activity. This includes attitudes, values, beliefs, and relational skills. In the Stellar Approach, we focus on cultivating three key virtues: courage, creative joy, and perseverance.

Annotations

Check-in

1. See Chenoweth & Stephan (2011).

Introduction

1. We initially focus on sustainability here, because it is perhaps a more familiar concept when speaking of possible responses to the climate crisis. In the following chapters, we'll discuss its limits and how it differs from a regenerative economy.
2. Liu & Raftery (2021).
3. We wish to add that digitalization, as it drives the rise of Artificial Intelligence (AI), is now also partially perceived as a threat to the survival of humanity.
4. In practice, it's not necessary to involve all teams. It's also possible to apply the approach in only parts of the organization (see p. 104).
5. A distinction is sometimes made between "weak sustainability" and "strong sustainability." The concept of strong sustainability prioritizes the essential ecological sphere over economic gains, thereby aligning closely with regenerative thinking. In German, the term "echte Nachhaltigkeit" (true sustainability) is sometimes used to imply that classic sustainability, focused on minimizing harm, doesn't go far enough (e. g., Beck & Buddemeier, 2022).

Between the "No More" and the "Not Yet"

1. de Yonge (2022).
2. Oxfam (2023).
3. As of 2023. Europe, however, is heating up much faster than other continents, and warming there is already averaging 2.2 degrees. See https://wmo.int/media/news/wmo-confirms-2023-smashes-global-temperature-record and https://climate.copernicus.eu/copernicus-2023-hottest-year-record (Retrieved 24.01.2024).
4. As of January 2024. Projections are based on the Sixth Assessment Report of the IPCC from March 2023. Current data available here: https://www.mcc-berlin.net/en/research/co2-budget.html (Retrieved 24.01.2024). Generally, we should avoid adopting the narrative of "We have x years left." In some countries the full force of the climate catastrophe may not have been felt yet, but in others (especially those in the Global South) it has already significantly disrupted lives and living conditions. Instead of a countdown of years, we believe a more useful attitude for spurring change is to accept that we already find ourselves in an unfolding climate catastrophe and are now shaping our response to it.
5. Sharpe (2013).
6. This term is from our friends over at arkH3: www.arkh3.com
7. Some of these positive effects are neatly summarized in Hans Rosling's book "Factfulness" (Rosling, Rosling Rönnlund & Rosling, 2018).

Annotations 341

8. This brief historical overview draws on the insightful report "Welcome to the Great Unraveling: Navigating the Polycrisis of Environmental and Social Breakdown" by the Post Carbon Institute (Heinberg & Miller, 2023).
9. For the sake of completeness, it's worth noting that there are different types of finance capitalism, such as democratic capitalism and authoritarian state capitalism. Ultimately, however, all types of capitalism are interconnected via the global market and therefore follow the same set of rules.
10. See Fraser (2022).
11. Estimates suggest that between 1990 and 2015, the Global North appropriated 242 trillion dollars worth of embodied raw materials, energy, land, and labor from the Global South (see Hickel et al., 2022).
12. Some also argue that the production of renewable infrastructure, such as solar panels and wind turbines, requires so much energy and rare raw materials that it again merely hastens the destabilization of ecosystems and postpones problems for future generations to solve.
13. Parrique, Barth, Briens, Kerschne, Kraus-Polk, Kuokkanen & Spangenberg (2019).
14. Vogel & Hickel (2023).
15. Olk, Schneider & Hickel (2023).
16. https://www.finanzwende-recherche.de/unsere-themen/finanzialisierung (Retrieved 01.11.2023).
17. Some ancient economic systems had a simple mechanism to try to curb increasing financialization: Every 49 years there was a "jubilee year," where all debts would be forgiven and land returned. This meant that capital could generate income for roughly the length of a human lifespan, after which the slate was wiped clean and the clock reset. (Sedlacek, 2012, p. 104)
18. This refers to distorted perceptions as described in cognitive psychology, for example caused by biases and stereotypes, cognitive assumptions, in-group favoritism, fundamental attribution error, or confirmation bias.
19. For example Bauhardt (2015), Fraser (2012), Jaspers, Ryland & Horch (2022), Kortendiek, Riegrad & Sabisch (2019).
20. In his book "The Economy of Society", Luhmann writes about the generalization of money as being both symbolic and diabolic. Because money is such a universal medium of communication, it replaces other symbols and "dries them up" (Luhmann 1988, p. 242), thereby making traditional relationships less significant in comparison (Simon, 2009, p. 51)."
21. Later on, we'll discuss the limitations of linear thinking and the importance of systemic thinking in more detail (see p. 64).
22. The risk for such aberrations is especially high if incentivized by subsidies or other attempts to steer behavior.
23. https://www.nationalgeographic.de/wissenschaft/2020/12/menschengemachte-masse-auf-der-erde-bald-schwerer-als-biomasse (Retrieved 24.01.2024).
24. Strictly speaking, this means there are no "finite resources" as long as the cycles of creation, utilization, and regeneration of a resource are synchronized. For example, had we humans paced our extraction of oil to match the rate at which nature creates it, natural

oil reserves would have replenished themselves, and emissions from burning oil would have likely been inconsequential over this longer timeline. Unfortunately, if we wanted to make up for the rate at which we've extracted oil over the past few decades, we'd now have to wait millions of years.
25. Graeber (2019).
26. The concept of "nature" is one we could discuss at considerable length. When we say that humans are in a mutually dependent relationship with nature, it already indicates that, of course, we are also part of nature. The dichotomous view of humans on one side and nature on the other unravels when in regenerative thinking. To make this clear, some authors also use terms like "non-human" nature, or "more-than-human nature" (to emphasize that nature consists of trillions of non-human organisms). To understand this better, Gregory Bateson's "Steps to an Ecology of Mind," published in 1972, is well worth reading. He explains from a systems theory perspective how deeply the narrative of "man versus nature" is embedded in our modern narrative of civilization (Bateson, 1972).
27. Richardson et al. (2023).
28. The concept of planetary boundaries also features in the thinking around Science Based Targets and Science Based Targets for Nature. They aim to ensure that corporate ecological objectives are formulated as absolute targets, consistent with scientific findings and within the budget of natural resources. Such fixed targets are needed in ecology because relative goals often result in overstepping the limits of nature (see p. 69).
29. As an example, consider Paul Polman, the former CEO of Unilever. By demonstrating the potential of responsible and sustainable business practices for long-term growth and shared value creation, he managed to convince investors to reinvest financial capital into natural, social, and cultural capital.
30. Naturally, we need to recognize that this very much embodies the view of the industrialized Global North. In many cultures, especially indigenous ones, networked and cosmic thinking
is far more prominent than in Western-influenced societies.
31. Kumar (2017).
32. Scharmer (2016).
33. Breidenbach & Rollow (2019). See further thoughts in Greenwood (2023) and Ahmed (2023). See also "What about our feelings?" on page 84.
34. The systemic viewpoint inherent in these models is compelling, but in practice there are still several open questions. In the business sense, capital is always tied to ownership and the right of disposal. And while a balance sheet can only show capital that a company owns, people and natural resources cannot be listed as assets by companies – thankfully. These models superimpose the economic concept of capital to a company's environments, without sufficiently distinguishing between the nuances. A more promising approach might be to define prices for various services performed by stakeholders, and closely monitor where these prices are missing or markedly low.
35. Konietzko et al. (2023).
36. E. g. point 31 in the CSRD.
37. In our view, to see an impact on actual daily business, we'd be far better off adopting a truly holistic assessment of success and adjusting existing corporate accounting

systems accordingly. So just as we need to debate the suitability of Gross Domestic Product as an indicator of societal success, we should also challenge the suitability of traditional accounting and controlling as holistic reflectors of business success. As long as business accounting practices remain stagnant with some new frameworks for impact measurement, sustainability control, or purpose assessment merely tacked on as an afterthought, economic concerns will continue to steer people's behavior toward all-too-familiar results. Please see more on this in the book New Finance (Lerche, 2023) and in the third part of this book, which examines the concept of a life-centric organization.

38. Dixson-Declève, Gaffney, Ghosh, Randers, Rockström & Stoknes (2022).
39. This kind of self-restraint should not be confused with total abstention. Limits are good, because they encourage the generation of diverse solutions. Without boundaries, we tend to follow our same old familiar paths, only deviating from them when limits challenge us to innovate new solutions. From a mathematical-physical perspective, we can term this phenomenon "folding." (Levermann, 2023).
40. From a systems theory perspective, psychological systems are not part of the organization, but psychological and organizational systems act as mutual environments for each other. Seen through this lens, it's clear that internal aspects like mindset and culture can't be directly changed by the organization's rationality. Things get tricky for individuals (psychological systems), when there's growing conflict between the demands of the organizational environment and the demands of other environments, like natural systems. This is why it's crucial for regenerative development that organizations become proficient in processing these contradictions and dilemmas in their operations. Otherwise, the chasm between employees and the organization can grow so wide that it erodes the motivation and emotional connection of employees, resulting in poorer performance that hurts the organization too.
41. For example Maté & Maté (2022).
42. Growth That Matters, AB (2021).

How Organizations Can Contribute to Regenerative Change

1. We're not the first to come up with this idea. For example, in his 2015 white paper "Regenerative Capitalism," John Fullerton summarized eight key characteristics and universal patterns of a regenerative economy that would enable shared prosperity on a healthy planet. Many of these ideas can also be found in the Stellar Principles and in our thoughts on a "life-centric organization" (see p. 284).
2. To understand this personally, consider the following – rather illuminating – thought exercise: Write down whom you were "dependent" on during any given day. For example, if you took a tram on that day, ask yourself: Who drove you? And who built the tram and laid the tracks for it? Where did the steel for the tracks come from? Or, if you bought a new pair of shoes, ask yourself: How did the shoes get to you? Where did the material come from? Who sewed them together? Picture all these people who contributed to enabling an average day in your life. How many are there? 100? 1 000? 100 000?
3. Coulon (2023).

4. Regarding embedding the Stellar Approach into the overarching transformation architecture, see p. 256.
5. In systemic organizational development, this is called "working with fractals."
6. The only aspect that we can be certain of today is that planetary boundaries are non-negotiable. This means that a regenerative economy must always operate within their limits.

Preparing for the Stellar Journey

1. The Stellar Virtues are based on the Inner Development Goals, but we've greatly narrowed them for our purposes (Growth that Matters AB, 2021)
2. We first came across the concept of tension-based work in Holacracy (Robertson, 2015). If you'd like to dive deeper into our approach to tension-based work, we suggest reading the relevant chapter in our book, "The Loop Approach" (Klein, Hughes, 2019).
3. The model is based on Stephen Covey's Circle of Influence, and we'll go into it in more detail in the second practice (see p. 157).

The Stellar Journey: Modules and Methods

1. In the final chapter of this second part, we'll take a closer look at how the Stellar Journeys of teams can be embedded among other workstreams of the regenerative transformation.
2. The founding father of systems theory, Niklas Luhmann, identifies four different decision premises in organizations: programs, communication channels, personnel, and organizational culture. Decision premises shape how decisions are made, thereby mitigating the chaos that would ensue from everyone acting independently. Unlike the first three premises, he characterizes culture as "undecidable" – it can't be deliberately chosen but emerges on its own, in a self-organized and spontaneous manner (Luhmann, 2000).
3. Please note that although we describe the workshop exercises as occurring in a physical setting, such as a meeting room, they can all be conducted just as well remotely via digital means.
4. You may remember that we described the doughnut concept in more detail in Part 1 of the book, on page 60 onwards. The key information can also be found in a concept card in the appendix.
5. The following exercise stems from the methods of the Doughnut Economics Action Lab (DEAL), though we've adapted it slightly for our purposes. It's particularly powerful when done in a physical space. https://doughnuteconomics.org/tools/172 (Retrieved 20.09.2023).
6. Global and national level data can be accessed here, for example: https://goodlife.leeds.ac.uk/national-trends/country-trends (Retrieved 29.09.2023).
7. The exercise is based on the "Wheel of Power, Privilege and Marginalization" by Canadian illustrator Sylvia Duckworth, which was further developed by Sigi Lieb: https://www.gespraechswert.de/intersektionalitaet (Retrieved 22.10.23). It illustrates where we might experience discrimination or benefit from privilege. Age has been deliberately left out of this wheel, as unfortunately both the young and the old may experience discrimination.

8. The Regenerative Business Canvas provides an initial foray into circular thinking, a topic we'll dive deeper into in the fourth Stellar Practice. The four cycles are most relevant for products, but teams providing services can also apply them to the upstream products or processes they need.
9. Sometimes it can be useful to complement the RBC with the concept of *scopes 1, 2, 3* to understand where the biggest potential for impact lies. This is a framework for classifying and monitoring greenhouse gas emissions in organizations. Scope 1 covers direct emissions from company-owned sources like cars or trucks. Scope 2 covers indirect emissions from buying electricity and heating. Finally, scope 3 covers all other indirect emissions, such as from supply chains, business travel, and the use of the company's products. And it's this last category that usually makes up the biggest share of total emissions. One important note regarding the scopes is that they primarily relate to CO_2- or CO_2-equivalent emissions, meaning to only one planetary boundary. To learn more about the scopes, please see the appendix.
10. We'll explain what we mean by safety concerns later when discussing the regenerative integrative decision making process (see. p. 204).
11. Regarding possible changes to the organization's purpose, please see the chapter "The Big Picture: The Stellar Approach as a Part of the Regenerative Transformation" on page 256.
12. We know that some teams may not be used to this, and there's certainly no pressure for anyone to force exuberance. That said, we do believe that light-heartedness and joy are helpful on any change journey. So, our advice is to take whatever chance you get to celebrate with your team.
13. "(…) resilience is best defined as an outcome of successful adaptation to adversity. Characteristics of the person and situation may identify resilient processes, but only if they lead to healthier outcomes following stressful circumstances." (Zautra, Hall & Murray, 2010, p. 3).
14. https://the-long-time-academy.simplecast.com/episodes/human-layers-W7vRUWu7 (Retrieved 20.09.2023).
15. How far forward can the team realistically try to look? This greatly depends on the team, industry, and business model, but usually the minimum should be five years.
16. If you'd like to dive deeper into role-based work, we suggest reading the relevant chapter in our book "The Loop Approach" (Klein, Hughes, 2019).
17. These perspectives are based on 4D mapping roles (Hayashi, 2021, p. 72–73), which in turn are inspired by Otto Scharmer's "Three Divides" (Scharmer, 2016).
18. More on *False Hope* and *Constructive Hope* here: https://www.frontiersin.org/articles/10.3389/fcomm.2019.00020/full (Retrieved 20.09.2023).
19. Pfeifer (2019).
20. Pfeifer (2019), p. 5.
21. Rieß (2010).
22. This was demonstrated in experiments conducted at the Stanford Graduate School of Business, explained here by Jennifer Aaker in her talk "Harnessing the Power of Stories": https://www.youtube.com/watch?v=9X0weDMh9C4 (Retrieved 25.09.2023).
23. Heath & Heath (2010).

24. This method was partly inspired by Thomas Pyczaks "Sparkline" https://www.strategisches-storytelling.de/sparkline-die-struktur-ueberzeugender-vortraege/ (Retrieved 03.01.2024)
25. See Breidenbach & Rollow (2019).
26. Schmid & Hipp (1998, p. 11).
27. Varga von Kibéd & Sparrer (2000).
28. Baldwin (1998).
29. There's more background information on the concept of "Infinite games" in the appendix.

The Big Picture: The Stellar Approach as a Part of the Regenerative Transformation

1. Some of these success factors also came up in our book "The Loop Approach," which focuses on agile transformation (Klein, Hughes, 2019). Similar to the Stellar Approach, the Loop Approach is also a team-based transformation curriculum, which is why some of the success factors are relevant to both.
2. Based on Beck & Buddemeier (2022).
3. To avoid any misunderstandings, we want to clarify that by "profit" we mean a company's EBIT or EBITDA. And we naturally understand that a private business must be able to finance itself to ensure its long-term survival in its environments.
4. We'll revisit the concept of purpose and principle of meaning in the last part of the book, when we discuss the idea of a life-centric organization.
5. You can find more information on the concept of Science Based Targets (for Nature) in the appendix.

The 5+1 Model: The Life-Centric Organization

1. We would like to once again emphasize that all theories and models are to the world what maps are to terrain, or what menus are to dishes. "The map is not the territory (…) because there's a substantial loss of meaning between symbols and things. (…) Maps that bear no relation to the real world are useless and misleading, which is why people should distrust the cognitive maps in their heads and constantly verify how accurately they depict reality" (Weick, 1995, p. 355f).
2. Luhmann, 1995, p. 433.
3. The biologist Humberto Maturana calls this behavior of systems "structural determination" (cf. Maturana & Varela, 1987).
4. See Lerche (2023) for more details.
5. https://purpose-economy.org/ (Retrieved 11.10.2023).
6. More on these organizational elements from the Doughnut Economics Action Lab (DEAL): https://www.doughnuteconomics.org/news/50 (Retrieved 29.01.2024).
7. Lerche (2023).
8. Klein, Hughes, Fleischmann (2023).

Appendix

1. Costanza et al. (2014).
2. Ripple et al. (2017).
3. Carse (1986).
4. Sinek (2019).

Image Credits

Image page 30: Graphic from https://www.ey.com/en_ro/sustainability/the-ceo-imperative-how-can-you-put-regeneration-at-the-heart-of-creating-value, based on data from the Global Footprint Network, Living Planet Index, and Materialflows.net.

Image page 56: Based on Reed, B. (2007), Shifting from "sustainability" to regeneration, Building Research & Information, 35(6), 674–690, https://doi.org/10.1080/09613210701475753 und Wahl, D. C. (2016), Designing Regenerative Cultures.

Image page 150: Based on data from the Stockholm Resilience Center and Stockholm University, 2023 (Planetary Boundaries) and from the Doughnut Economic Action Lab, 2015/2017 (Social Foundation).

Image page 155: Based on the by Sylvia Duckworth, further developed by Sigi Lieb (https://www.gespraechswert.de/intersektionalitaet).

Image page 187: Based on Achterberg, Hinfelaar & Bocken (2016). Master Circular Business With The Value Hill and Potting et al. (2017), Circular Economy: Measuring Innovation In The Product Chain.

Image page 240: Based on Schmid & Hipp (1998), Power and Powerlessness in Dilemma Situations.

Contributors

Although only three authors are listed on the cover, many others have also been indispensable in making this book:

First, we'd like to express our gratitude to the Stellar team: To Nabil Ranné, who has time and again shared crucial impulses that have lifted the Stellar Approach to the next level. To Rebecca Weisl, who has made significant contributions to the development of the Stellar toolkit. To Theresa Sauter, who has shaped the Stellar Approach's distinct visual identity from the start and made even the most theoretical concepts visually accessible. And to Julia Dappa and Kai Goldhorn, who were part of the Stellar team's journey for a good chunk of the way. Thank you for all the energy, passion, and love you've poured into this project.

We also wish to thank everyone who gave us helpful and precise feedback on the manuscript, especially Frederik Fleischmann, Constanze Bürkner, Andreas Lerche, Felix Rübcke, and Karoline Rütter.

Thank you to Josephine Belke for her valuable input on resilience models, and to Marcel Sydow for his support in researching and finalizing the manuscript.

Many thanks also to the authors of the Loop Approach, first developed some years ago at TheDive. Its methodological approach enriches many parts of the Stellar Approach.

Thank you to our interview partners and experts, including Lisa Ertl, Tim Riedel, and many others.

We're also deeply grateful to our wonderful illustrators, Danika Baker-Sohn and Jana Stolz, who designed the book, and once again to Theresa Sauter, who held the various threads of the design process together throughout. Without all of you, the book would be a mere lifeless desert of text.

Finally, we wish to extend a huge thank you to the entire team at TheDive. You're the ones who make it possible to again and again dream up new solutions and share them with the world!

About the Authors

Simon Berkler (Ph. D.) is a co-founder of TheDive with over 20 years of experience as an entrepreneur and organizational consultant. He has studied media and communication science and holds a doctorate in media economics. Trained in systemic and integral organizational development, he has a long track record in supporting transformation processes at large and mid-sized companies. At TheDive, he focuses on the question of how the economic system can be developed in a life-serving direction.

Ella Lagé (M. A. Design) worked for many years as a service designer in innovation projects at large corporations, focusing on creating lasting changes to established behaviors. Today at TheDive, she explores what organizations need in order to foster renewal and embrace it as something positive. Her focus areas include agile methodologies, leadership development, and the design of the sustainable-regenerative transformation.

About the Authors

Ben Hughes (M. Sc. Tech.) is a speaker, author, and leader. A former management consultant, he spent ten years building and leading the content team at the Berlin-based start-up Blinkist. Based on his experiences with self-organization there, he co-authored the book *The Loop Approach*. He speaks about hybrid leadership, self-organization, and the regenerative transformation.

The Stellar Approach was developed at TheDive, where since 2015, people from different backgrounds have been exploring how to shape the future of work and the economy:

How can organizations help bring about a world that serves humanity, society, and the planet? How can organizations continually renew themselves in these turbulent times? How can transformations succeed that harness the innovation potential of the entire organization?

The Stellar Approach provides a clear framework for regenerative change. It builds on many established concepts in sustainable and regenerative economic activity and enhances the organization's competence in finding regenerative solutions. And just as the field of regenerative economic activity continues to evolve over time, so too does the Stellar Approach.

In addition to the Stellar Approach, TheDive has also developed the Loop Approach, which helps teams and organizations stay adaptable and work effectively together in these complex times.

A further topic that TheDive is contributing to is New Finance, which endeavors to find a modern approach to financial management, processes, and KPIs. For more information on TheDive, please see https://www.thedive.com/en.